LEARN AMERICAN CALLIGRAPHY

OTHER BOOKS BY MARGARET SHEPHERD

Learning Calligraphy (revised in 2001 and reissued as *Learn Calligraphy*)

Using Calligraphy

Capitals for Calligraphy

Borders for Calligraphy

Calligraphy Made Easy

Calligraphy Projects

Calligraphy Alphabets Made Easy

Calligraphy Now (reissued in the UK as *A Manual of Modern Calligraphy*)

Basics of the New Calligraphy

Basics of Left-Handed Calligraphy

Modern Calligraphy Made Easy

Calligraphy for Celebrating Your Wedding

Calligraphy for Celebrating Your Newborn

The Art of the Handwritten Note

The Art of Civilized Conversation

The Art of the Personal Letter

Learn World Calligraphy

Song of Songs

contributor to *Almost Lost Arts*

The Alphabet Advent Calendar

The ABC Advent Calendar

LEARN AMERICAN CALLIGRAPHY

The Complete Book of Lettering, History, and Design

Margaret Shepherd

author of *Learn Calligraphy*

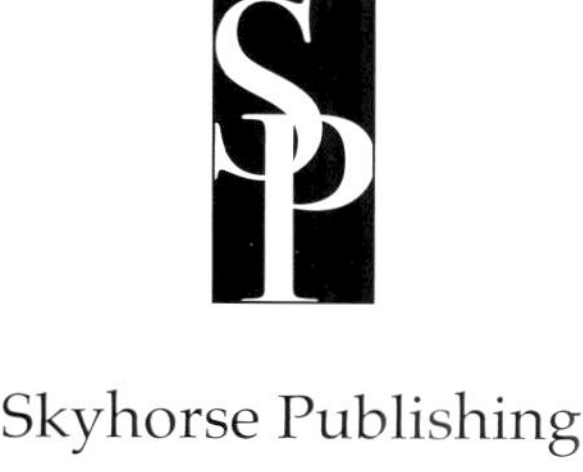

Skyhorse Publishing

Skyhorse Publishing books may be purchased in bulk at special discounts for sales promotion, corporate gifts, fund-raising, or educational purposes. Special editions can also be created to specifications. For details, contact the Special Sales Department, Skyhorse Publishing, 307 West 36th Street, 11th Floor, New York, NY 10018 or info@skyhorsepublishing.com.

Skyhorse® and Skyhorse Publishing® are registered trademarks of Skyhorse Publishing, Inc.®, a Delaware corporation.

Visit our website at www.skyhorsepublishing.com.

10 9 8 7 6 5 4 3 2 1

Library of Congress Cataloging-in-Publication Data is available on file.

Cover design by Kai Texel
Cover image by Getty Images
Book design: Robin Brooks
Design layout: Sr. Anna-Hope Mitchell, Sr. Martina Albro

Print ISBN: 978-1-5107-7202-1
Ebook ISBN: 978-1-5107-7786-6

Printed in China

Contents

Thanks

I WANT TO THANK THE MEMBERS of my book team:
Skyhorse editors Nicole Mele and Lilly Golden,
picture researcher Debby Paddock, agent Colleen
Mohyde, and book designers Sr Anna-Hope Mitchell
and Sr Martina Albro. Robin Brooks created the
book's basic layout.

My family and friends helped me to start,
finish, and debug this book. My husband David
Friend read through its early drafts. Richard
Herold contributed tech support. Zoë Friend
made drawings to order. Steve Dunwell shot the
photographs on pages 19, 34, 86, and 133.

More help, information, pictures, and
encouragement came from Marilyn Brandt, Nancy
Netzer, Anne Bromer, Karen Boss, Cat Schaad,
Carl Lazarus, Pam Steel, Rosalie Davis, Liza
Ketchum, Mary Jaffe, Joyce Serwitz, Sarah Friend,
Todd Light, Rolena Adorno, David L Frye, Matt
McArthur, Randall Hasson, Jennifer Parkhurst,
Ian Staber, Jasper Friend, Lydia Savage, Bryan V.
Platt, Huy Huang Dao, Jay Boggis, Miriam Butts,
Suanne Stange nee Miss Peterson, Karin Clark,
Winifred Kelley, Tamara Plakins Thornton, Lou
Roberto, Shelley Payette, Beth Harris, Jake Rainis,
Tom Ukena, Denny Cooper, Richard Sheaff, Pierce
Hofman, Gordon Hofman, Brigid Cowdrey, Don
Meeker, John Downer, Florence Shepherd, Dennis
Stephan, Chris Skillern, Monique Ortman, Jonathan
Appell, John Murray, and Pat Vinter.

The handwriting on page 53 came from Carol
Christmas, Gordon Shepherd, Cheryl Cipro, Molly
Henessey-Fiske, Alison Lewis, Mark Peterson, Annie
Zeybekoglu, and Rachelle Flowers.

Many curators helped me find just the right
objects: Lisa Minardi at Historic Trappe Museum,
April Harper at Letterform Archive, Hannah
McAuley at Speed Museum, Barry Mickey at
Heritage Museum, Tom Clabaugh at Shelby
Museum, and Doug Greenway at the Corn Palace.

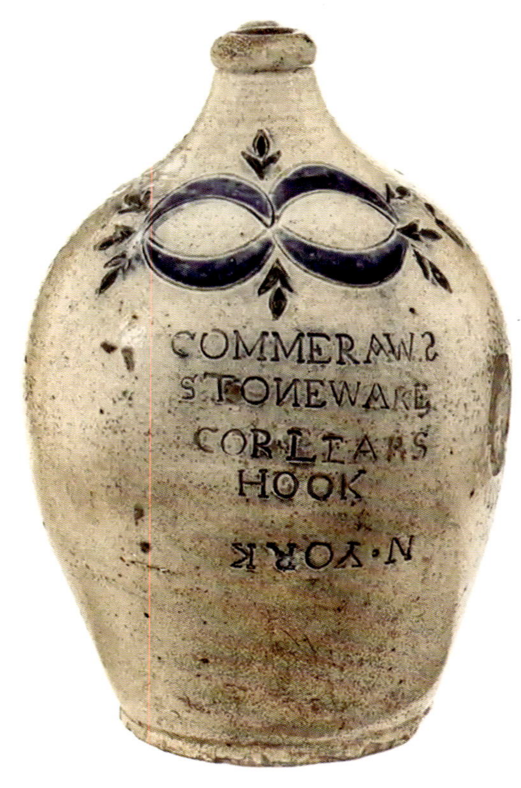

*Stamped Roman letters identify a ceramic creamware
jug made around 1800 in New York City by Thomas
Commeraw, Black businessman, activist, and
expert potter. Image: New-York Historical Society*

PREFACE

LIKE MANY BEGINNERS IN CALLIGRAPHY, I was happy at first to simply copy alphabets from the bygone Roman empire, the Middle Ages, and the Renaissance. They teach the basics of letter construction and map the roots of today's alphabet, while they evoke the time and place of the scribes who wrote them.

As I learned more about these traditional letters in pen and ink, however, I kept wondering "What about *now*!?" and "What about *here*?!" When I chose American writers, the mismatch between words from the New World and alphabets from the Old World left me unsatisfied. Instead of sticking with formal alphabets of the past, I wanted to include calligraphy from my own era and country. Meanwhile, I began to notice American letter artists in related fields who wrote with completely different letters and materials. I genuinely admired their work: graffiti filled the gray cityscape with color; the heroes of comic books spoke in lively American accents; eccentric scrawls felt more personal than standard cursive. And for decades, every lemonade stand and protest march offered dynamic letters that spoke earnestly for the amateurs who had invented them.

The important thing is never stop asking questions.
~ *Albert Einstein*

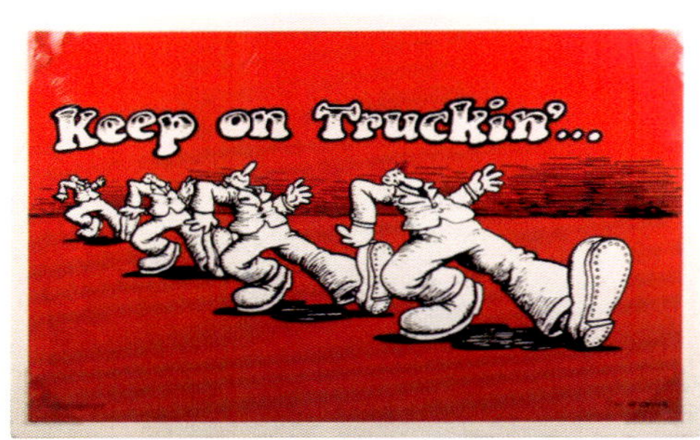

These letters look like fat-footed Cooper (see page 85) but they also have roots in graffiti (see page 35) and comics (see pages 125–127). From Zap Comix, *first issue, 1968. Artist, Robert Crumb. 22" x 34" (60 cm x 92 cm). Used with permission.*

Letter arts in America echo its music, philosophy, language, cuisine, and poetry. One by one, such original thinkers as Ralph Waldo Emerson, Martha Graham, E. E. Cummings, Aaron Copland, James Beard, Buckminster Fuller, and Duke Ellington declared their independence from the ideas they had inherited, and struck out on their own path. Calligraphy too has matured from its colonial past, to become, in the words of the man who created Spencerian handwriting, "even more American."

I have spent years, maybe decades, looking at American letters and wishing someone would write about them. Eventually, as Nobel Prize–winning author Toni Morrison puts it, "If there is a book you want to read and it doesn't exist, then you must write it." This is that book. Using photos, diagrams, art, and words, it redefines American calligraphy from many new and different perspectives.

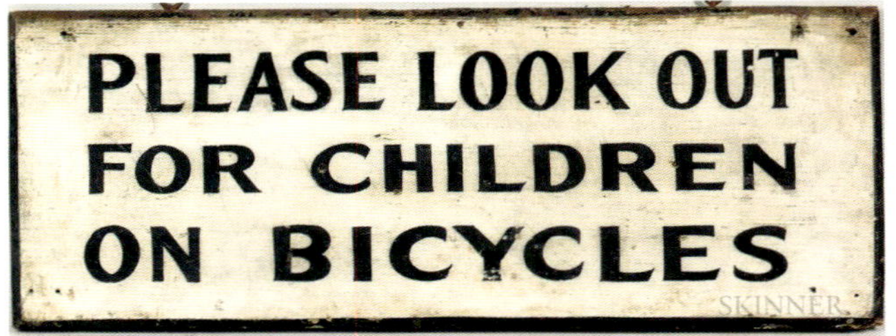

In this minor masterpiece of the sign-painter's art, block letters (see page 109) have been narrowed or widened to fit the margins. Their strokes have a hint of thick and thin, but they lack the complex letter families that govern Roman capitals. Early twentieth century. 9" x 24" (23 cm x 60 1 cm). Courtesy of Richard Herold.

The stories and images I have chosen come from a lifetime of looking at calligraphy. They are not a neutral overview but reflections of the most important and most interesting facets of American letters. Of course, I have many stubborn opinions and a few blind spots. Inevitably, I have chosen some alphabets that readers won't warm to, and have left out some of their favorites. I have shortened many complicated backstories to make them fit in. The people I spotlight are not always the usual suspects. I like to reverse the clock by turning type back into pen and ink letters. Readers will also soon figure out that my own hand is far from steady; I flunked handwriting in the third grade and I still have to work hard to learn any new style. Some of my model alphabets look like rough drafts because they are; I'm still discovering what is the essence of each style. I trust my readers to look past the flaws of what I write and try to see what I see.

This book can be read with or without a pen, by visitor or citizen, master scribe or beginner, aspiring artist or skeptical engineer. I hope the letters here, and the stories behind them, will help illuminate the past and future of American calligraphy.

Margaret Shepherd, Boston, 2024

INTRODUCTION

WHILE MANY PEOPLE ENJOY learning calligraphy because it helps them express their own thoughts, they are often surprised to find that it can also teach them about their own country. For decades, American calligraphers have focused on centuries-old traditional scripts that they inherited from Europe. Although they started out with alphabets from the Old World, once they unpacked this legacy of historical scripts, the letters evolved in new ways. Many of these alphabets, and the local styles that they blended with, did not even fit the old definitions of calligraphy.

This book has an expansive view of letters in America, not just by calligraphers but also by protest marchers, quilters, sign painters, and graffiti artists. It offers examples from every era of the last five hundred years and includes letters by people of every age, ethnicity, and skill level. Scripts brought by recent immigrants have mingled with local alphabets to invent hybrids. A few letters from Canada and Latin America are part of the story, too. And everyone can learn from writing systems of the Indigenous people who predated the first settlers.

Some three dozen American letter styles display their variety and depth here in full-page alphabet models. Simple diagrams explain how they are made, and creative designs show how they are put to use. Each alphabet has a story to tell, with its own drama and its own heroes. Together, they take the reader on a visual trip around the United States, with stop-offs in many locations and insights on every page.

Some of these alphabets have been hiding in plain sight since the nation's founding—and before—while others have been created within recent memory. All are rewarding to meet and get to know. You'll never look at the ABCs the same way again.

A hand-lettered sign from a cafeteria in Colorado. Graphic artist Ben Shahn was inspired by amateur lettering like this (see pages 131 and 137–40).

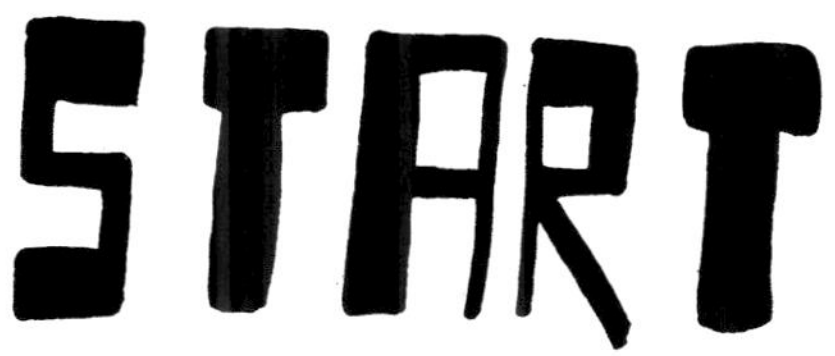

"The discernment of truth . . . comes from listening to many voices."
~ *David Quammen,* Breathless

FIRST AMERICANS

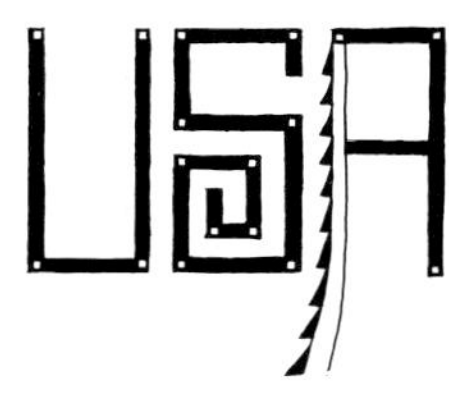

THE FIRST EUROPEANS TO REACH THE WESTERN HEMISPHERE some five centuries ago encountered people who had already been living there for thousands of years. Indigenous people had adapted to many different climates, spoke diverse languages, grew unique plants, migrated across open plains or settled in cities, and lived under political systems that ranged from tribes to federations to empires. The only thing the original Americans had not invented before contact was a phonetic alphabet, but they created many other kinds of writing to narrate tribal stories, practice religion, record events, transact business, sign treaties, decorate everyday objects, explore artistic vision, and express powerful philosophical ideas.

Much of the interest in Indigenous writing systems and culture came after contact with outsiders had virtually wiped out the people who created them. With few exceptions, Europeans routinely imposed their own alphabet to spell out the Native languages they heard. Invasive diseases decimated whole populations and left tribes vulnerable to more cultural erosion. And US government policies of the past actively tried to prevent Native people from writing or even speaking their own languages.

Nevertheless, Indigenous artists spent decades on the margins of American culture. Their symbols were widely dismissed as merely decorative, pigeonholed in anthropological museums, parodied in mainstream art, or crudely mass-produced for sale in souvenir stands. Outsiders freely stole ideas and made bad imitations.

In the twentieth century, many Native Americans exerted political pressure to protect their language, culture, and rights. Artists and craftspeople have begun to reclaim their languages and heritage, and much-needed laws now regulate how their artifacts can be labeled and sold.

"We will be known forever by the tracks we leave."

~Dakota Tribe

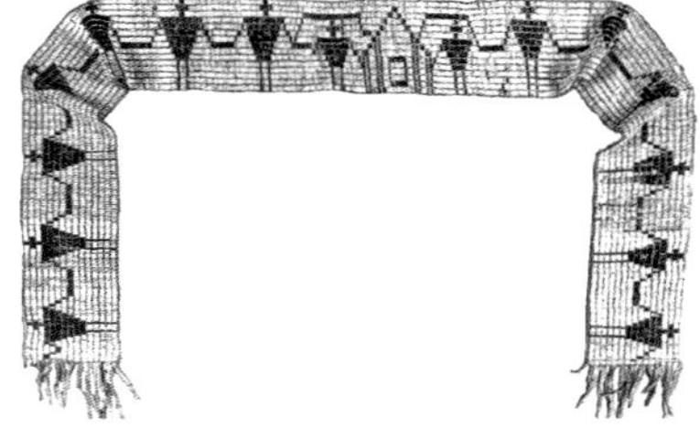

↑ *The six-foot-long George Washington Belt was given to the Onieda to solemnize the Canandaigua treaty of 1794. Two tribal gatekeepers flank a central house, with the other thirteen men representing the colonies*

Indigenous artifacts, especially those that kept records, are cherished today by scholars, curators, and tribe members. They offer a rich legacy for all American artists and a unique cultural treasure for the world. They broaden the definition of writing itself, encouraging calligraphers to integrate these ideas from the first Americans into their own art. The half-dozen writing systems shown here are a small sample from the 576 distinct tribes in North America alone.

1. Federations

The political structure of many tribes impressed early New England settlers so deeply that they included its core concept of equality in the constitution of Massachusetts, which later was a model for the United States Constitution. Many Native Americans used wordless but eloquent visual language in ceremonial belts woven with "wampum" beads, to formalize important treaties and events. These symbols, as well as the beaded medium itself, illustrate how individual, equal parts can add up to a unified design. The national motto *e pluribus unum*, or "from many, one" was eventually chosen by the founders.

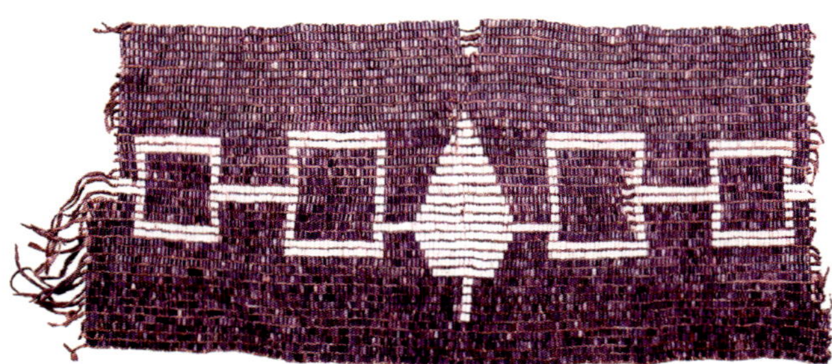

↑ *A 1450 alliance known as the Haudenosaunee Confederacy, or Five Nations, was made up of Mohawks, Oneidas, Onondagas, Cayugas, and Senecas, and commemorated by the so-called "Hiawatha Belt." Its joined squares and central polygon portray a federation of equal individuals, not a hierarchy.*

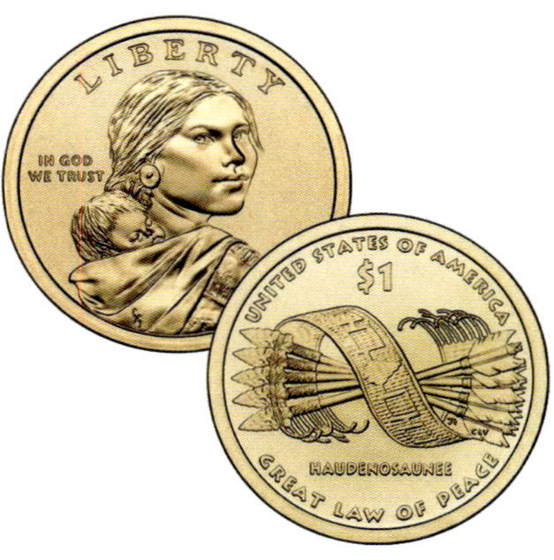

↗ *The dollar coin honoring Sacagawea in 2000 featured the Hiawatha belt on its reverse.*

2. Type

Sequoyah, a Cherokee Indian, observed his Tennessee neighbors reading printed words on book pages, which he called "talking leaves." Although illiterate himself at first, in the 1820s he devised a syllabary—symbols not for letters but for syllables—for the Cherokee language, to make it easy for his own people to read, too.

While some of the characters seem to resemble Roman letters, their pronunciation and purpose are different. Because this writing was logical and easy to learn, it united the Cherokee nation, which was scattered during the forcible relocation and repression of the Trail of Tears.

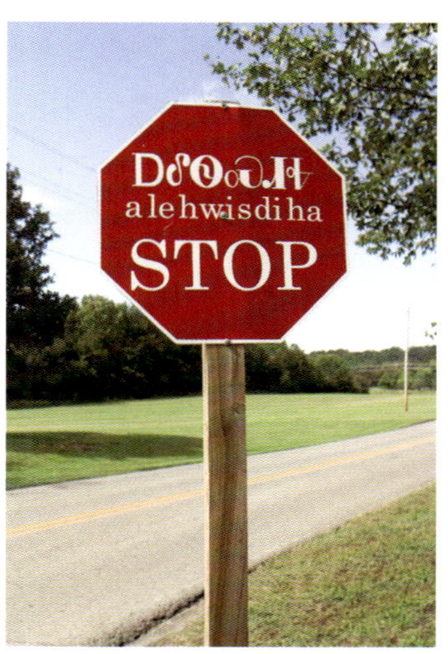

Cherokee dual-language street sign with transliteration. ↑

The Cherokee Syllabary

Nearly two centuries after its invention, Cherokee leaders initiated a redesign of their syllabary. With under two thousand fluent speakers remaining, they needed modern materials for teaching the language to the estimated 328,000 other members of their tribe. Designer Mark Jamra modernized the type, removed serifs, added boldface and Italic versions, and gave extra attention to spacing. Other graphic artists have explored lowercase characters, acceents, numerals, and punctuation.

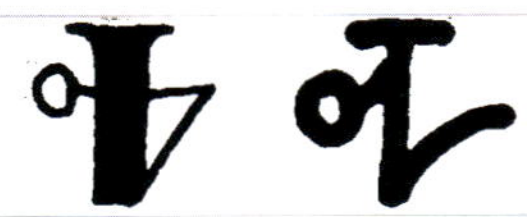

Original   Modern

Modern Cherokee type, adapted here for calligraphers, has no thicks and thins or serifs.

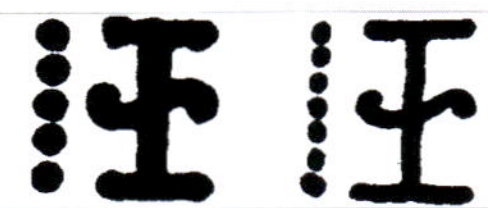

Bold   Regular

Speedball B pens make heavy or light letters, using the guidelines on page 9.

a	e	i	o	u	v
a	e	i	o	u	v
ga ka	ge	gi	go	gu	gu
ha	he	hi	ho	hu	hv
la	le	li	lo	lu	lv
ma	me	mi	mo	mu	
na hna nah	ne	ni	no	nu	nv
qua	que	qui	quo	quu	quv
sa s	se	si	so	su	sv
da ta	de te	di ti	do	du	dv
dla tla	tle	tli	tlo	tlu	tlv
tsa	tse	tsi	tso	tsu	tsv
wa	we	wi	wo	wu	wv
ya	ye	yi	yo	yu	yv

Variations

"Thank you" in Cherokee is "wado."

Cherokee designer Chris Skillern intended "Meli," type for children's books.

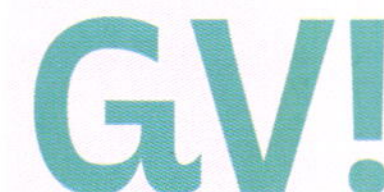

"Kamama" type by Monique Ortman evokes Cherokee rivercane basketry.

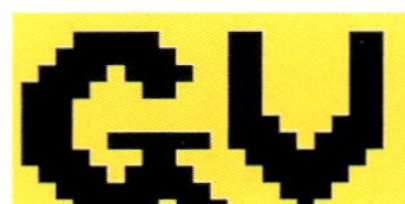

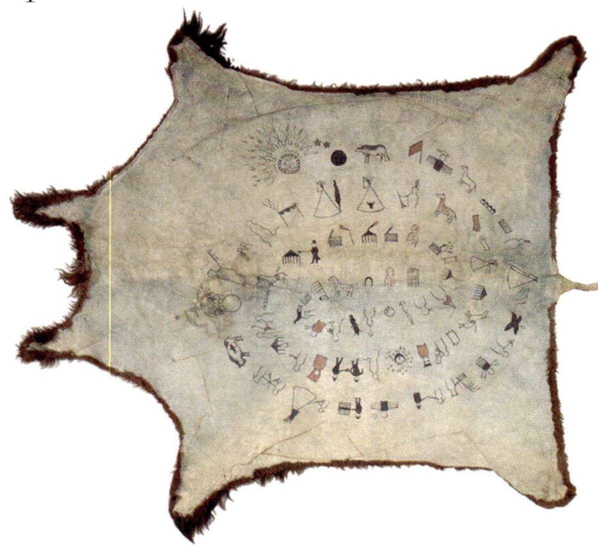

3. GREAT PLAINS

THE LAKOTA TRIBES made annual narratives they called "the winter count." As each year ended, the tribe gave it a title and made a pictograph to remember it by; for example, the year when they first acquired horses, or the year of a spectacular meteor shower. Mnemonic devices rather than literal documents, they were meant to help a designated "keeper" recite the tribe's oral history

↑ *A winter count on buffalo hide, written in a typical spiral.*

The Lakota drew this dramatic image to mark the year 1880–1881, when their children were forcibly taken away to school. Detail. →

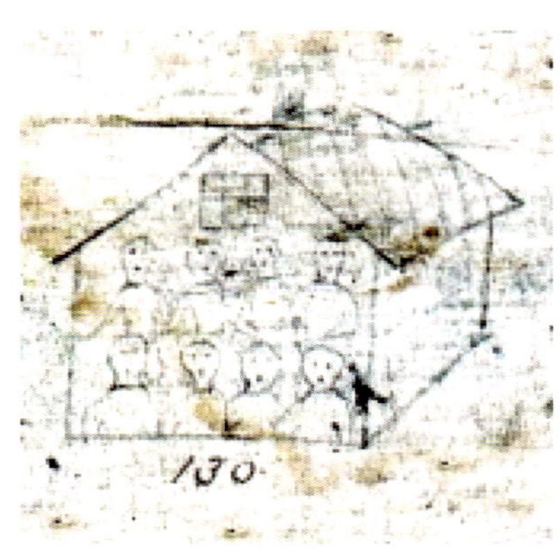

4. SOUTHWEST

OTHER TRIBES devised their own symbolic languages, which ranged from detailed animal pictures to medallions to decorative bands.

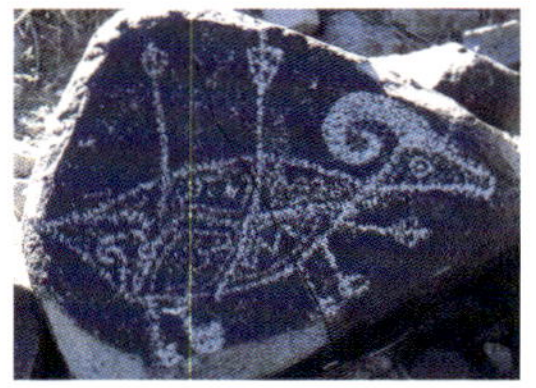

The Mogollon people left 21,000 petroglyphs that visitors can see up close in the Three Rivers area of New Mexico. Some artists carved animal pictures that seemed to hold special meaning, but scholars still puzzle to figure them out. Others drew stylized hands, the sun, or humans in ritual costume.

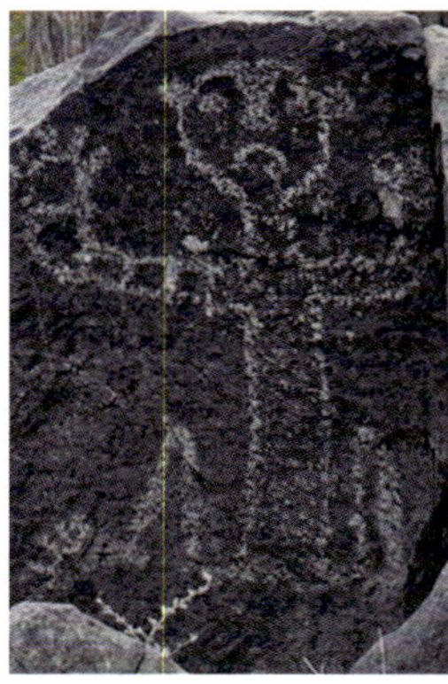

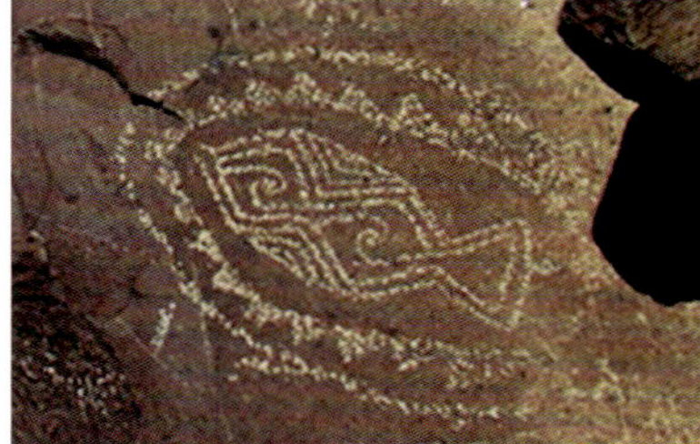

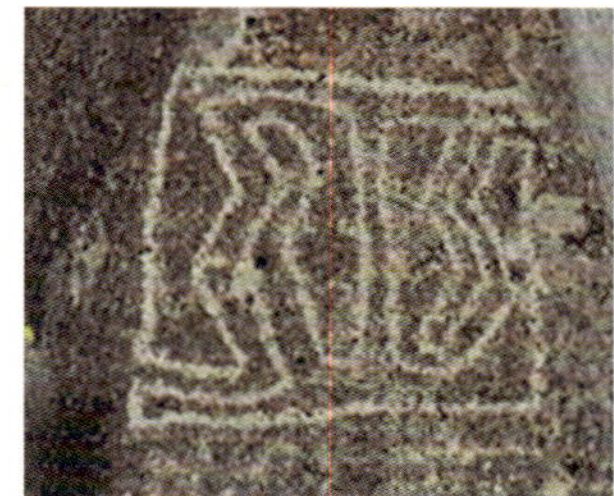

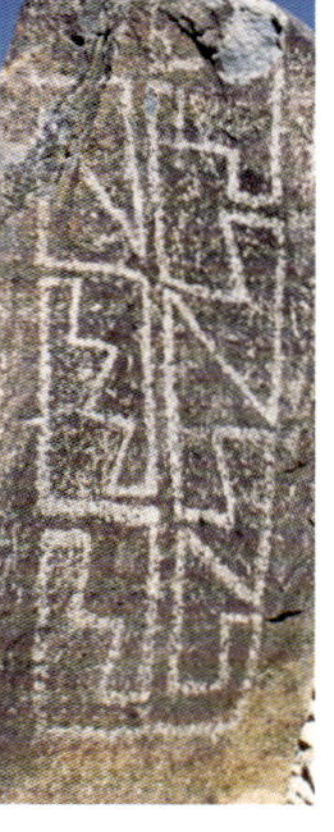

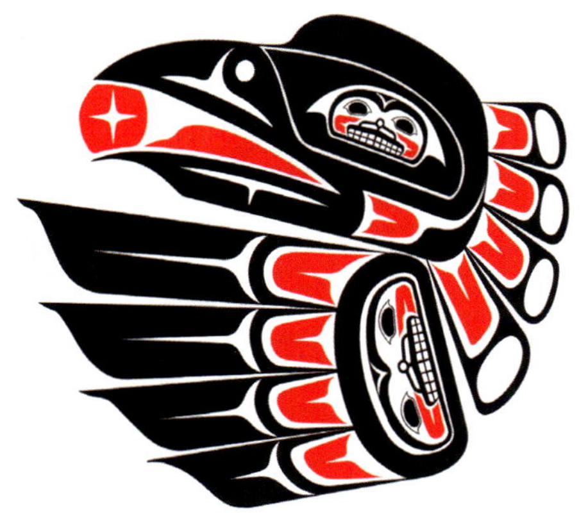

A modern design by Haida artist Lon French features the legendary trickster Raven whose story defines the tribe.

5. PACIFIC NORTHWEST

NATIVE AMERICAN ARTISTS from northern California to Alaska carved and painted in a style now called "formline," which balances black shapes against white spaces. These flowing lines swell or shrink organically, while the "finelines" stay at a constant width.

The distinctive color scheme of Pacific Northwest artists was limited to red, gray and black, plus a little blue-green or yellow, until outside contact introduced them to new new pigments. Their favorite motifs for pottery, masks, canoes and totem poles are stylized eagles, orcas, feathers, bears, ravens, and symmetrical faces.

BASIC OVOIDS

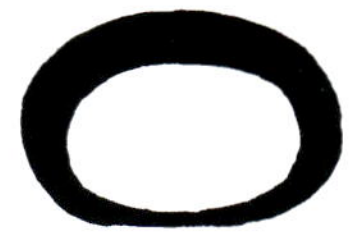

↑ Formline

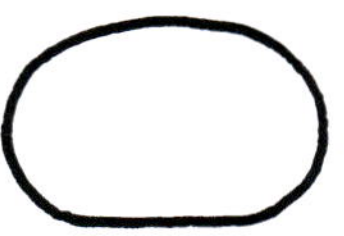

↑ Fineline

BASIC U SHAPE

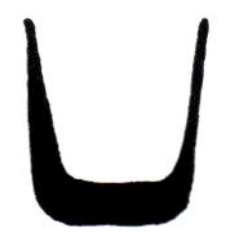

This rounded U is one of two basic shapes that can be manipulated, rotated, and repeated, to construct many alphabet letters (a few samples are shown below). Inner spaces can hold crescents, trigons, and quadrons. →

INTERIOR SHAPES

Crescent   Trigon   Quadron

A FEW MADE-UP ALPHABET LETTERS   A B C D E   M W

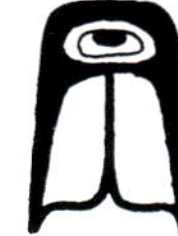 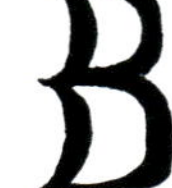 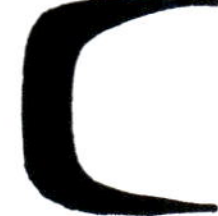 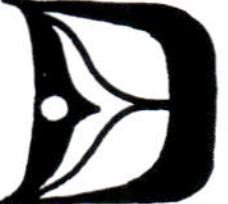 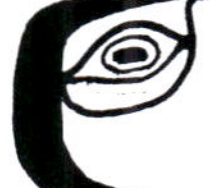 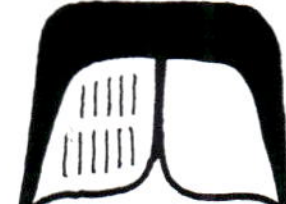 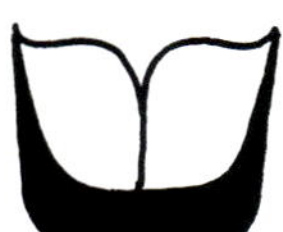

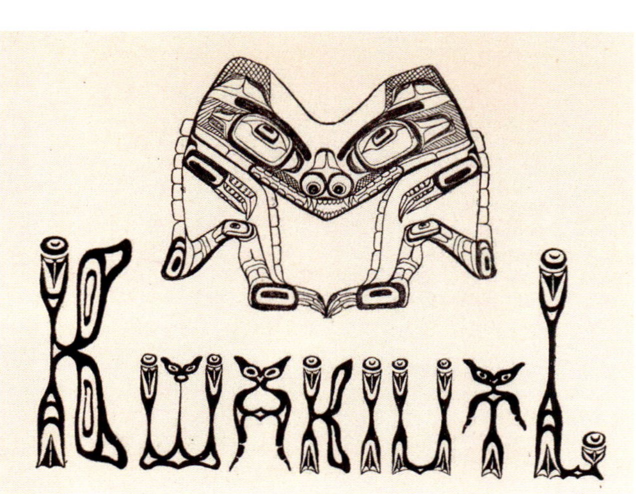

← In 1905, artist Angel DeCora (see page 7) used basic elements of Pacific Northwest art— ovoids and U shapes—to build an alphabet in the style then known as Kwakiutl. Today, this tribe prefers the name Kwakwaka'wakw.

6. HAWAI'I

NATIVE HAWAI'IANS, like many other precontact island peoples, carved petroglyphs and stick figures in stone or painted them on bark cloth. Missionaries introduced the Roman alphabet around 1820. For decades after that, letter designs came from mainland fantasies rather than island art; hula girls and visiting sailors often shared a generic tropical landscape with vaguely Japanese and Chinese writing.

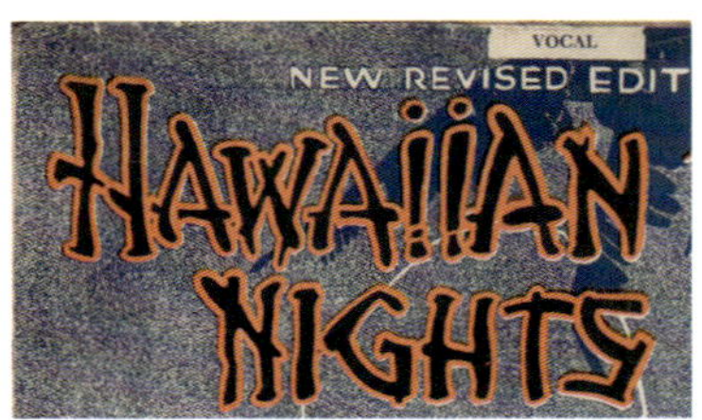

↑ *Letters from a 1919 sheet music cover evoke Hawaii with exotic motifs and colors.*

COMBINING ABCs WITH INDIGENOUS STYLES.

AUTHENTICITY WAS A MAJOR PROBLEM for artists who tried to give their letters the flavor of America's first inhabitants but did not really know much about their traditions. Designs by non-Indians ranged from the well-meaning to the truly cringe-worthy. Some simply threw in all-purpose symbols such as tomahawks, tepees, and feathers. Some touched up basic block letters to imitate more subtle hand-hewn materials. As racist attitudes slowly softened, artists began to use subtler motifs, such as local pigments and abstract borders, to suggest regional and tribal styles.

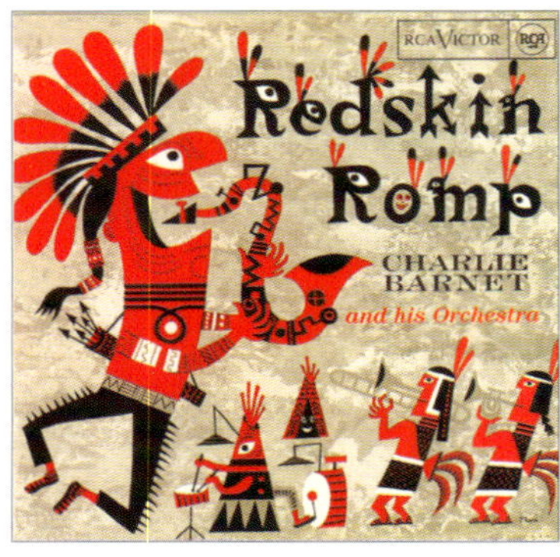

↑ *Crude in both words and pictures, this kind of casual racism was still common in 1950s America. Designer Jim Flores.*

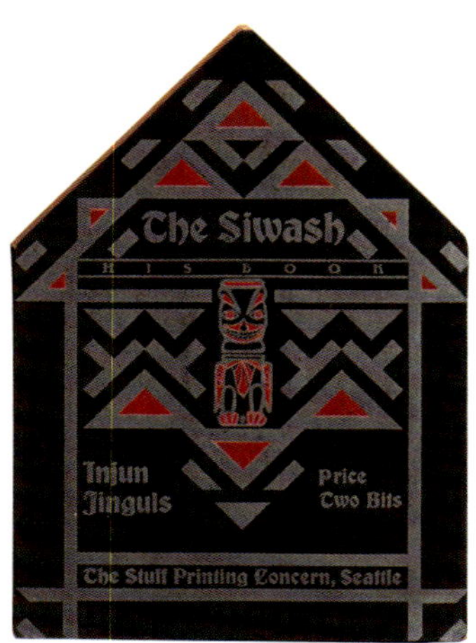

↑ *Even though the design and colors of this 1909 booklet cover seem inspired by Tlingit art, its title and subtitle use common racial slurs from a century ago. Designer Will Bradley.*

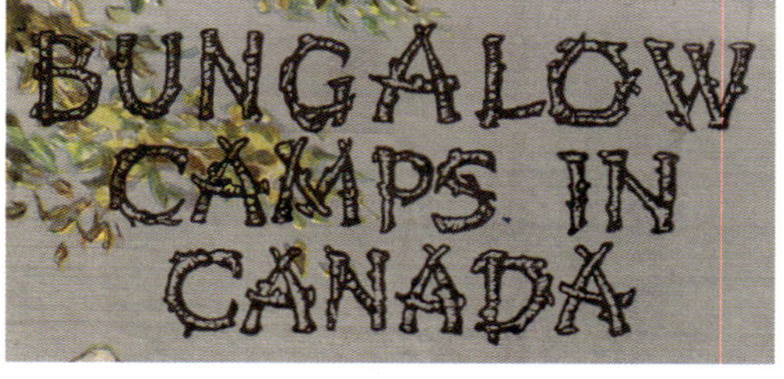

↑ *Letters made out of birch twigs evoke a pleasant vacation in the woods.*

→ *An imitation of weathered woodgrain creates a general impression of the northwest.*

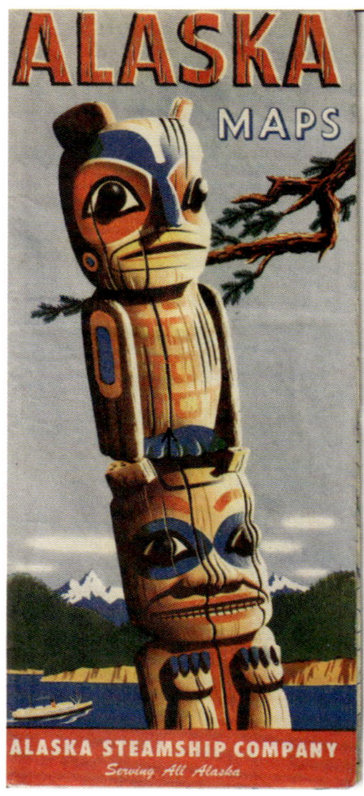

THE BEST WAY TO ACHIEVE AUTHENTICITY is to look at how Indigenous people themselves have already chosen to blend their art with the alphabet. Angel DeCora, for instance, was a graphic designer born into the Hochunk tribe in 1871. In an era of relentless prejudice against women and Native Americans, her unmistakable early talent helped her gain an education. Although she studied painting and illustration at Boston's School of the Museum of Fine Arts, Smith College, and Drexel University, she still managed to keep her own roots alive and teach herself the visual traditions of other tribes. She went on to design highly regarded Indian-themed book covers, title pages, and illustrations that reflected her deep understanding of letterforms and tribal customs.

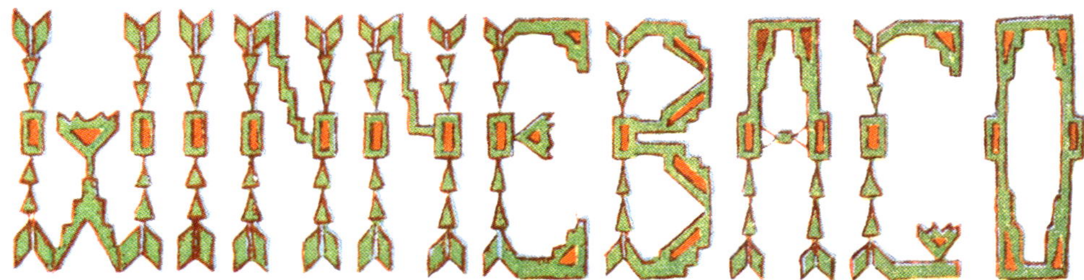

↑ *In dozens of titles for the widely popular* The Indians' Book *of 1907, Angel DeCora shaped the letters of each tribe's name to suggest the style of its art. A fellow designer remarked, "Whoever did that lettering is a genius!"*

In articles and lectures, Angel DeCora articulated her belief in a middle way between assimilation and isolation, exemplified by artists who could absorb outside ideas without losing their own core identity. Ahead of her time, she also called for better opportunities for Native Americans and women.

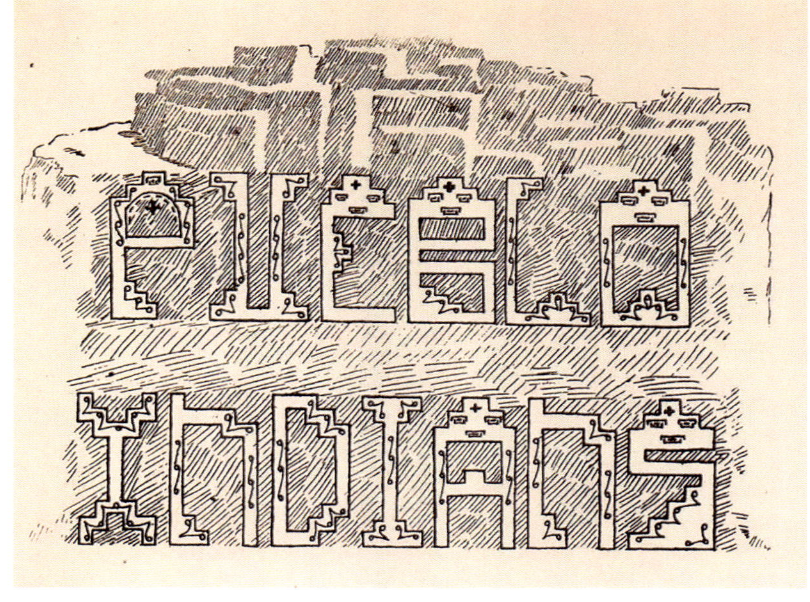

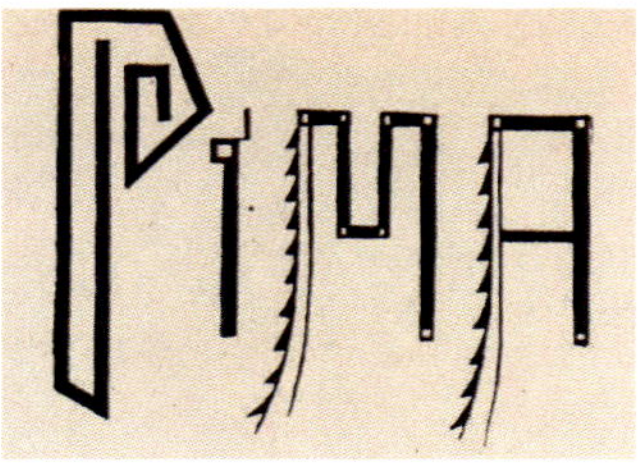

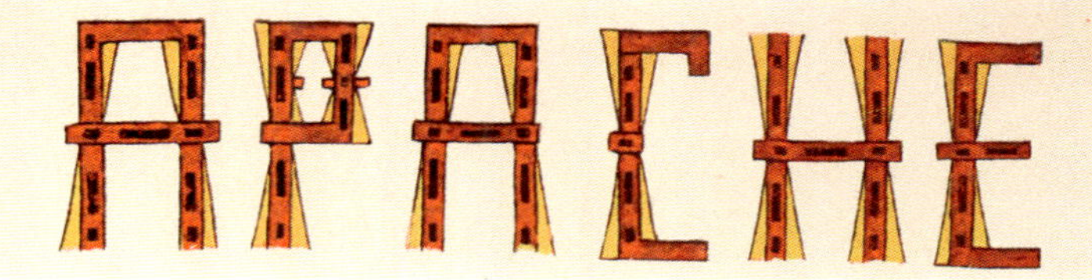

Next

A new generation of Native Americans from a variety of tribes have kept their languages alive, preserved their customs, and reinvigorated their traditional art—all in spite of 250 years of the ignorance and interference of outsiders. Today they form a bridge between tradition and modernity. They create blended typefaces, logos, syllabaries, and signs that serve to spread their visual culture to the larger world.

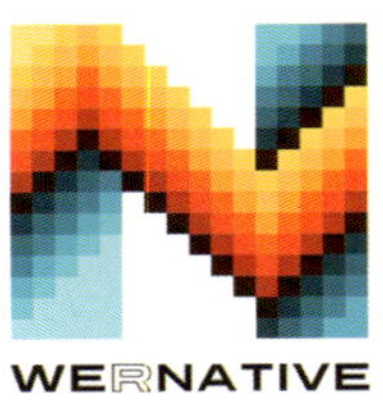

↖ Earth pigments and turquoise are a tradition of many tribes. The grid suggests the craft of beading. The diagonal line of the N also looks like part of a larger W.

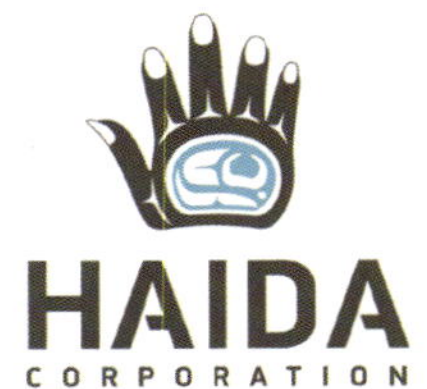

← Haida-Tlingit forms in the shape of a hand are echoed in the alphabet letters of this Alaskan company.

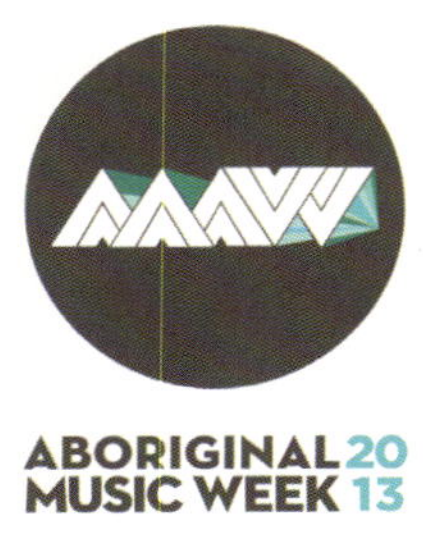

↙ The initials for Aboriginal Music Week evoke not only the Canadian mountains where the festival began, but also the tribes of America's west and beyond, to music of the whole world. Designs by digitalnavajo.com

America is home to many groups who have merged their own art with the alphabet, so that hybrid ABCs have grown to be the country's new normal. After 500 years, immigrants and their alphabets are finally learning from Indigenous people and their symbols, the way they should have done from the start.

These calligraphic swashes, and →
their coloring, suggest an eagle
diving past the sun. The Thunder
Bird of Old X. T. C.
© 1999 by Cree artist Alvin Constant.

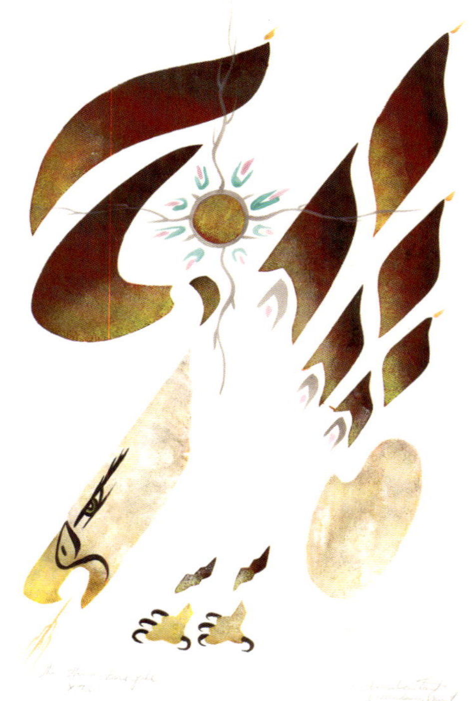

Blunt marker or Speedball B

GOTHIC

MOST AMERICANS CAN RECOGNIZE GOTHIC (even if they do mislabel it "Old English") as the spiky, old-fashioned letters that they see on diplomas and newspaper mastheads. This angular Gothic dominated the Middle Ages for four hundred years in northern Europe. In Spain, however, it followed a separate path, absorbing Moorish influences that softened its corners, widened its letter bodies, and lengthened its swashes. The conquistadores brought this Spanish version of Gothic, in Christian scriptures and imperial decrees, to the West Coast of the Americas as early as the 1530s. Eventually the style spread to the American Southwest.

While Gothic letters were putting down roots in New Spain, they continued to fade away in Old Europe, eclipsed by the revival of Roman capitals and the evolution of small letters during the Renaissance. By the time the earliest Pilgrims and Puritans emigrated in the 1620s to Massachusetts Bay, although they were still reading Gothic in their King James Bibles, the first books they printed for themselves were set in Roman type. Even professional scribes used Gothic only sparingly for emphasis and ornament.

Gothic lettering had come to symbolize everything the colonists wanted to escape—the unquestioned doctrines, hierarchical church governance, overwrought cathedrals, and ornate manuscripts of the Middle Ages. The clarity of humanistic Roman typography and carving seemed a better way to express their new ideals of independent conscience and rational thought. In the United States, it appeared, Gothic was gradually becoming a relic of the past along with superstition, monarchy, feudalism, and state religion.

Although American letter artists had grown out of Gothic, they just couldn't let it go. Always looking for something vivid and exotic to catch the reader's eye, they kept going back to Gothic calligraphy, five more times. Every new revival of Gothic in this chapter shows that even well-worn letters can offer fresh forms if a new generation writes them in a new place for a new purpose.

"How medieval do you want to be?"
~ *Patrick O'Donnell,*
The Knights Next Door

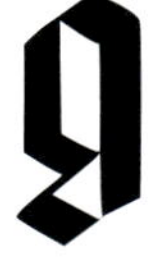
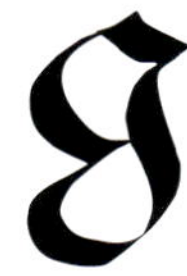

Gothic letter **G,**
from northern
and southern Europe

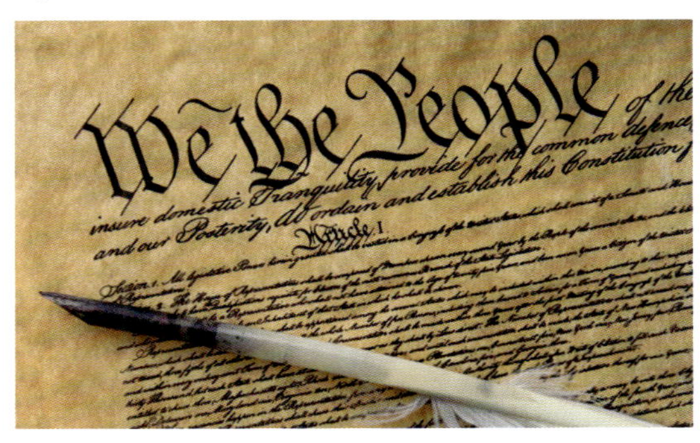

Gothic, a relic from the Middle Ages

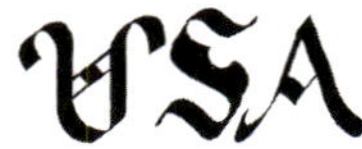

"they have all
come to add
more burdens on
the Indians."
~ Felipe Guamán
Poma de Ayala

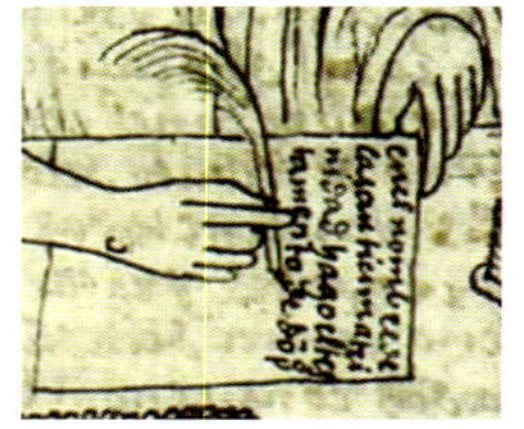

*The flexibility of a
quill pen helps to
shape the stroke ends
(detail).*

NOT LONG AFTER COLUMBUS'S FINAL VISIT, Gothic calligraphy was brought to America by the Spanish conquistadors, a band of opportunists who were mainly motivated by plunder. They overthrew the Incas of Peru in 1532; within eighty years Quechua artist Felipe Guamán Poma had written a book-length letter, "Nueva Corónica," to protest their mistreatment of his countrymen. In 1,200 pages of detailed maps, ethnological profiles, charts, individual portraits, local scenes, and eloquent prose, he pleaded with King Philip III to right this wrong. Guamán Poma, who came from an aristocratic Incan family, drew with a keen eye and lettered with a vigorous hand. His pages resemble illuminated manuscripts. He had created this calligraphic masterpiece before the first Pilgrims arrived in New England.

The lettering in his New Chronicle had Spanish roots in the Rotunda style of Gothic. Like many American versions of old-world art, these Spanish letters had taken on new vigor in the New World. Most of the capitals are typical of medieval Versals, based on rounded Roman letters but executed with the straight pen strokes, sharp corners, and narrow proportions of Gothic. A few letters are complete inventions, though, with their own strange forms, and most of the capital letters appear in a variety of shapes. Readers today will enjoy deciphering this book, if they allow for its abbreviations, phonetic renderings,

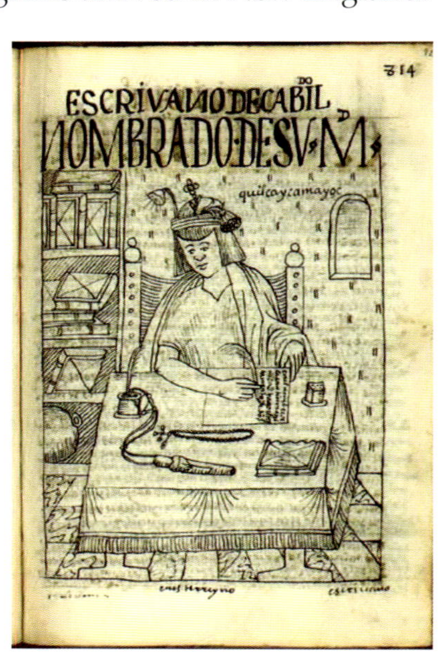

*Quechua scribe drafting a will,
c 1600 (detail to left).*

archaic Spanish spelling (**G** for **C**, for instance, and the reversed **N**), and underlying Quechua syntax. For sheer virtuosity, it has no peer.

Centuries of repeated conquest, conversion, and colonial rule spread the Spanish Gothic style all around Latin America. Until 1848, this visual culture included parts of Mexico that are now the states of New Mexico, Arizona, and southern California. Today this unique Inca book is part of the greater American visual heritage.

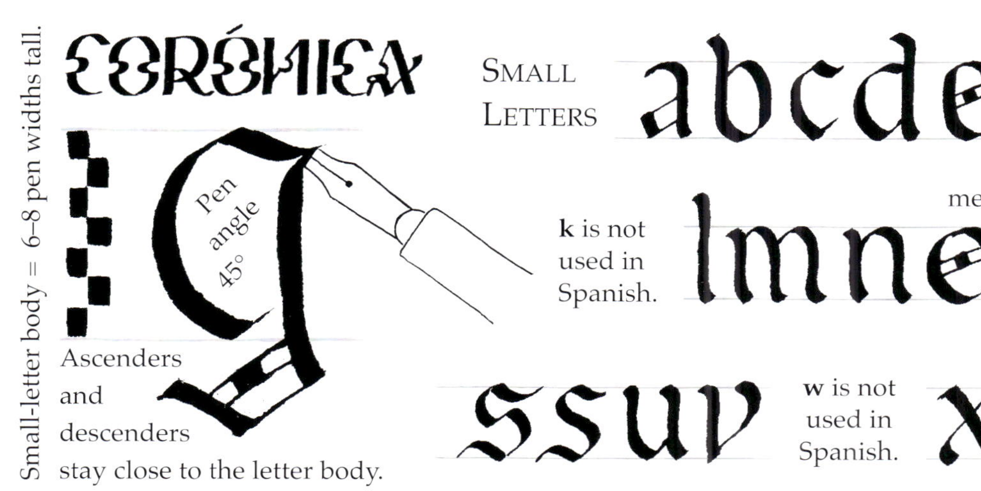

Small-letter body = 6–8 pen widths tall.

Ascenders and descenders stay close to the letter body.

Small pen mark indicates an abbreviation.

A medley of methods add variety: curlicues; built-up serifs; interior strokes; small half-circles; drawn contours.

Capitals = 8–10 pen widths tall.

0° (flat) and 45° (diagonal) pen angles.

45°

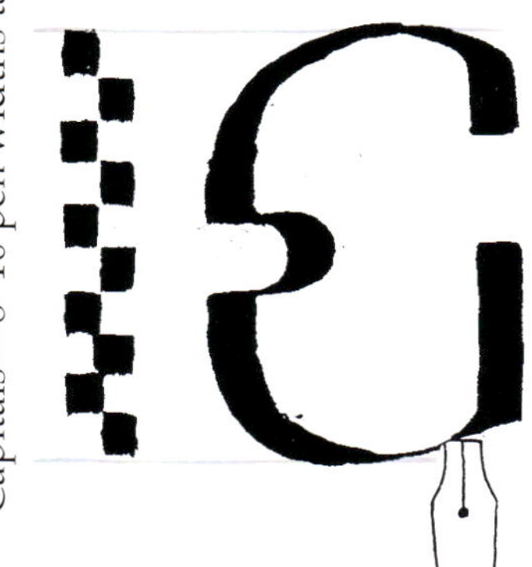

Small
Letters

k is not used in Spanish.

medieval letter **r**

w is not used in Spanish.

z is rare in Spanish.

"Mundo," has forms for **U** and **N** → that are unusual today but were common in the Spanish of 1600.

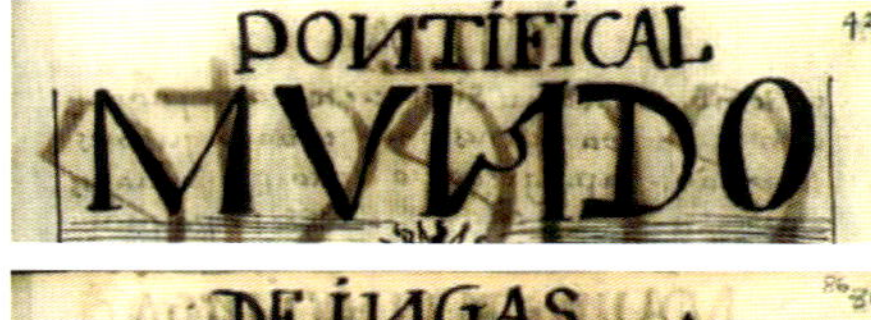

"Manco Capac Inca," is typical of → the complicated, built-up capital variants in the alphabet below.

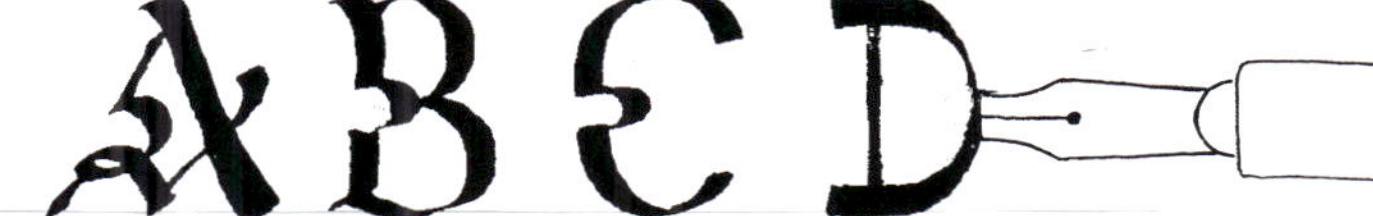

Capital
Letters

↑ A 90° pen angle writes the odd, unique strokes of D.

K is not used in Spanish.

The center of **S** can be one stroke or two.

W is not used in Spanish.

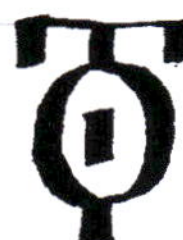

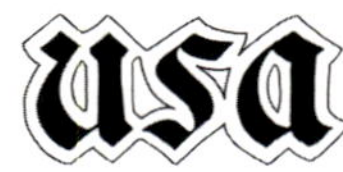

"Our new buildings
(in the . . . Gothic
historical style) . . .
seem to have added
a thousand years
to the history of
Princeton."
~ *Woodrow Wilson,*
then president of
Princeton, 1914

ALTHOUGH THE POINTED ARCHES AND LAVISH ORNAMENT of Gothic calligraphy had once been widespread in medieval England and northern Europe, the letters were reduced to largely ceremonial roles once they landed on America's East Coast. Ordinary people wrote practical scripts. The founding documents may have had handwritten Gothic headings, but they were typeset and printed in Roman to be circulated. Roman symbolized their democratic aspirations. Neoclassical public buildings were eventually carved in Roman capitals. In a nation that prided itself on rejecting old ideas and European influence, Gothic appeared to be reaching the end of its natural life as a script.

The pendulum, however, was just getting ready to swing back. Although they believed in a bright future, many Americans with European roots were nostalgic for the culture of a deeper past, whether real or make-believe. Cheap paper, made from America's abundant forests using a new sulfur process, enabled a surge of publishing that fed the new appetite for romantic novels in old-world settings. Gloomy tales by Nathaniel Hawthorne and Edgar Allan Poe unfolded in the ruins of crumbling abbeys. The Gothic Revival spread through architecture, too, soon buoyed by a wave of post–Civil War prosperity that fostered half a century of downtown construction. Gargoyles, vines, heraldry, and inscriptions covered new churches in Boston, new office buildings in Chicago, and new townhouses in San Francisco. Other parts of the country saw suburban bungalows in "Carpenter Gothic," and state university bell towers in "Cherokee Gothic."

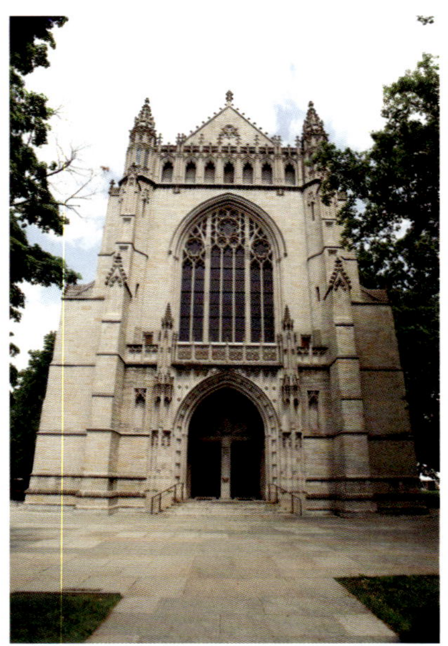

Letter artists felt free to load—and overload—their versions of Gothic Revival with their own fantasies, without ever looking at real medieval manuscripts or buildings. Artists and amateurs wallowed in exuberant color, florid decoration, and bogus heraldry, while legibility and authenticity took a back seat to mood and illusion. They brought fourteenth-century Gothic calligraphy back to life and pressed it into service for nineteenth-century enterprises such as Christmas cards, diplomas, advertising, and hobbies.

"Collegiate Gothic" buildings still
dominate university campuses today.
Princeton University Chapel, built 1928.

By the 1850s, American calligraphers were copying copies of Gothic letters without understanding them. Sometimes they went further astray by simply outlining the text letters with a thin pen and filling them in, thus losing all connection to the natural strokes of the broad-edged pen. They inevitably added their own odd quirks, which other calligraphers faithfully copied.

American calligraphers were careless with Gothic letter basics: the equal width of white spaces and black ink strokes; the sharp corners; and the absence of thin strokes. Once the letters had sprawled, the square stroke was replaced by two longer, very un-medieval strokes (circled below). This alphabet's basic flaws make it a bad model for learning today's Gothic, but a good illustration of what to avoid.

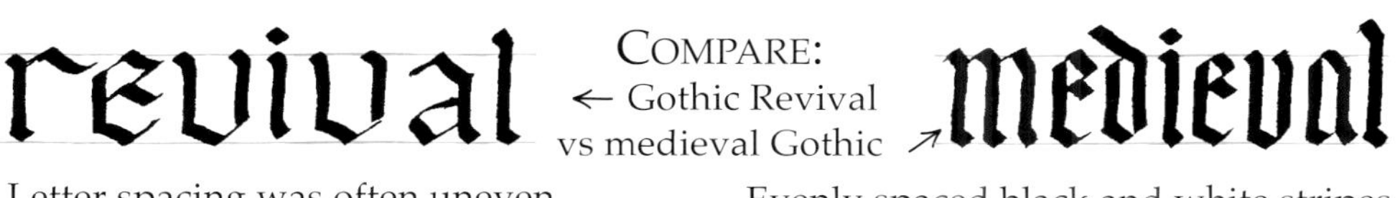

Letter spacing was often uneven.
Evenly spaced black and white stripes.

Gothic Revival basic strokes

Medieval Gothic basic strokes

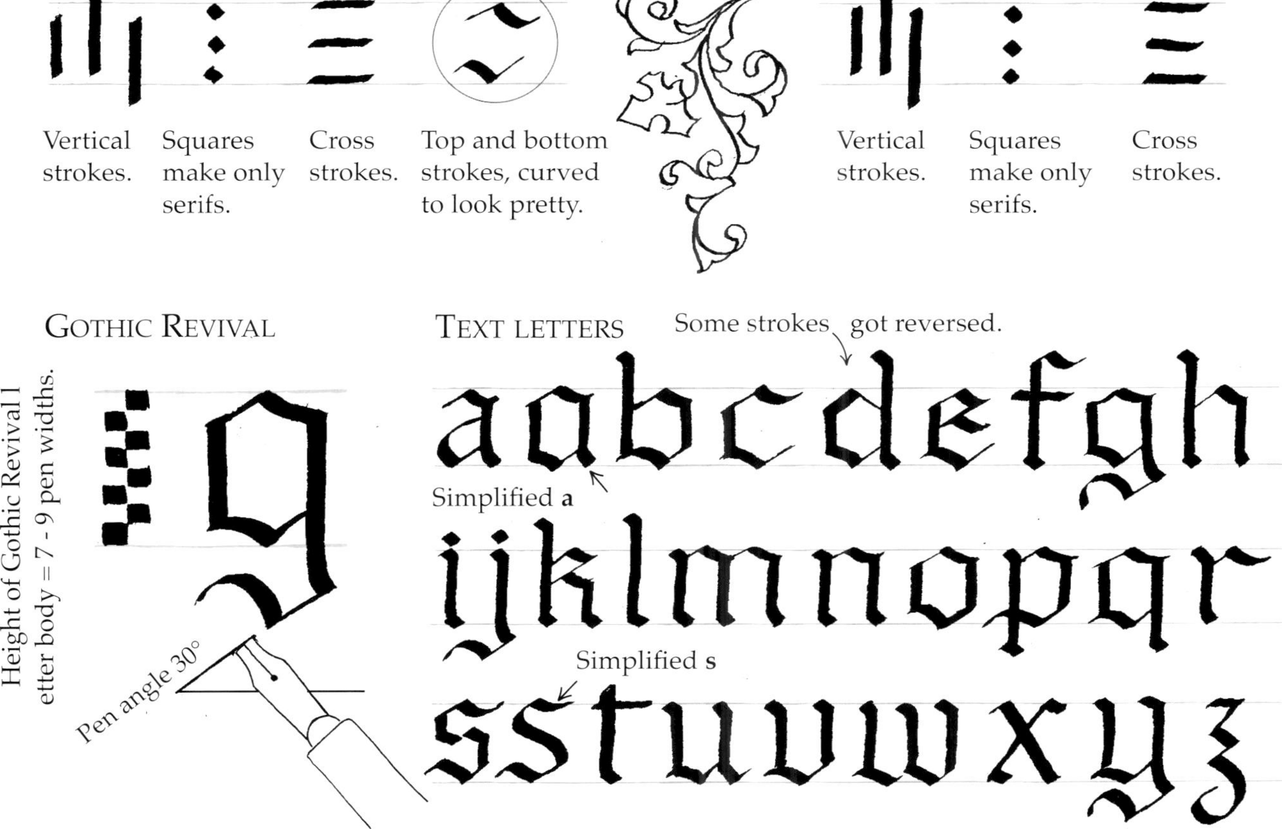

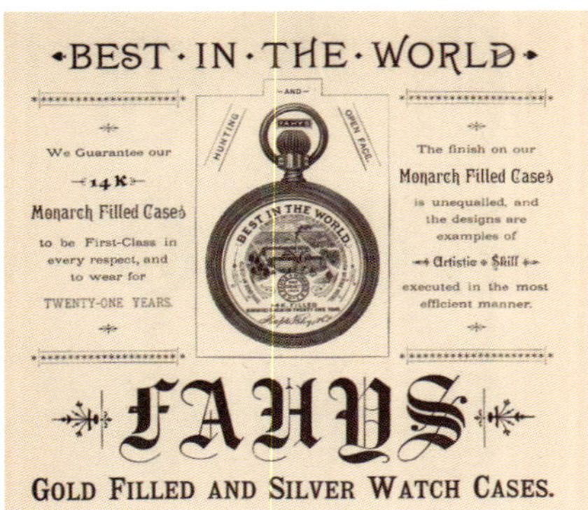

An advertisement from the 1890s displays the business name, Fahys, in nearly unreadable pen capitals.

PEN CAPITALS HARMONIZE WITH TEXT LETTERS because they are written with the same broad-edged pen, at the same scale, using the same pen angle. Just because pen capitals sort themselves into letter families based on some similar strokes and shapes, it is tempting to treat them like a type font. But pen capitals are divas rather than team players, and they hate to share the stage with each other. They like to be the one big letter that leads a word or sentence of small letters. Unlike drawn capitals (page 17) they should not be used to spell out whole words. and medieval scribes wisely never used them this way. Gothic Revival calligraphers, however, just couldn't resist.

3 MAIN BODY SHAPES:

Most letters are built from left to right, as well as from inside to outside.

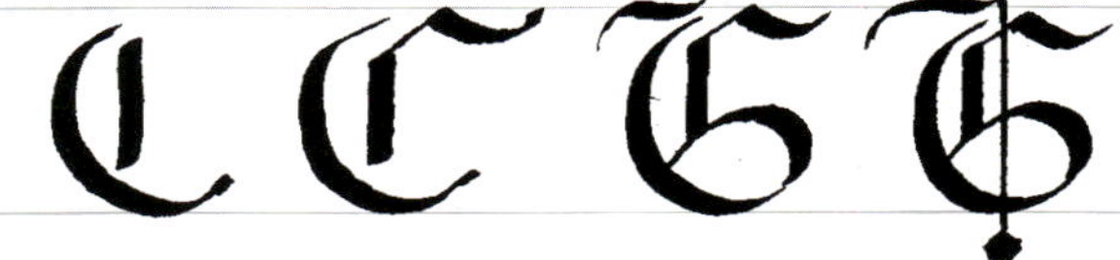

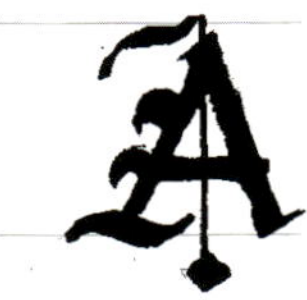

B D F H I J K M N P R V and sometimes **E W Y** are straight on their left.

C G O Q U and sometimes **E T W Y** are curved on their left.

A S X Z are diagonal.

Typical capital, with stroke order. Extra strokes can be omitted on smaller letters.

Letter height = 6–8 pen widths.

45° pen angle

Thin strokes require using the corner of the pen or a different pen angle.

PEN CAPITALS

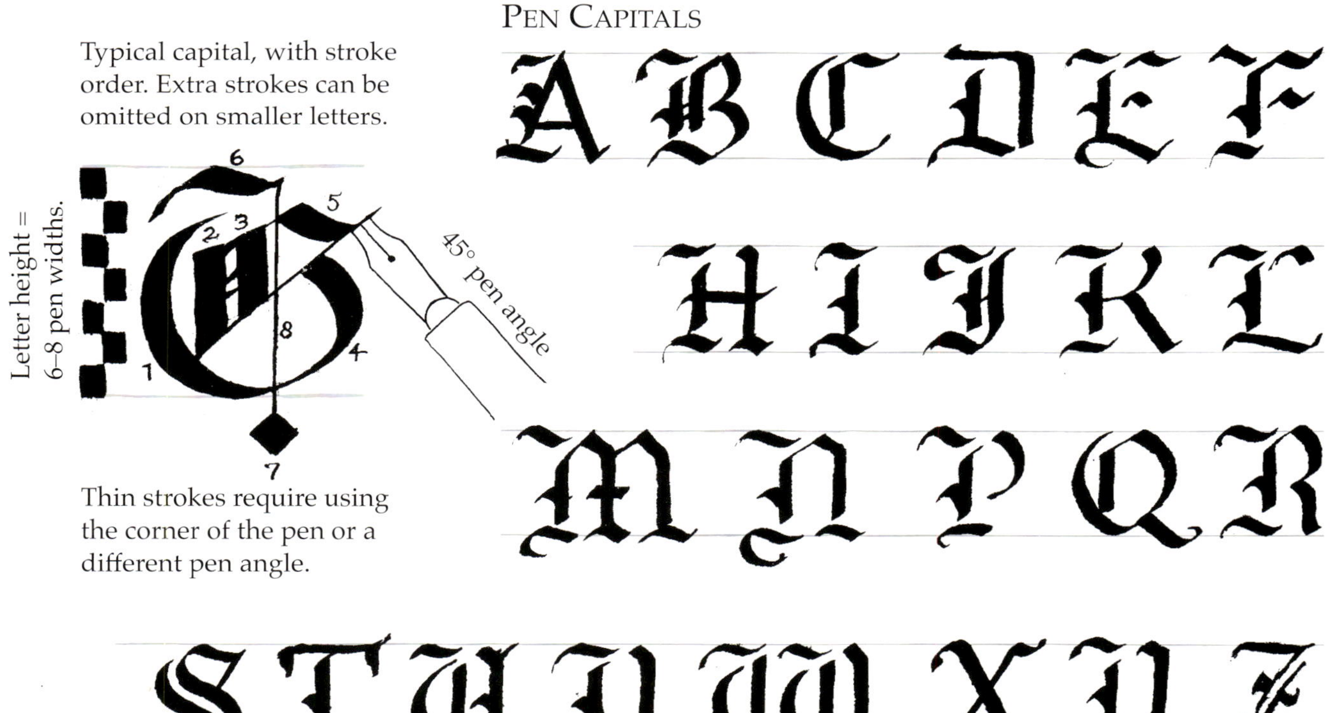

DRAWN CAPITALS, WHICH ARE OUTLINED with a thin pen and filled in with color, are in some ways easier to design with than pen capitals. Like a versatile performer, they can be a prima donna in the spotlight, but they don't mind singing in the chorus. Gothic Revival scribes adored them.

The curves of drawn capitals can be a welcome relief from all the stiff strokes and sharp corners of Gothic. The letters can be enlarged or reduced, widened or narrowed, dashed off or labored over, and filled in with any pattern or color—and they will still combine readily with other letters.

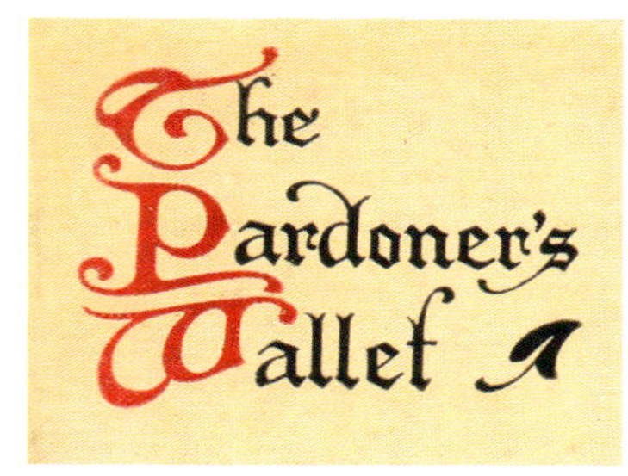

The drawn capitals of this 1905 book cover stretch themselves into shapes influenced by Art Nouveau.

STEPS IN CONSTRUCTING A DRAWN CAPITAL

Built from inside to outside, and left to right.

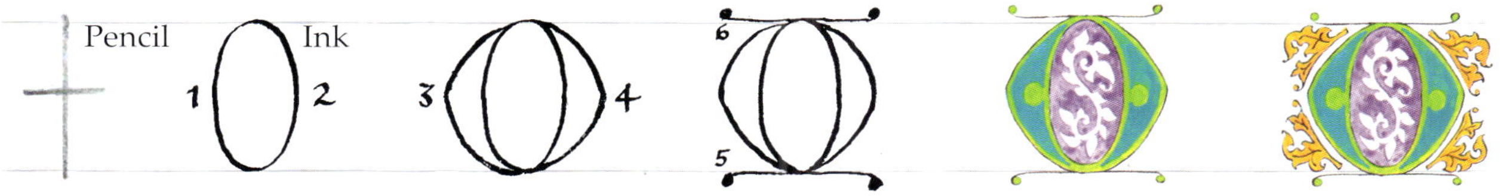

Pencil   Ink

Axes of symmetry — Inner space is an oval. — Inner space is an oval. — Outer curves are slightly pointed. — Pictures and patterns were rendered in colors from 1880, not 1380.

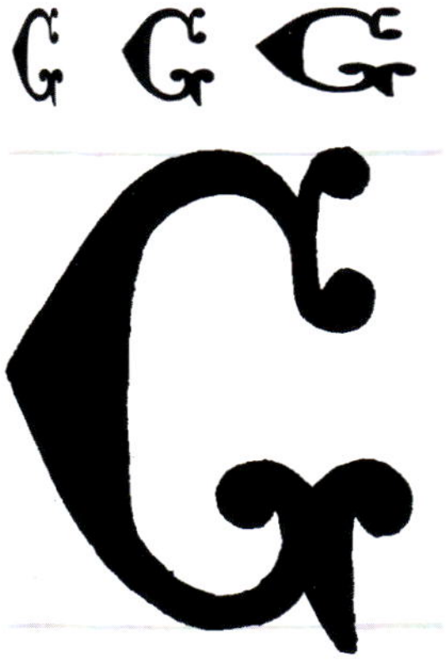

DRAWN CAPITALS

Thin lines can end in small circles.

Letter width can vary: narrow, square, or wide

This line helps tell **H** from **N**.

Horizontals widen the narrow letter **I**.

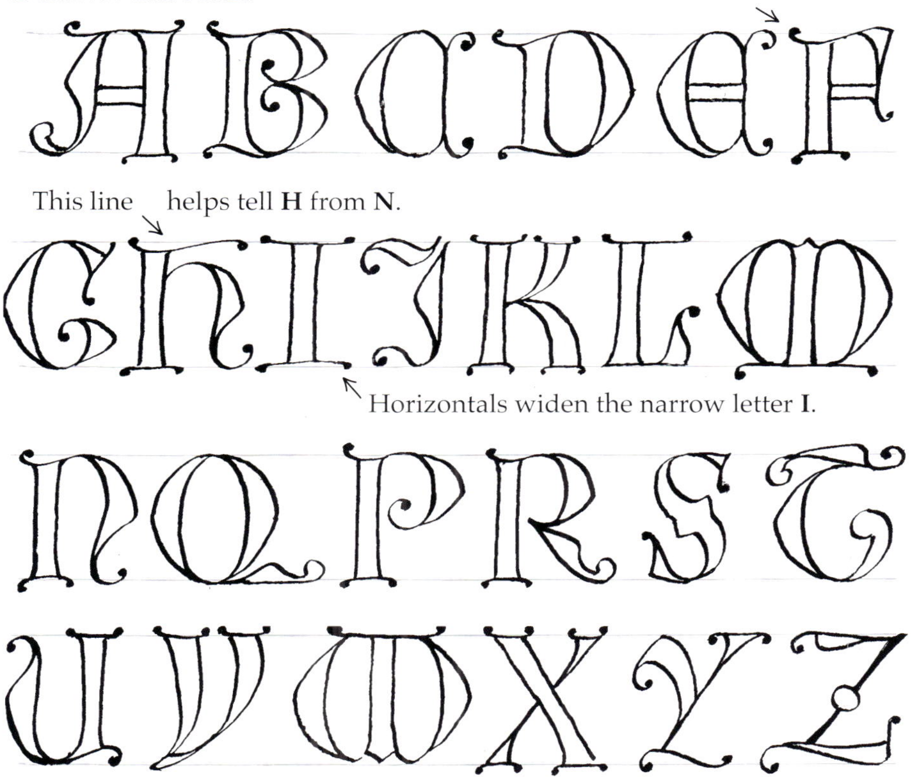

These letters are similar: **M W; C D E; O Q;** and **H N U.**

GOTHIC REVIVAL ON THE PAGE

MUCH OF THE DISTINCTIVE CHARM OF GOTHIC REVIVAL came from the unique ways that American calligraphers put it to use. It reached new audiences through advertising, permeated Christmas, covered buildings, saturated academic life, and created a rewarding hobby for a generation of amateurs. Newly improved printing technologies such as steel engraving and photo-offset helped Gothic reach more people, in more places, with ever more complicated letters.

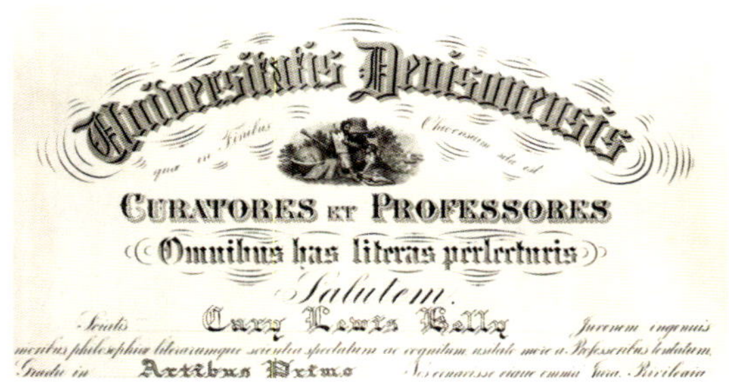

These 1899 letters follow along an arch, a Gothic Revival innovation that was a favorite with diploma designers, and still is.

INNOVATIVE CALLIGRAPHERS re-arranged Gothic letters into layouts unknown in the Middle Ages: curved lines; paragraphs with ragged-right margins; or words scattered around the page rather than tightly packed in a block of text.

ADVERTISING let calligraphers join a brand-new American industry. To sell things in a competitive marketplace, simple readability was no longer enough; calligraphers had to catch the customer's eye among a crowd of competing words and images. Always looking for new ways to grab attention, they made elaborately engraved copies of Gothic letters, added even more decoration, then arranged them into unusual layouts—what one jeweler hyped as "new novelties."

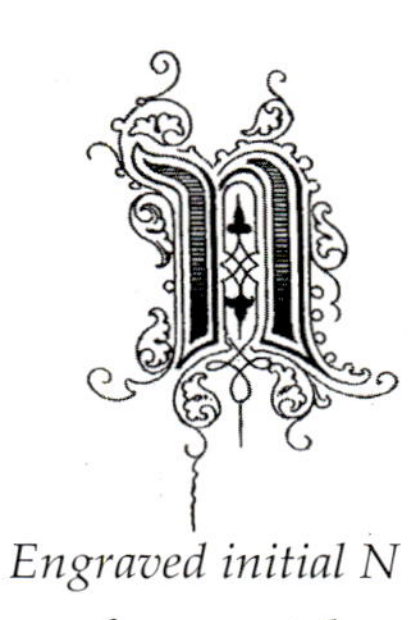

Engraved initial N from a catalog.

ELABORATE IDENTITY MARKS gave calligraphers the chance to design monograms for engravers, who routinely helped their clients choose from catalogs of ornate capitals in all 325 possible letter pairs (plus quite a few three-letter combinations) for interlaced monograms on jewelry, medals, pocket watches, and household silver.

CHRISTMAS AND GOTHIC REVIVAL CALLIGRAPHY were linked together in the late nineteenth century. Puritans had disapproved of celebrating Christmas, condemning it as a pagan holiday; but tastes changed. Greeting cards, adapted from Europe, included images of medieval castles, saints, cherubs, plants, snowy landscapes, Father Christmas, and, usually, Gothic lettering. The first printed American Christmas card was designed by German refugee Louis Prang in Boston in 1874. He established an annual competition and published the winning designs, many of them by women artists. Today the United States Postal Service estimates that it delivers some two billion Christmas cards each year—many of them printed with the still-customary Gothic letters.

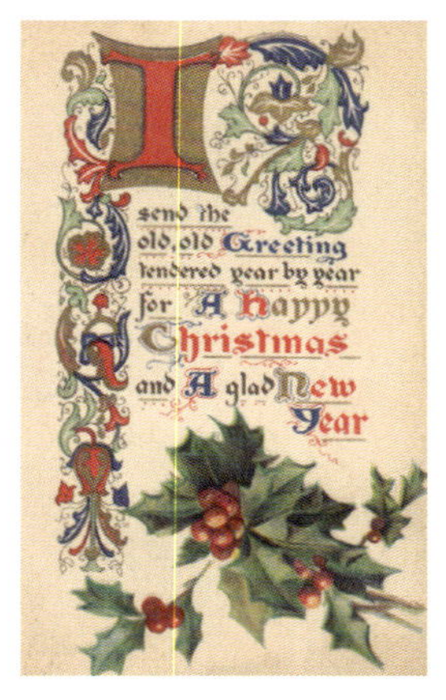

Typical Christmas card.

SPECIAL TECHNIQUES made an intricate style even more intricate. Using double-pointed "scroll" pens to write outlined letters, scribes and engravers found dozens of ways to fill them with pattern and contrasting colors; drop shadows or extra outlines added a 3D effect.

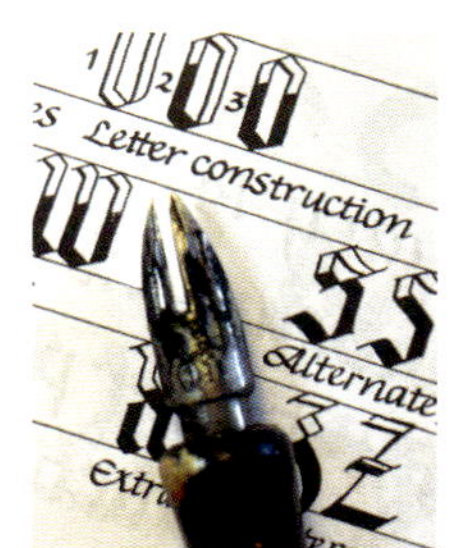

A metal split pen

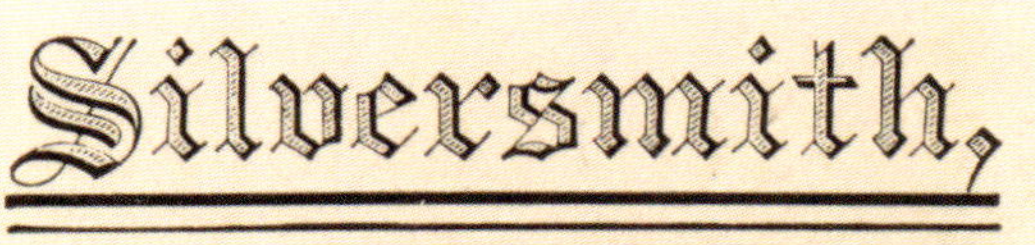

These split-pen letters from the 1890s are filled with tiny hatch lines.

ARCHITECTURE welcomed the Gothic Revival. And even though most medieval Gothic buildings did not in fact include inscriptions, five hundred years later no American Revival church was complete without one or two— or many.

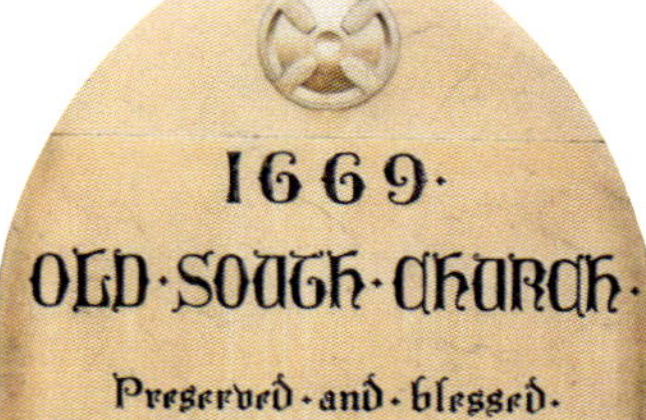

A panel of Gothic from the 1890s, in Boston's Old South Church, offers graceful Versal capitals.

AMATEURS embraced the idea of making books by hand. In the classic *Little Women*, set during the Civil War era (1861–1865), Louisa May Alcott describes artistic Amy's handmade contribution to a crafts fair:

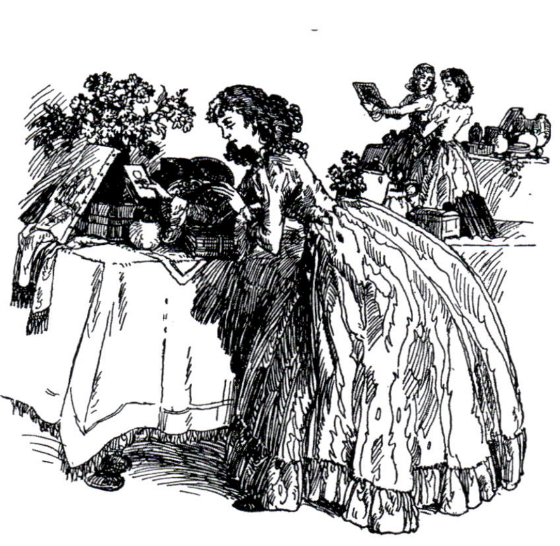

"[. . .H]er pet production—a little book, the antique cover of which her father had found among his treasures, and in which, on leaves of vellum, she had beautifully illuminated different texts. . . . Framed in brilliant scrollwork of scarlet, blue, and gold, with little spirits of good will helping one another up and down among the thorns and flowers, were the words; 'Thou shalt love thy neighbor as thyself.'"

—*From* Little Women,
illustration by Louis Jamber, 1947.

The small **e** *and* **r** *have such similar forms that they are often hard to read.*

IN THE HANDS OF BOTH HOBBYISTS AND PROFESSIONALS, Gothic Revival dominated American calligraphy until the end of World War I. Then American life changed again, expanding to include a larger population from a wider world, ready to invent their own new interpretations of Gothic.

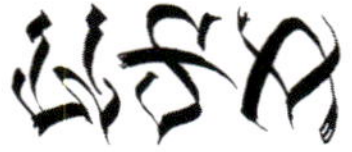

"I believe that any drawn line that speaks about identity, dignity and unity . . . that line is art."
~ *Chaz Bojórquez*

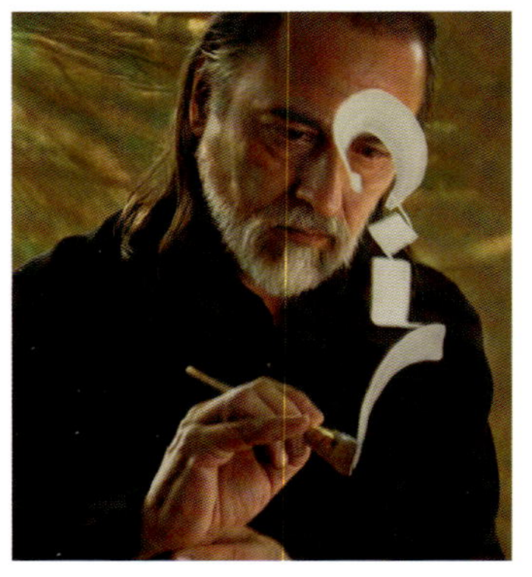

Chaz Bojórquez, a prolific letter artist known as the godfather of cholo, has likened its earliest inscriptions to a "pledge of allegiance."

WHILE GOTHIC HAD TO WAIT for its own nineteenth-century revival on America's East Coast, it was already part of visual culture on the West Coast, where it lived on in churches, graveyards, and official documents. Just before World War II, young Latino men in Los Angeles began writing slogans on walls in letters evocative of Spanish Gothic style, declaring loyalty to the local gangs that distinguished them from the Anglo population. They were labeled "cholos," a term first used in 1616 in race-conscious Peru as a slur that meant "mutt" or "mestizo." The young men, however, and a few young women, transformed it into a badge of Latino pride.

Over the decades, cholo artists have reached beyond graffiti to create distinctive book designs, clothing styles, car decorations, fine art, music, and tattoos. Today's artists have broadened the style while also deepening its Spanish, Latin American, and Indigenous cultural roots. Recently it has absorbed the meditative influence of Asian brush calligraphy and has thereby energized street writing in Japan.

Most cholo letters share these characteristics:
- The writer controls the thicks and thins by changing the position of a flat brush, pen, or marker. The pen angle is mainly a reverse 45°. ≥
- Letters are built up of a few basic strokes.
- Some serifs are as long as strokes, and some strokes are as long as swashes. Accents often lengthen into ornaments.
- Spanish and English words are mixed and punctuated with Spanish inverted exclamation points (¡Hola!) and question marks (¿Que?).
- An austere color scheme of black and gray is often accented with a few touches of red.
- Tight spacing between letters and lines keeps the texture dense.
- Even the most daring cholo letter artists tend to arrange their words horizontally in an austere layout more like a rectangular document than a freeform wall mural.

Cholo graffiti also serves a different cultural purpose from its jaunty, colorful, extroverted Anglo cousin on the East Coast—less a unique expression of individuality and more a serious affirmation of group identity. Instead of declaring, "This is who *I am*," cholo graffiti says, "This is who *we are*."

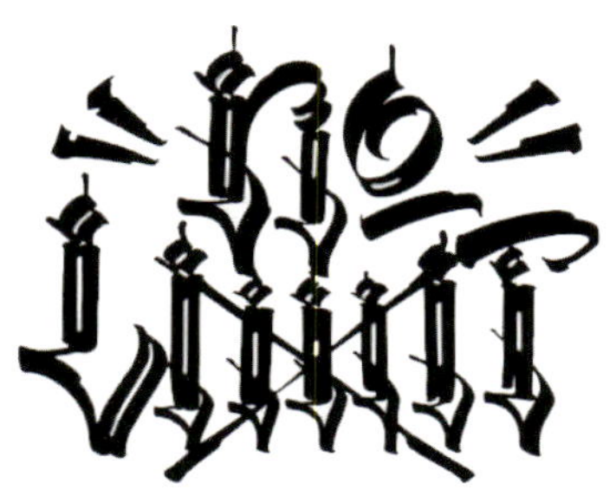

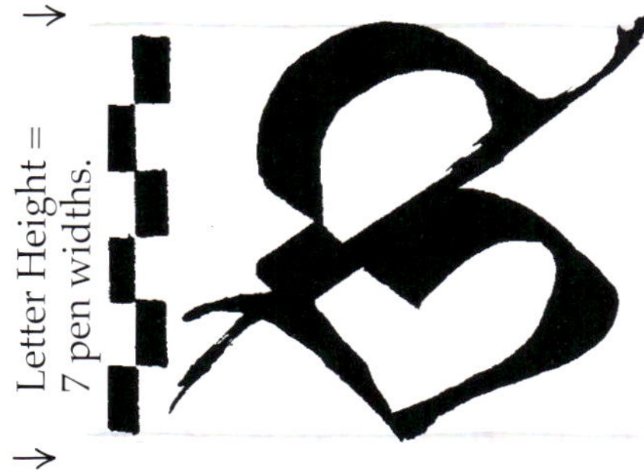

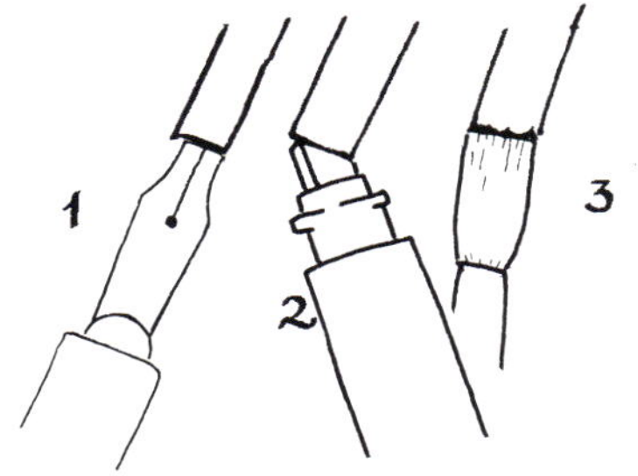

BASIC STROKES

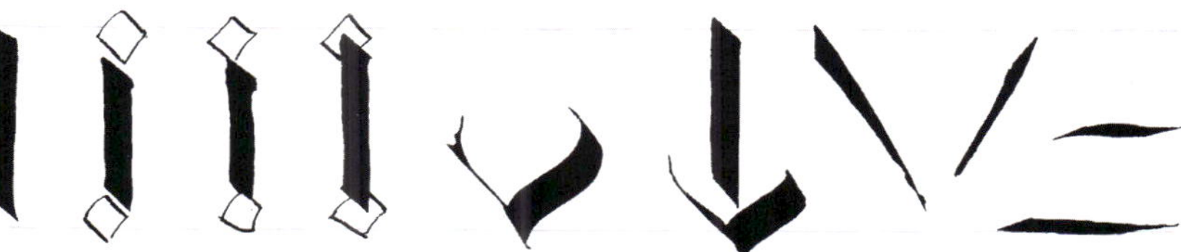

↗ A square serif can hover, touch, or overlap at either end of a stroke.

↑**V** serifs can finish some verticals.

Dragging one corner of the nib helps to make thin lines.

LETTER CONSTRUCTION

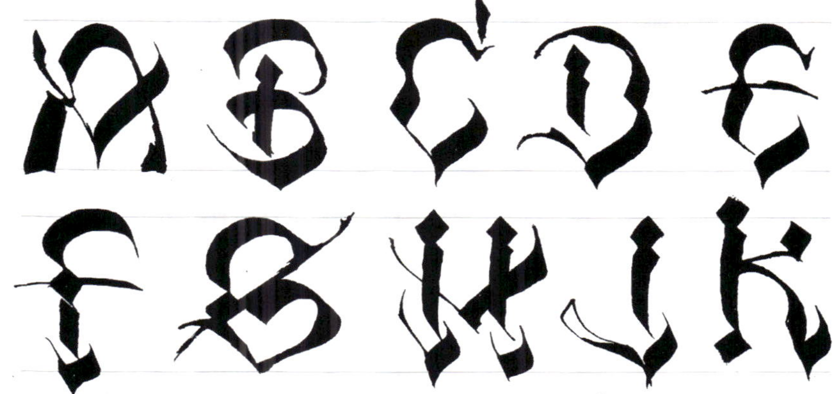

Lengthening this stroke ↑turns **I** into **J**.

HOW TO REVERSE THE 45° PEN ANGLE TO -45°

1. Right-handers can reverse their usual 45° pen angle by 90° with a slanted, wedge-tip marker on its long edge or its shorter flat end.

2. Most left-handers can use a square-cut pen, brush, or marker held in their usual hand position.

3. Either hand can hold a brush or marker upright on the writing surface. This allows changing the pen angle all through the stroke.

4. The paper can rotate without changing the pen position.

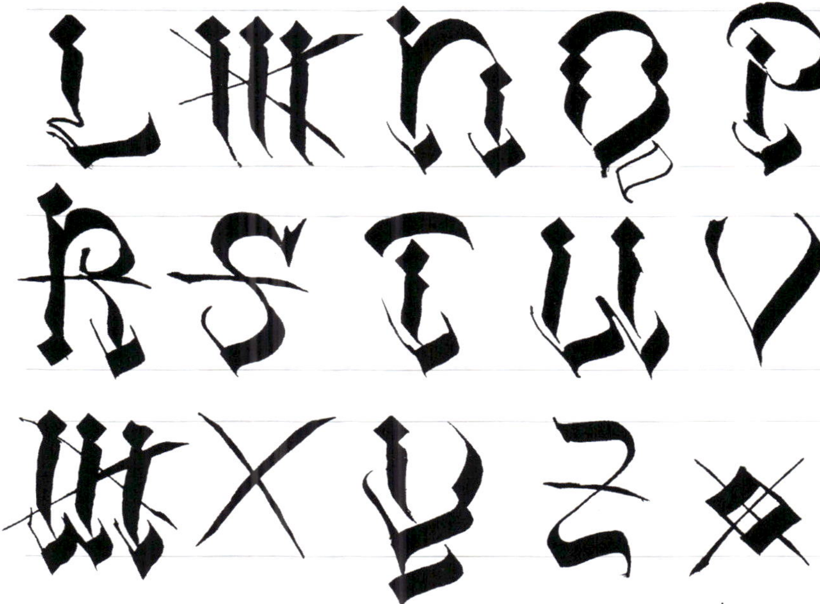

ACCENTS

CHOLO INCLUSIVENESS

This detail from a wall-size Bojorquez installation affirms that although cholo was originally Latino, today it is a blend of styles, with appeal for many artists.

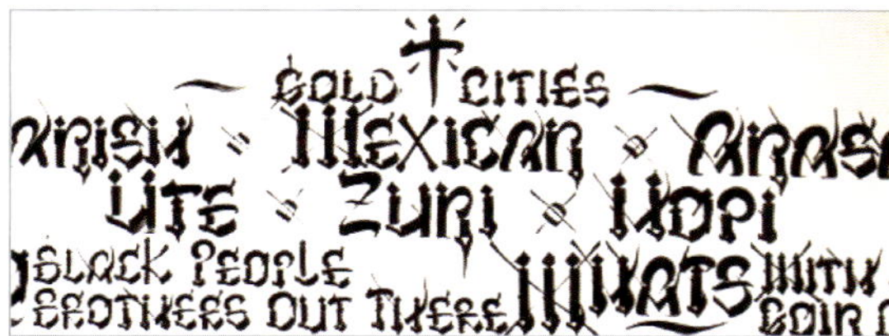

STYLE MOVES IN MYSTERIOUS WAYS. Eight hundred years after its heyday in the Middle Ages, and one hundred years after its first American revival, Gothic calligraphy came back to life, like a zombie, in a strange new incarnation called "Goth." Starting as a fringe movement in mid-century British music and clothing, Goth was promptly embraced in the United States as a symbol of ironic alienation. Like many other styles through the ages, it made a U-turn from the trends that came before it. Although Gothic calligraphy was shunned during World War II for its toxic Nazi associations, it was revived again, with an edgy, in-your-face version that appealed to a postwar generation of young people who did not mind being seen as the barbarians at the gates.

Goths adopted the barbed silhouette of traditional Gothic letters for their elaborate logos, clothing, music, band emblems, graffiti, and tattoos. Even the gloomy color schemes of Goth contrasted strongly with the sparkly, happy rainbow hues of disco and pop. The same love of irrational excess that had inspired Gothic Revival a century before also prompted late-twentieth-century Goths to push their designs to the extreme. They gave their digital fonts extreme names too, such as "Creepsville," "Fearless Vampire," and "Misfits." Although both cholo and Goth styles share a gloomy color scheme and a fascination with skulls, Goth also carries a disagreeable undertone of white nationalism from northern Europe.

Goth letter artists, particularly tattooists, borrowed heavily at first from Gothic Revival designs by making exact copies of pen capitals and text letters. As time went by, however, they tapped into wider trends, especially the late-twentieth-century fondness for vampires, zombies, witchcraft, occult magic, and the supernatural.

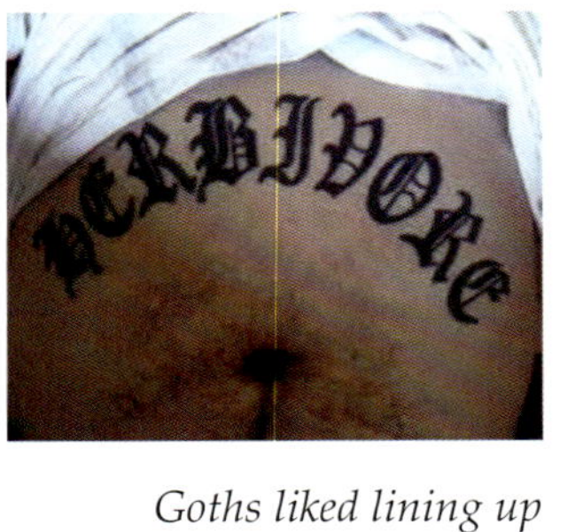

Goths liked lining up pen capitals to spell out whole words.

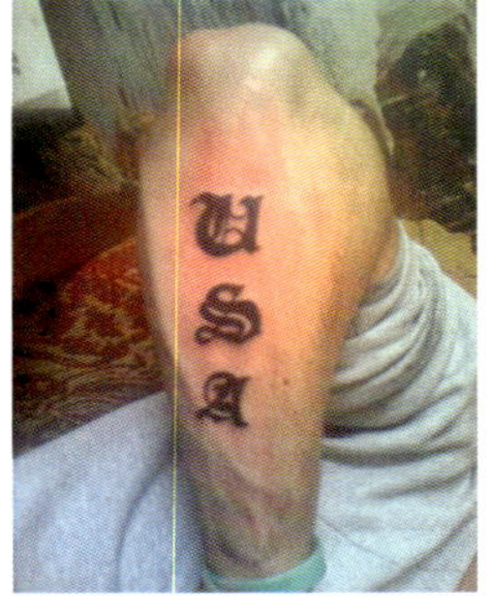

A few letter artists ventured to stack the capitals vertically, too.

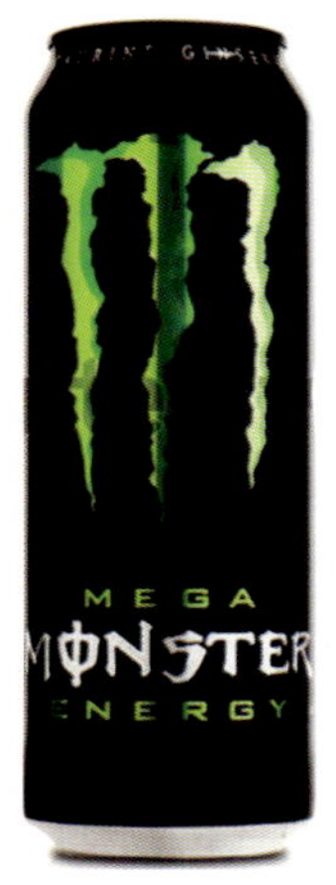

The logo for one of America's most popular energy drinks suggests the claw marks, or the claws, of a monster.

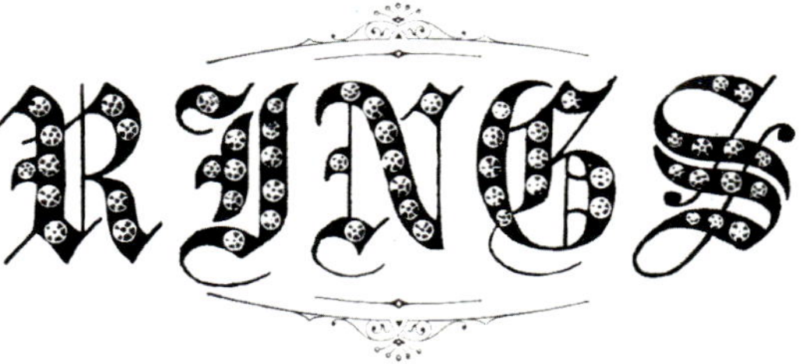

Spelling whole words with all-capitals has been popular throughout the revival of Gothic, as shown in a 1888 advertisement for RINGS.

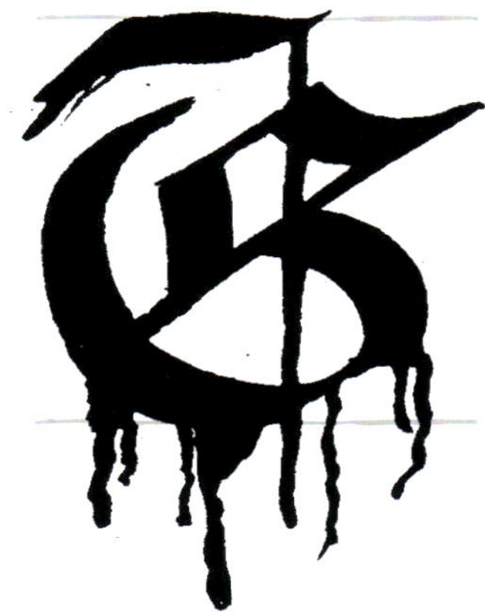

GOTH LETTER CONSTRUCTION

Transforming standard Gothic into ghoulish Goth is easy. Half the letters have open bottoms or descending strokes that can can be lengthened unevenly to suggest trailing cobwebs, jagged gashes, or rags in the wind. The other thirteen letters stay unchanged, providing context that helps the reader decode the exaggerated letters.

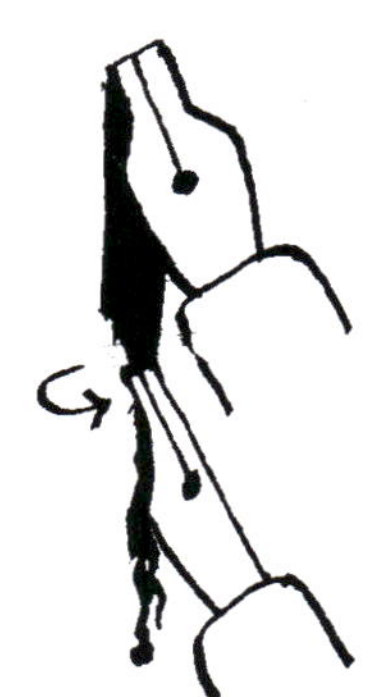

The pen uses one corner to pull a thin ink line down.

BASIC STROKES

Tilting the pen onto its corner will let ragged strokes meander down to different depths. A marker or Parallel pen makes this easier.

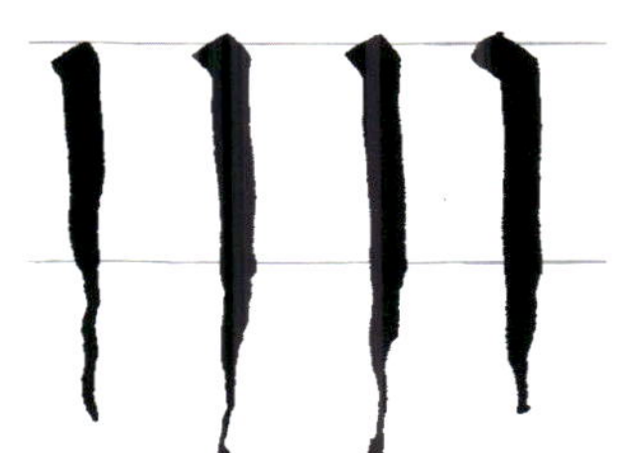

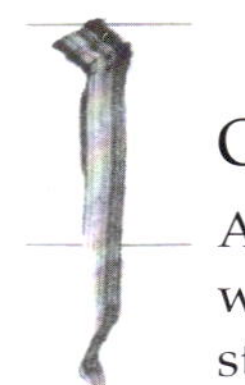

OPTIONAL:
A dry marker writes a ghostly stroke..

LENGTHEN THESE LETTERS:

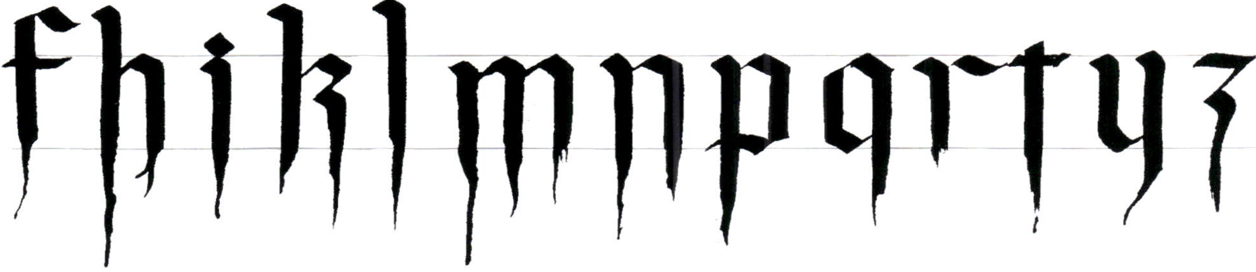

LEAVE THESE LETTERS UNCHANGED:

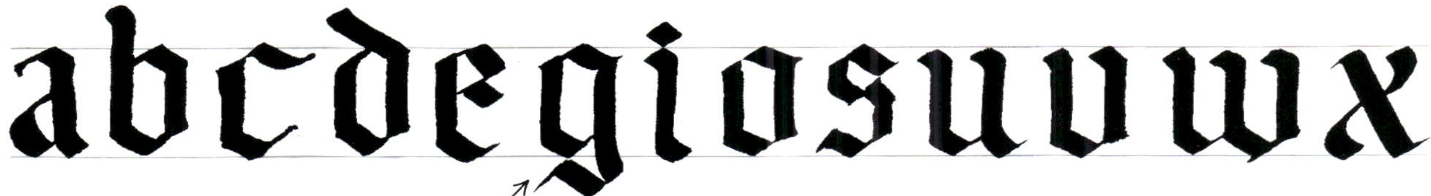

If lengthening **g**'s descender makes it look like **q**, better to leave it as is.

COLOR CHOICES CAN REINFORCE GOTH'S INNATE CREEPINESS:

Purple, gray, or the nasty red of dried blood. Any color on black, especially acid green.

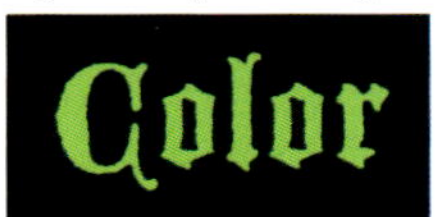

ART REVOLUTIONS SELDOM INCLUDE EVERYONE. There is usually a backlash for every bright idea—a *yin* for every *yang*. The same generation that resurrected the Gothic alphabet as "Goth" by deepening its gloom, alienation, and barbarity, also found a completely different way to revive it as "Ye Olde Gothicke" by focusing on its sunlit cheeriness, family fun, and good-natured improvisation. Since its founding in Berkeley, California, in the 1960s, the Society for Creative Anachronism (SCA) has dedicated itself to re-creating European customs and traditional crafts from before the Industrial Revolution. It is part of a broader cultural movement that recaptures the American past through living history locations and historical reenactments.

The Society and its many Renaissance Faires promote a late-twentieth-century version of medieval calligraphy that accentuates the positive. Their events began by reviving period dress and cuisine, without always bothering to pin down exactly *which* historical period. Unlike the Gothic Revival taste for romantic dramas in sinister ruins, the Cholo push for Latino identity in an Anglo nation, or the Goth pose of ornery opposition to social norms, this movement centered on everyday activities from the workshops, festival grounds, and village squares of the past. *The New York Times* called them "Woodstock with wimples." Participants in these fairs sought to retrofit America with an upbeat, invented past.

These freeform, inclusive gatherings, now reexported back to England and the rest of Europe, include a mix of medieval and Renaissance food, costume, heraldry, dance, drama, knightly tournaments, and, of course, calligraphy. Just as American scholars came to dominate the field of medieval studies in England, American reenactors came to define the popular view of the Anglo-Saxon part of America's past. Members like to call it "the Middle Ages as they ought to have been."

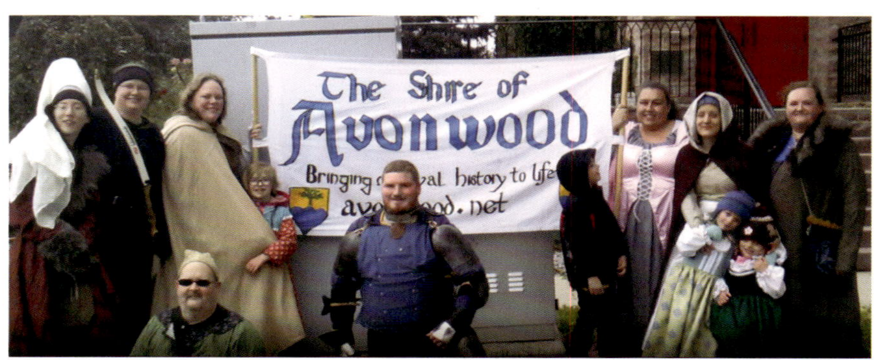

WHILE YE OLDE GOTHICKE CALLIGRAPHY has not yet produced a new direction in letter design, it has focused new attention on many issues of authenticity. It has drawn attention to the very American question about how much historical insight an amateur group can offer alongside the companionship and entertainment. Calligraphers who enjoy re-creating the Gothic era will benefit from considering the list offered here.

26 YE OLDE DOS AND DON'TS

A. When you demonstrate traditional calligraphy, show a few **authentic materials** too, to help your viewers picture the past.

B. Real medieval Gothic letters conform to one basic **body shape**, and most can be made from two main strokes. (See *Learn Calligraphy* by Margaret Shepherd.) Gothic Revival letters of 150 years ago are not the best models to copy.

C. You can **update** the most archaic text letters: **a d e j k u v x z.**

D. Rounding off the hexagonal letters' **sharp corners** will help new readers who may have never read Gothic before.

E. Do not use **pen capitals** to capitalize whole words. Drawn capitals cooperate with each other much better (see page 17).

F. Don't randomly misspell words or exaggerate courtly speech. Read up about **early spelling**.

G. Bear in mind that the letters that you write while you demonstrate to a **live audience** will not be nearly as good as the letters you write in your own studio where you have all the right materials, a comfortable desk, and no interruptions. Live demonstration is good, but if you prepare some accurate calligraphy handouts for your audience to take with them, you will spread good models.

H. **Parchment** and vellum were expensive; that's why Gothic scribes packed as many letters as they could into every page. Scraps may still be affordable to try out.

I. You can buy Pergamenta paper or print out **parchment backgrounds**. Avoid harsh yellowed shades.

J. **Paper** did not reach Europe until around 1300, and did not really catch on until the invention of moveable type in 1454. If you want Renaissance texture for your hand-lettered pages, use laid paper (above) rather than wove paper, which was available only after the 1780s.

K. If you want to make ordinary white paper look **old**, you can apply a wash of very diluted brown paint or ink, but not coffee or tea, which will eventually weaken the paper.

L. Don't go too far in **imitating age**, because Gothic scribes did all they could to prevent it. Don't burn the edges (a weird modern notion about aging) or crumple the paper. Instead, suggest the passage of time with the slight darkening that happens along a page's edge and corners, where readers' fingers have worn out and stained it.

M. Brown sepia ink, made from squid ink, did not come into use until paper was common c. 1500. Medieval scribes wrote with the blackest, densest ink they could make. Don't start with faded or brown tones. **Modern versions** of traditional handmade ink include India ink, sumi ink, walnut ink, and acrylic ink.

N. Demonstrating calligraphy with a metal or quill dip pen and a pot of ink can be a precarious activity if **children** participate. It is much better to offer them wide markers.

O. Medieval scribes wrote with quill pens made from the flight feathers of a large waterbird such as a swan or goose. (A **crow quill** is too small and flexible for Gothic letters.) Stripping off its picturesque fluffy fibers makes it easier to hold. Baking the quill in sand at low heat makes it flexible. Cut the tip square with a sharp penknife or X-Acto knife.

P. Metal **dip pens** from the nineteenth and twentieth century can approximate medieval quills. Broad-edged **fountain pens** or **markers** can also make authentic letterforms, though their ink is thinner and paler than India ink.

Q. Scribes have always had to squint. **Lenses** were first mentioned around 1290 but were not designed to be wearable until the 1720s. Glass bottles of water could magnify letters.

R. Interruptions, the main cause of errors, were reduced by the medieval scriptorium's rule of silence—still a useful idea today.

S. Two medieval techniques used **real gold**: either powdered gold paint in a suspension of egg white (glair), or a layer of gold leaf laid on a base of tacky gesso and then burnished to a smooth shine.

T. Today, **imitation gold** paints and inks are made from fine yellow metallic powders suspended in a medium such as gum arabic, glycerin, or acrylic.

U. Titles and **heraldry** don't have to be vague or whimsical; simple rules and specific Latin terminology govern this craft. Follow the color protocols, too, with basic hues of red, blue, and green interspersed with gold.

V. Medieval illuminators did not use **silver** (argent) on the manuscript page, because it not only tarnished easily but could spoil any pigments next to it. Synthetic silvery foil or aluminum paint are used today.

W. Keep your **illumination** simple. A decorative border can take ten times as much work as a decorated capital letter. Medieval scribes were skilled in copying long texts, but they usually left capitals and borders, as well as gilding and binding, to a team of other craftsmen.

X. The original Gothic letters were intended for **serious words** such as Biblical scripture, sacred music, or the start of a legal document. Guard against a frivolous modern use.

Y. Don't disparage the anachronisms of other calligraphers; **learn something** from them.

Z. Enjoy! Whether you are a beginner or an expert, just writing the letters by hand takes you on a trip into the **past**.

EVERY REVIVAL OF GOTHIC adds a new chapter to America's history, revealing how the country sees itself at that moment, where it wants to go, and what it would like to take with it from the past. The Gothic alphabet in its many versions lets people decide how medieval they want to be.

CORÓNICA   REVIVAL   *Broad-edge quill pen, metal dip pen, marker, fountain pen, flat brush, or Pilot Parallel pen.*

{ SMALL LETTERS

{ SMALL LETTERS

{ SMALL LETTERS

{ SMALL LETTERS

CORÓNICA   REVIVAL PEN CAPITALS   CHOLO CAPITALS   GOTH CAPITALS   *Broad-edge quill pen, metal dip pen, marker, fountain pen, flat brush, or Pilot Parallel pen.*   REVIVAL DRAWN CAPITALS   *Thin pen outline*

{ CAPITALS

{ CAPITALS

{ CAPITALS

GRAFFITI

AS OLD AS THE ART OF WRITING itself—maybe older—graffiti comes from people's basic need to tell the world who they are. Bravado urges them to write; innovation drives them to find a style they like; and their inner critic nudges them to try a slightly improved version. By repeating their favorite word, usually their chosen alias, they gradually shape it into art.

Good manners, however, used to say that "Fools' names and fools' faces are often seen in public places." Until recently, graffiti writers were seen as vandals rather than artists.

Graffiti started to influence American art and fashion in the early 1970s, following two decades of suburban prosperity that contrasted with urban decay. Graffiti created a visual language for small groups in the city, letting them feel heard, share their ideas, and bear witness to the lives they lived. The movement started in Philadelphia, showed up in the South Bronx, and then quickly spread to the blank walls of other cities, where graffiti artists wrote with markers and aerosol spray paint, both recent American inventions.

Elaborate letter art blossomed on subway cars and tunnels, where population density guaranteed a captive audience of thousands, public transit offered quick escape, anonymity was a fact of life, and law enforcement could not keep up. A dozen unwritten rules evolved to keep order among the writers, who already shared a community of hip-hop music, dance, and fashions.

Even while groups organized to scrub graffiti off their neighborhoods, critics found much to analyze and admire. Type designers embraced it. Sociologists focused at first on its bad effects, but gradually woke up to see its benefits. Calligraphers today who make the effort to look at graffiti with an open mind will discover that they, too, can learn a lot.

"The graffiti movement has become a greater thing than the Renaissance."
~Lady Pink

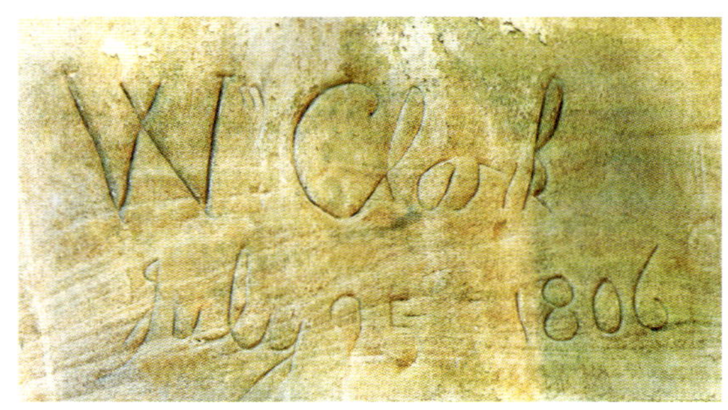

← *Decades before the internet, "Kilroy was here" went viral during World War II.*

↑ *This inscribed signature is the only physical evidence that remains from the eight-thousand-mile journey of the Lewis and Clark Expedition.*

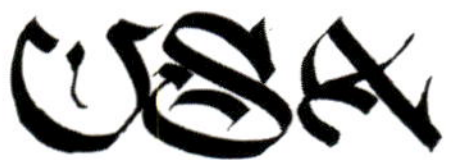

This chapter covers three main categories of graffiti letters: thick and thin; variable monoline; outlined. A few of these are written with the same marker pens that calligraphers use, but most rely on new writing tools.

WRITING LARGE LETTERS WITH A FLAT MARKER can help calligraphers reach back two thousand years to the roots of the traditional styles they may have learned as beginners, and scrawl short messages on walls the way the Romans did.

Easy-to-use wedge markers for thick and thin graffiti offer two line widths in one, just by rotating the pen 90°. For a wider line than 3" (7.5 cm) and letters taller than 15" (40 cm), graffiti artists use a bucket of paint and a flat brush. Just like the Romans.

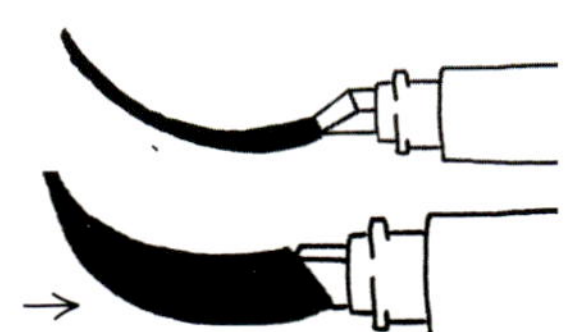

The same wedge marker, rotated. →

Graffiti is unlike any other letter art; it gives visibility to voices that have no other forum, off the page, in letters that readers may not like but can not ignore. While the US Constitution protects it as freedom of speech, the American Civil Liberties Union recognizes that "American society has always been deeply ambivalent about this question." Local laws, however, are often much stricter. The drips and extensions of the calligraphy itself reflect writers working at night, dodging the authorities, and often moving on in a hurry.

Along with what graffiti says and how it looks, where it appears is also important. Its writers take pride in finding public venues that are unexpected, ironic, and subversive.

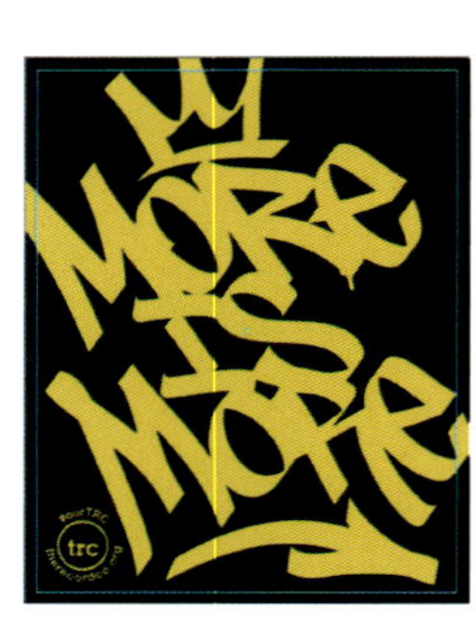

← The Record Company's motto emphasizes its commitment to abundance. The letters have heavy strokes, a strong backward letter angle, an arrow, and a crown on top.

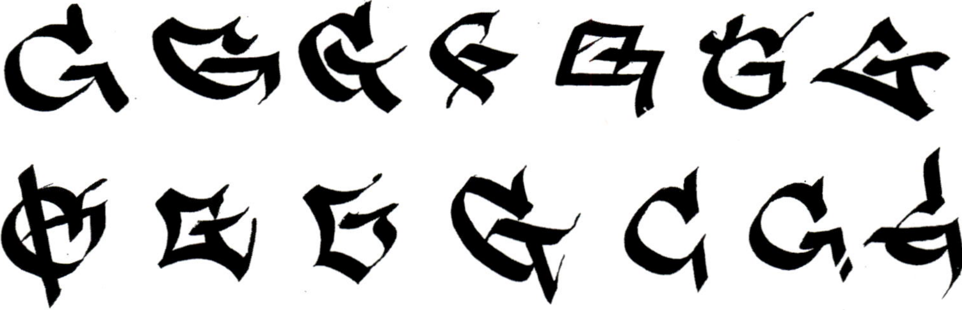

↑ One pen can easily make fourteen different versions of a single thick and thin letter (collected from local graffiti and online fonts).

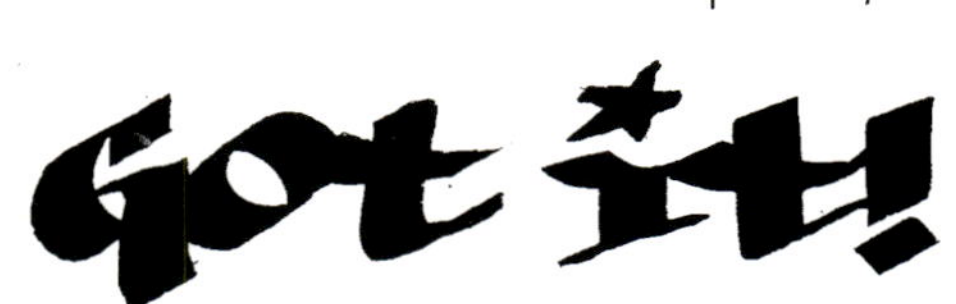

← Even extremely bold letters can still be readable. These are only 2½ times taller than the pen's width.

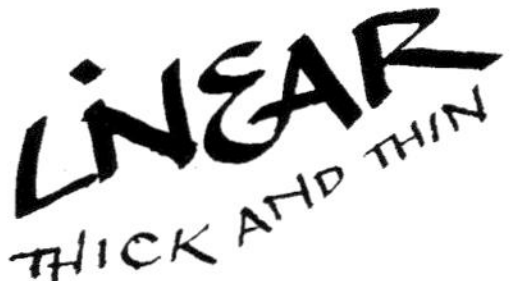

A tilted square can decorate a stroke.

Tilting the main strokes 10° backward and arching them adds energy.

Letters

For small practice here, then scale up for big letters outdoors.

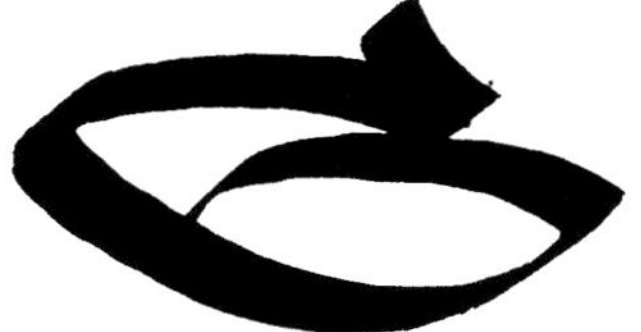 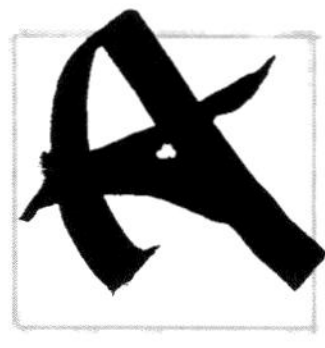 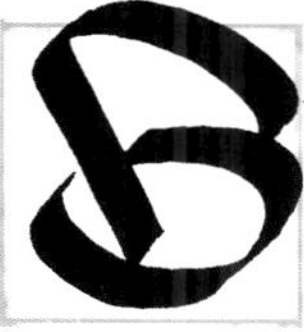 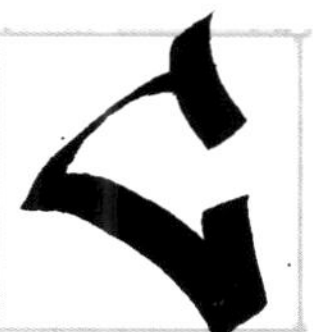 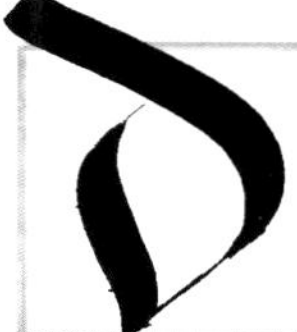 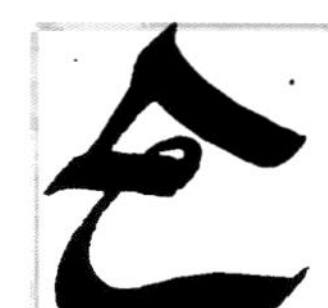

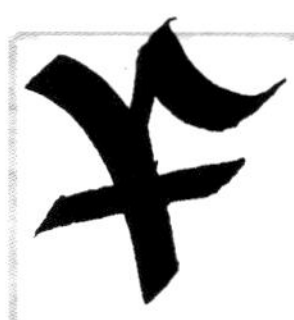 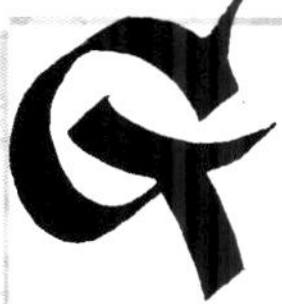 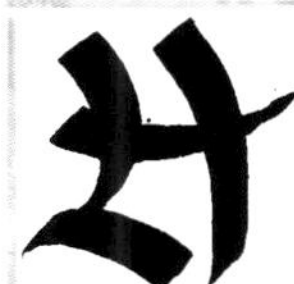 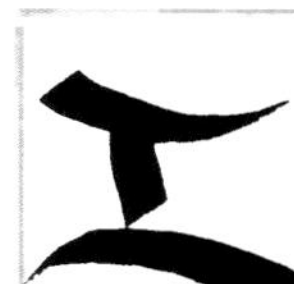 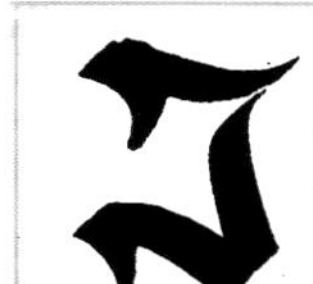

Unique graffiti serifs

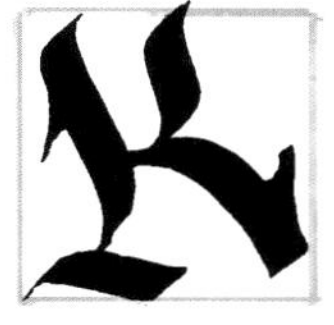 Serifs that "bounce" are a recent calligraphic invention. They make the pen's motion visible at the start or end of a stroke, and encourage the connections between letters.

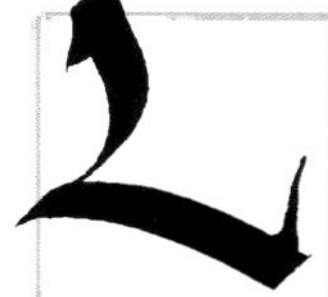 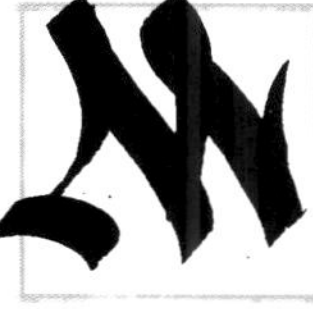 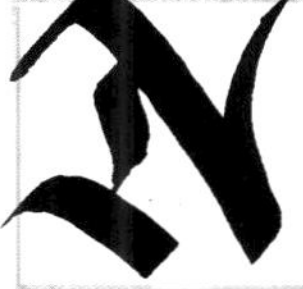 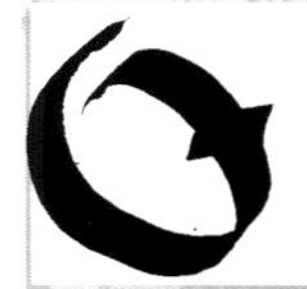 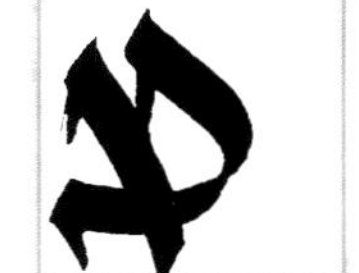

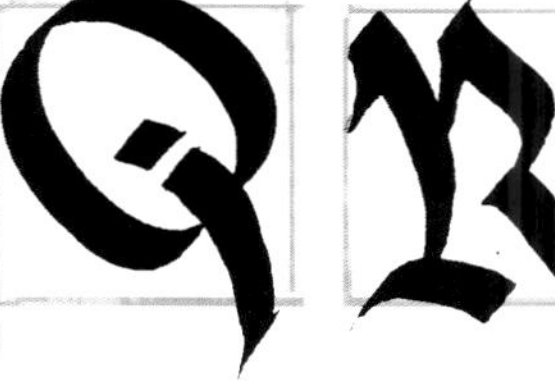 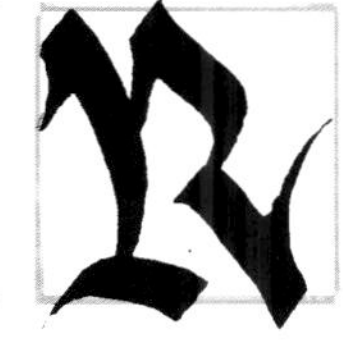 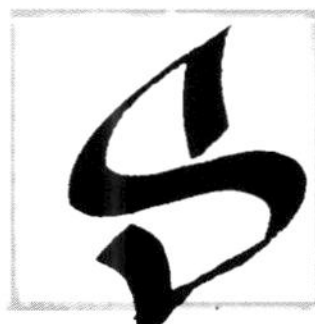 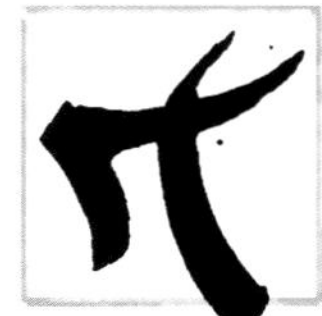 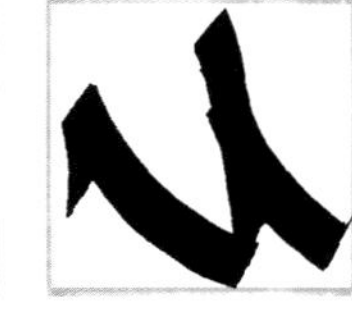

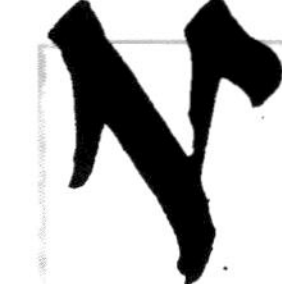 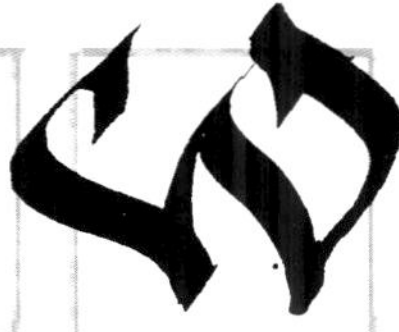 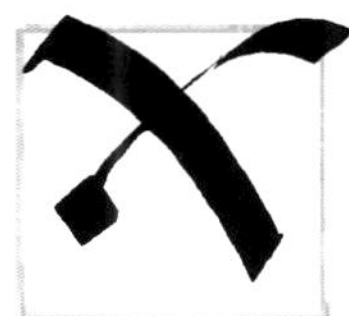 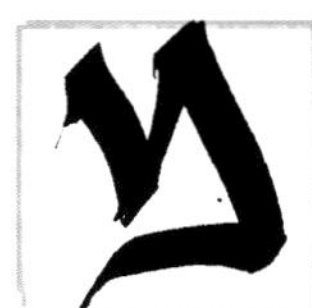 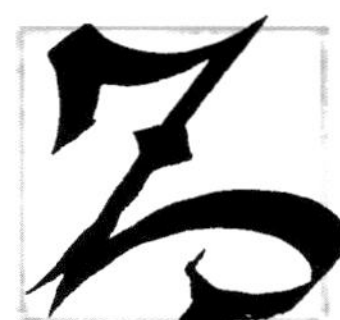

Dingbats

Punctuation, emojis, wingdings, swashes.

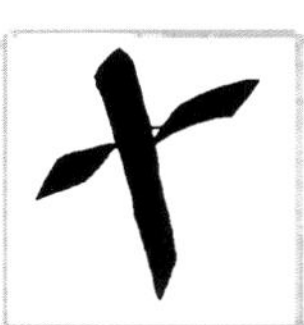 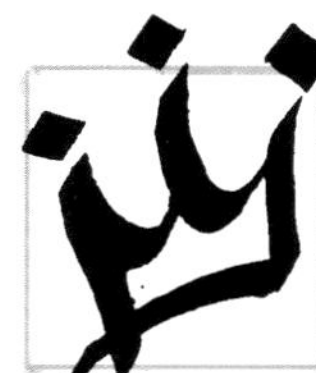 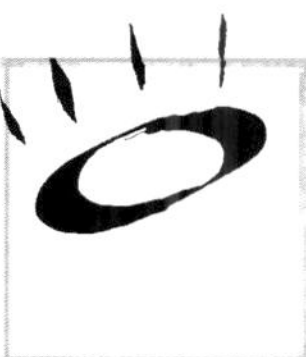 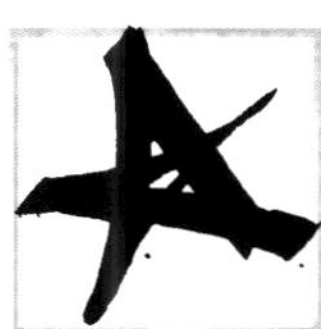 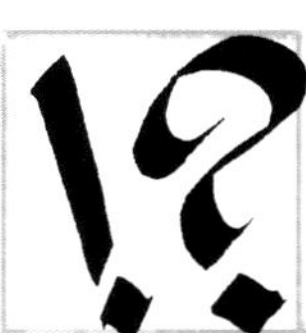 

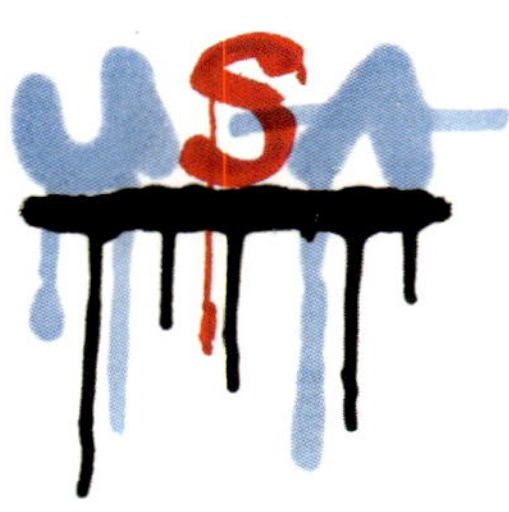

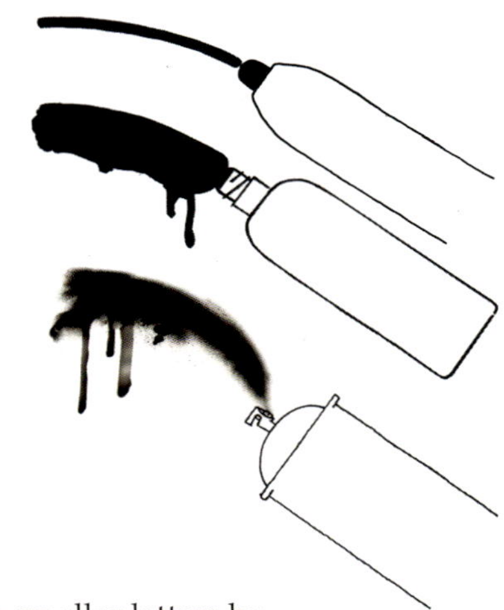

Monoline letters, with strokes of uniform weight, are familiar to graffiti artists and calligraphers when written with a blunt pen. But writing them with a sprayed line adds two unique factors: time and gravity. The spray widens and darkens whenever it slows down, while gravity makes the ink drip. In traditional calligraphy, ink drips would be a disaster, but they give graffiti the artistic animation of a Jackson Pollock painting.

"Capture a map of the gesture."

~ Aesop Rock, "Rings"

The spreads and drips of sprayed graffiti can be evoked in smaller letters by using squeeze pens with spongy mop tops. Unless the calligrapher owns an air compressor and an airbrush, the only other way to get these speed-related effects is to imitate them on a tablet with a digital stylus.

↓ In this emphatic 2012 graffiti, the exclamation point, the quotation marks, and a dynamic coil add energy. A slight pause made a little drip at the bottom of **A** *and* **R**.

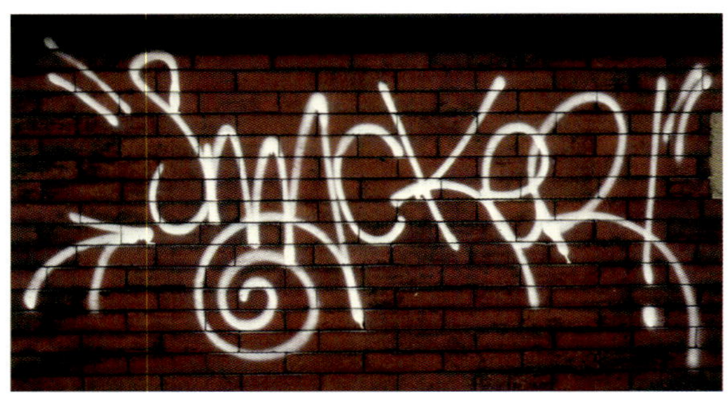

↓ A sprayed line gets denser whenever the flow pauses to change direction.

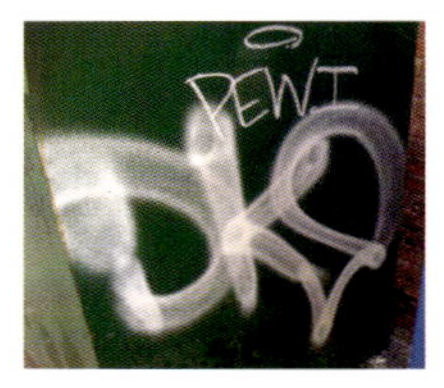

↑ Very slow spray makes long, dramatic drips.

→ Sprayed lines have two more distinctive variables; the angle and distance from the surface matters too. Pulling the spray nozzle back widens and blurs the stroke as shown here in the letters **L N A S.**

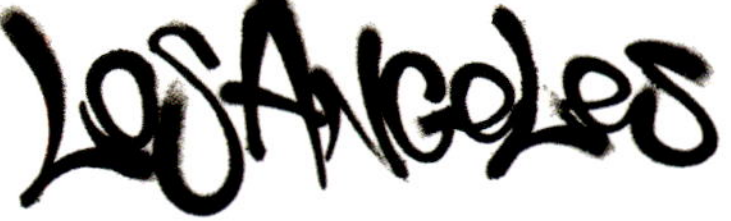

Because urban graffiti consists of so many codes, symbols, and aliases, pedestrians have gotten used to tuning out any spray-painted writing that they don't quite understand. Thus most of them walk right past the spray-painted language of "utility graffiti," the national system that cities have used for fifty years to warn workers where not to dig up the sidewalk. Sprayed fast and repeatedly by non-artists, this cousin of graffiti is worth noticing for its fluid line.

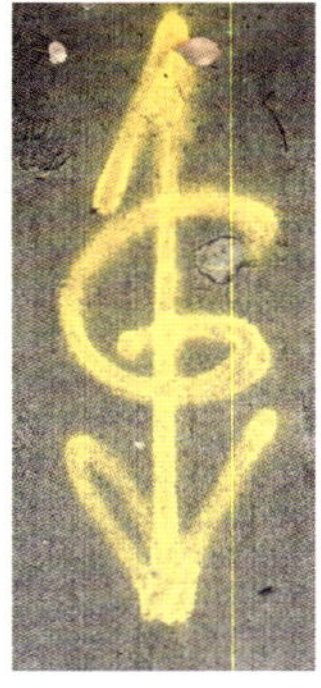

← Location of a gas main is painted on a city sidewalk. A special nozzle works even when the can is held upside down. The paint is formulated to weather away in weeks.

MONO LINE

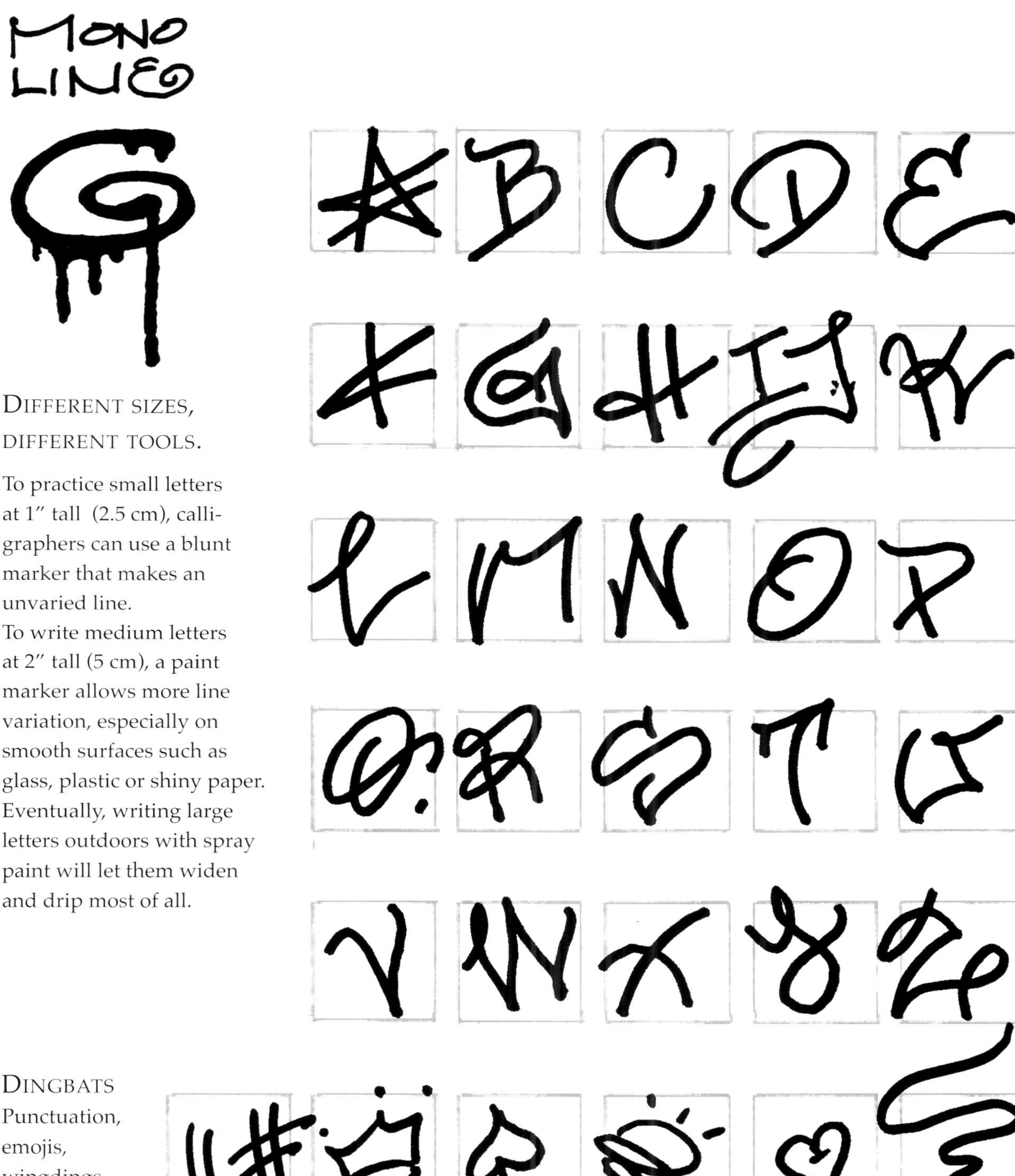

DIFFERENT SIZES, DIFFERENT TOOLS.

To practice small letters at 1″ tall (2.5 cm), calligraphers can use a blunt marker that makes an unvaried line.

To write medium letters at 2″ tall (5 cm), a paint marker allows more line variation, especially on smooth surfaces such as glass, plastic or shiny paper. Eventually, writing large letters outdoors with spray paint will let them widen and drip most of all.

DINGBATS
Punctuation, emojis, wingdings, swashes.

CAUTION: Aerosol paint should be used only outdoors or with good ventilation. Indoors, artists should use only water-based markers. Indelible markers containing xylene or certain dry-erase markers should be used only outside or while wearing a respirator. Labels are required to include a warning.

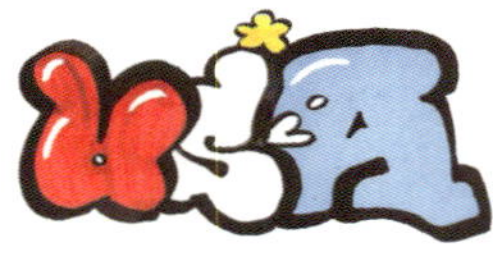

"If . . . you came to New York and you didn't paint a train, it's like you just wasted a trip."
~CES aka Robert Michael Provenzano

OUTLINES SHOW THE LETTER'S EXTERNAL CONTOURS, allowing artists to control every feature of a letter, deciding its weight, size, color, slant, proportions, and historical style. They can make infinite variations, unrestrained by the pen's geometry. And while outlined letters are fun on their own, the final step of filling them with color, ornament, and images can take them to a higher level of creativity through teamwork, thus continuing a tradition that started with the illuminated, inhabited initials of medieval manuscripts.

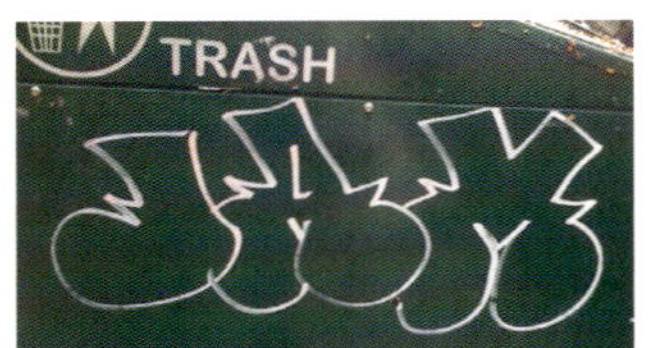

OUTLINE, FILL, OVERFILL

← *Some letters puff up so soft and squishy that their internal spaces squeeze shut. The little elbows here add energy. c 1990.*

↓ *These concave letters are all awkward elbows and knees. Graffiti from Boston, 2021.*

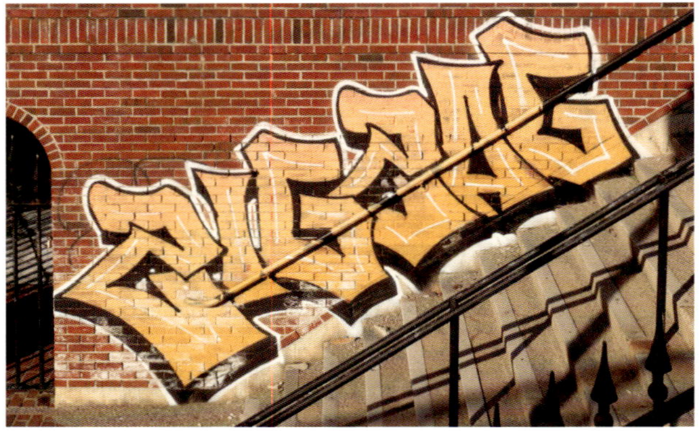

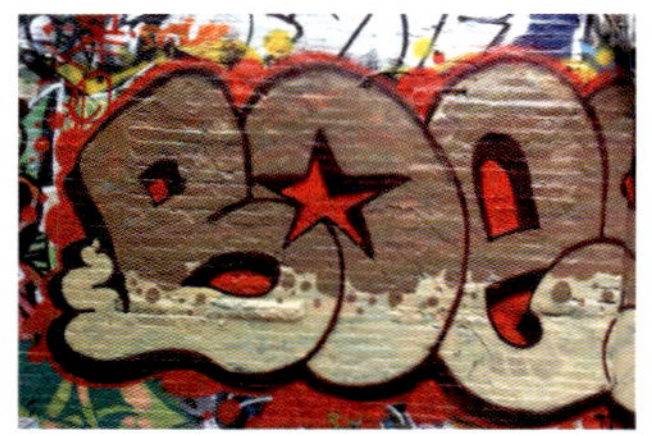

← *This elaborate 2005 design adds a tail to B, turns the interior space of O into a star, puts foaming bubbles inside the letter strokes, and gives them the illusion of three dimensions.*

In the 1970s, subway cars in New York City were the favorite place for graffiti artists to display their names, as with "Freedom." →

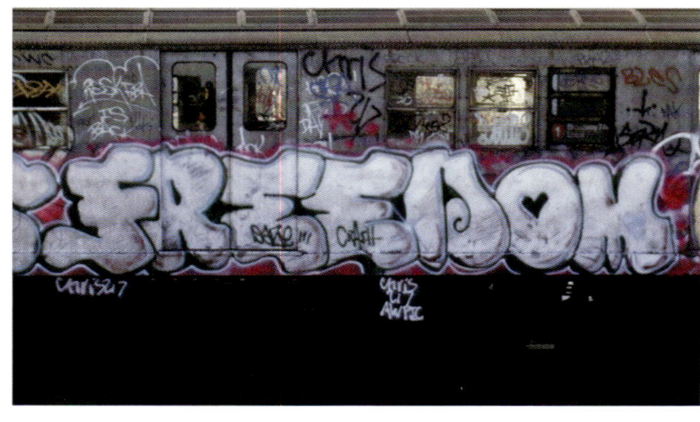

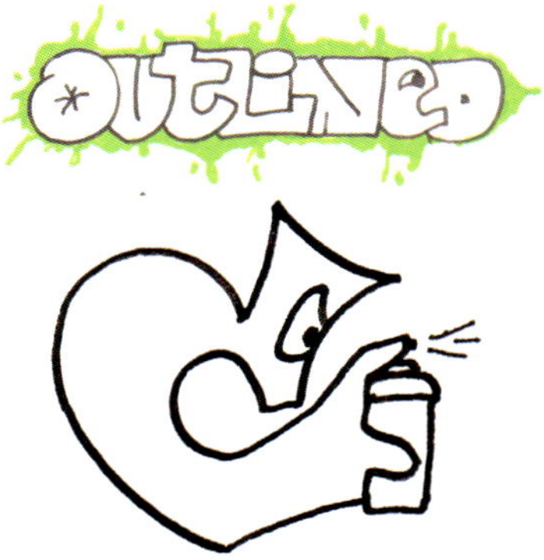

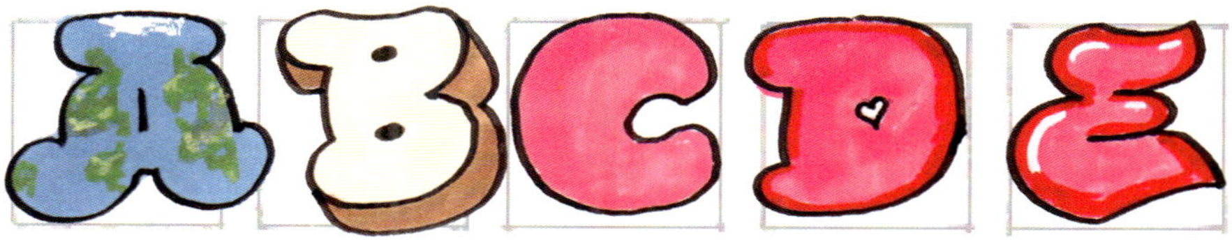

Whole earth · **3D solid** · **Flat color** · **Contour** · **Contour + highlight**

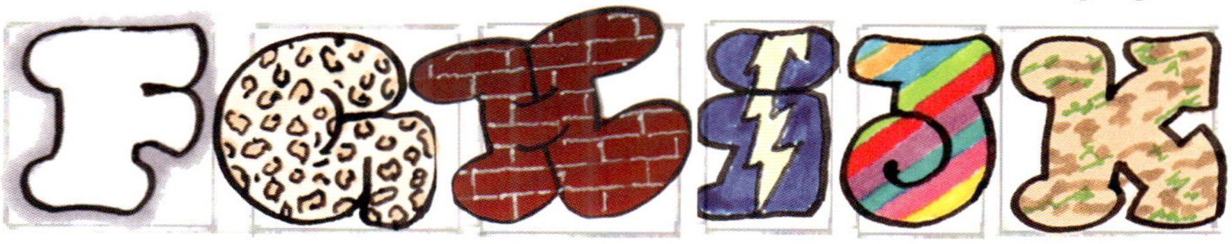

Aura · **Leopard** · **Brick** · **Lightening** · **Rainbow** · **Camo**

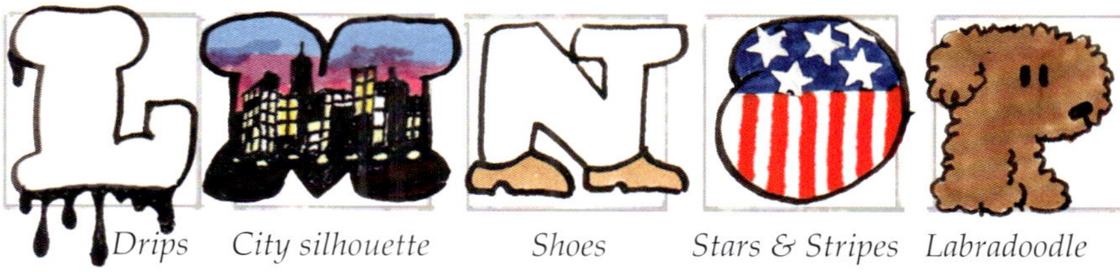

Drips · **City silhouette** · **Shoes** · **Stars & Stripes** · **Labradoodle**

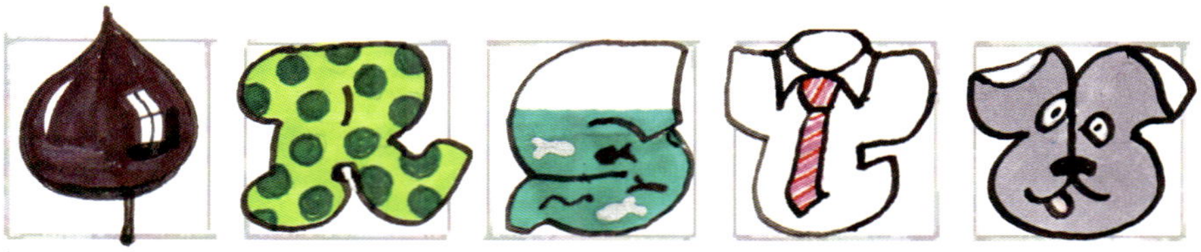

Big Drip · **Polka Dots** · **Aquarium** · **9 to 5** · **Doofus Dog**

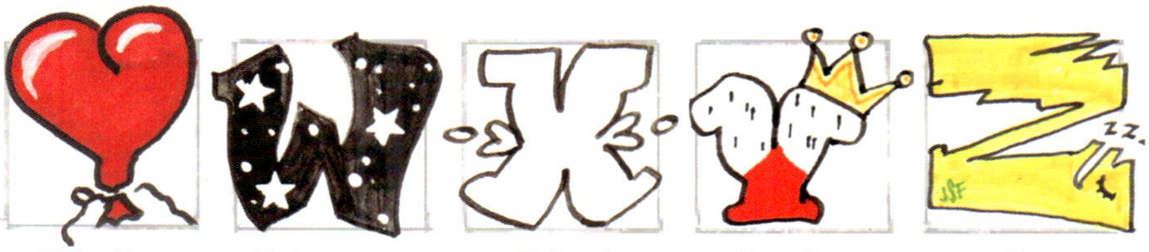

Valentine balloon · **Outer space** · **Sploosh** · **Royalty** · **Zag**

FILLED IN 26 + WAYS

Outlined letters have soft bodies, but they grow from firm bones. They squeeze against the letters next to them.

Graffiti artists sketch out their large letters before painting them. They use mostly capitals, plus a few small letters such as **a e i t**.

Letters contain extra tags, comments, and decorations.

DINGBATS

Punctuation, emojis, wingdings, swashes.

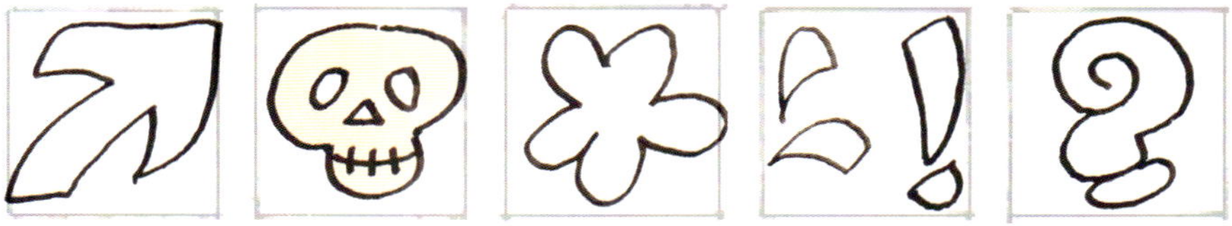

HUMANOIDS

Because letters are people, too.

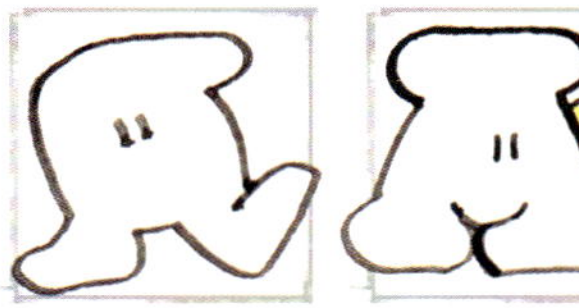 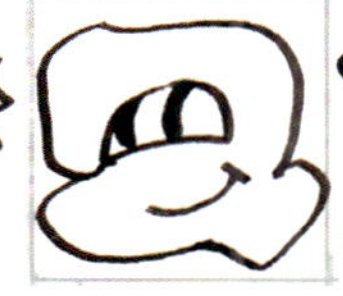 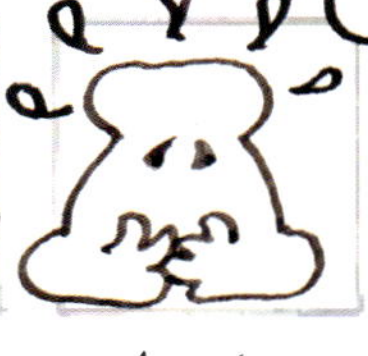 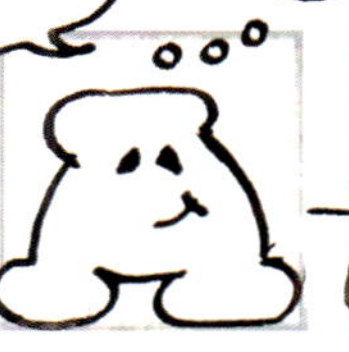

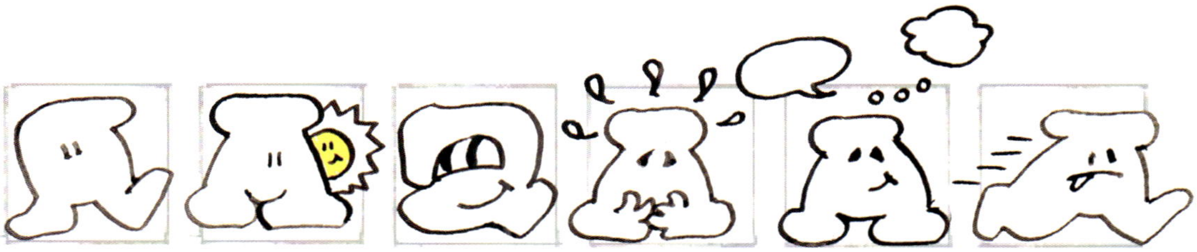

Fat Feet · **Buddy** · **Expression** · **Angst** · **Opinions** · **Sprint**

GRAFFITI, ACCORDING TO *THE NEW YORK TIMES*, went "from vandalism to art to nostalgia." By the late 1990s it was tame enough to provide art for galleries, typefaces for advertising, and logos for hip urban fashion. Some critics said that graffiti had been co-opted for profit; others insisted that it was just evolving to reach a wider public.

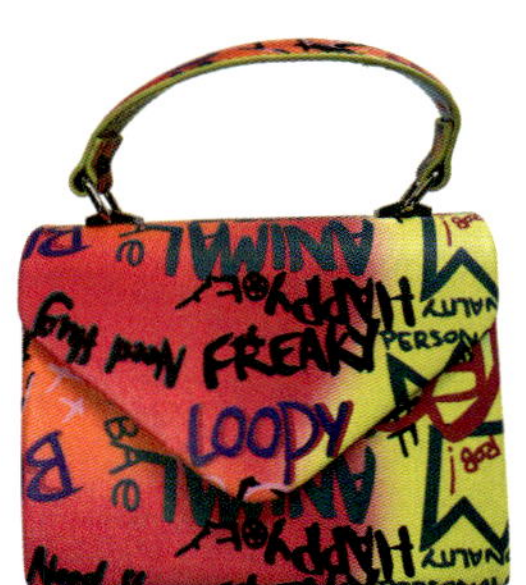

Designers decorated high-fashion handbags with their idea of graffiti letters.

Everyone piled onto the graffiti bandwagon: sociologists, law-enforcement experts, gallery owners, city planners, art schools, and art historians—even publishers of coloring books. Exploiting urban graffiti's edgy intensity was a hallmark of twenty-first-century branding that soon became a cliché.

Meanwhile, graffiti's original creators grew up and moved on. New writers came from different backgrounds, driven by different needs and reaching different readers. In cities such as present-day Miami and East Los Angeles, both cities without subways, letters on walls are no longer a sign of urban decay but a tool that can revive a declining neighborhood. Backed by corporations or civic groups, this graffiti appeals to residents, fellow artists, and tourists. It draws foot traffic that makes the area feel welcoming for block parties, pedestrians, parks, restaurants, boutiques, and art galleries, and ultimately, revived housing.

Graffiti gave the world a powerful visual metaphor for both the vitality and the ugliness of late twentieth-century life in urban America and a tool for shaping it. Like other major movements in art, it also influenced artists in many fields and changed the way people looked at the calligraphy that came before and after it. America's graffiti represents a place and a moment for the rest of the world, which, in the words of chronicler Henry Chalfant, "sees in the giant across the Atlantic the image of their own future, like it or not."

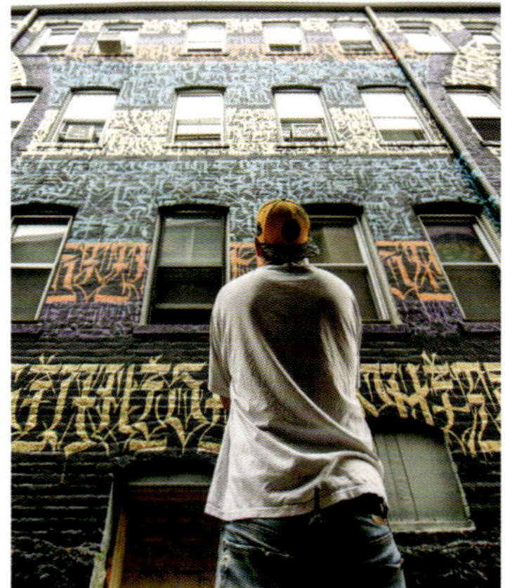

Much of today's street art aims for appeal beyond the group who writes it. Ian Staber, architect, uses "calligraffiti" for his designs. In 2018, his mural at the Punto Urban Art Museum, Salem, Massachusetts, enlivened the district and celebrated his Hispanic heritage, with a custom script that fuses Gothic calligraphy and graffiti lettering.

For planning and keeping favorite graffiti letters.

HANDWRITING

Americans have their own special handwriting, which came from old-world calligraphy but developed along its own path. Social mobility, marketplace forces, and new materials transformed it into a unique compromise between the ideal and the real.

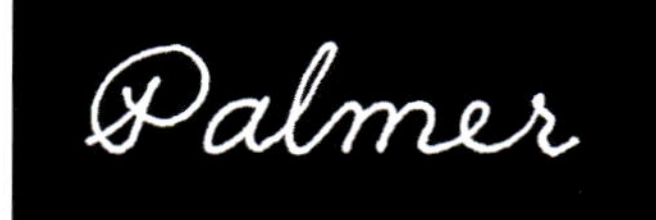

Copperplate was better suited to the skilled engraver than to the average American citizen.

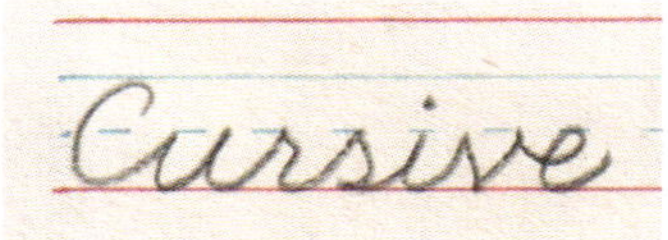

By the mid 1800s, prosperity reshaped American handwriting. Penmanship teachers strove to make good writing accessible, most notably through **Spencerian** script.

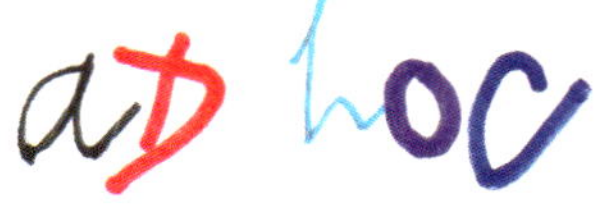

In the 1890s **Palmer Method** claimed to streamline handwriting, tailoring it for stylus, chalk, pencil, and fountain pen. By 1920 its trademarked lessons were taught in most of the country's primary schools.

Mid-century schools next tried teaching six-year-olds to read and write separated letters first, then **cursive** letters later, hoping to make the eventual transition easier. Meanwhile, ballpoint pens made everyone's writing worse.

Popular interest in **Italic** calligraphy in the 1970s briefly made instruction better in a few American schools, but it could not stop the general decline. People were learning to type at an ever-younger age.

Today, keyboards have mainly replaced pens, so that people rely on an **ad hoc** scrawl for the infrequent signature or jotted list.

Each style of American handwriting adds to the story about the first five hundred years of the country's history.

"As those who aim at perfect Writing by imitating the engraved copies, tho' they never reach the wish'd for Excellence of those Copies, their Hand is mended by the Endeavor."
~ *Benjamin Franklin,
in* The Autobiography of Benjamin Franklin

U. S. A.

COPPERPLATE ARRIVED WITH the first English colonists and went right to work in daily life. Like other luxuries from the Old World, however, it had to be modified to serve the harsh realities of the New. Book designers had accustomed the English public to a rich diet of copperplate text, titles, pictures, and decorative flourishes that proved to be unsuited to life in a new settlement. The script got simplified from ideal to real.

Although most early colonists learned to read, about half could barely write. While an agrarian society did not need much paperwork, a growing population sorted itself into more specialized jobs, which did. Social distinctions began to matter; writers had to choose whatever variant of copperplate would be appropriate to their job, gender, and social class.

And most of all, proper copperplate demanded real skill. The writer fashioned a quill pen from a large feather, burnished the paper surface smooth, and mixed a small supply of ink from powder. In summer that ink had to be guarded against mold, and in winter against freezing.

Copperplate scripts of the period 1620–1850 all faced this central problem; how to adapt an idealized script made for a printing plate so it would fit the handheld pen of a right-handed writer. Citizens who could read and write were crucial to the prosperity and equality that the founders had envisioned. The reform and spread of handwriting, to make it accessible to everyone, became the underlying patriotic task of the next fifty years.

← *Thomas Jefferson wrote the last draft of the Declaration of Independence and pasted it together, but Timothy Matlack,* → *though not a professional scribe, was picked by the other delegates to make the final copy, because he had the best penmanship of the group.*

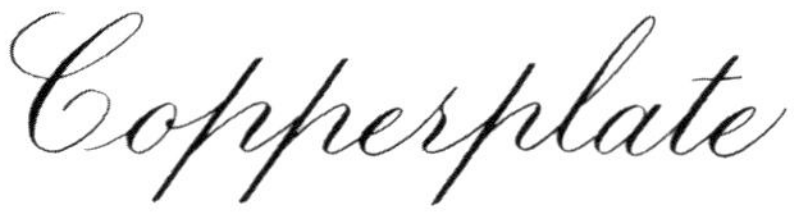

Copperplate

Letters slant
at 55°–65°

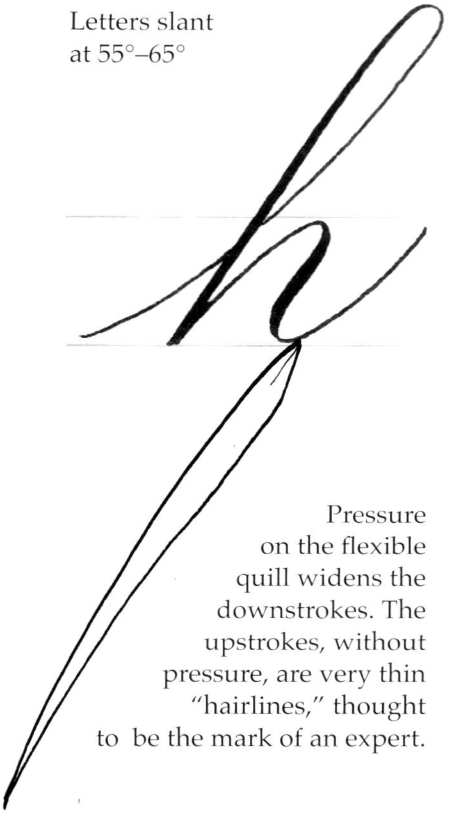

Pressure
on the flexible
quill widens the
downstrokes. The
upstrokes, without
pressure, are very thin
"hairlines," thought
to be the mark of an expert.

WARM-UPS   Repeat twenty-five times

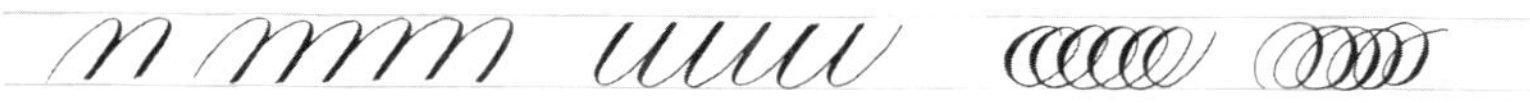

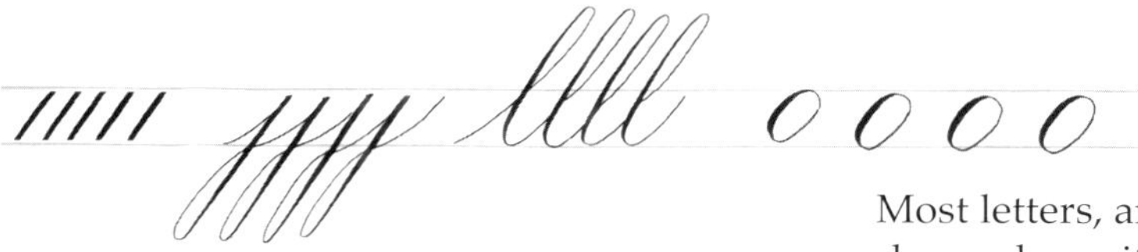

Most letters, and many
words, can be written with
one continuous stroke.

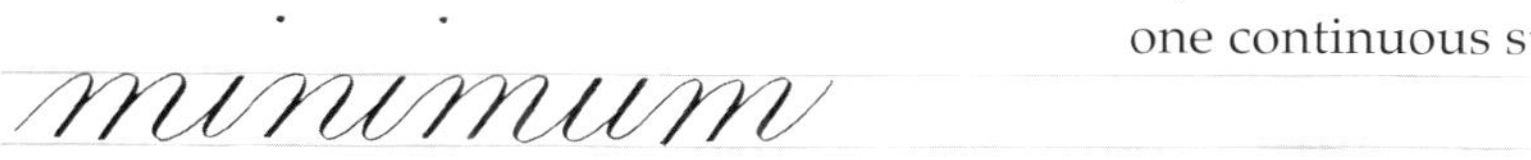

minimum

SMALL LETTERS

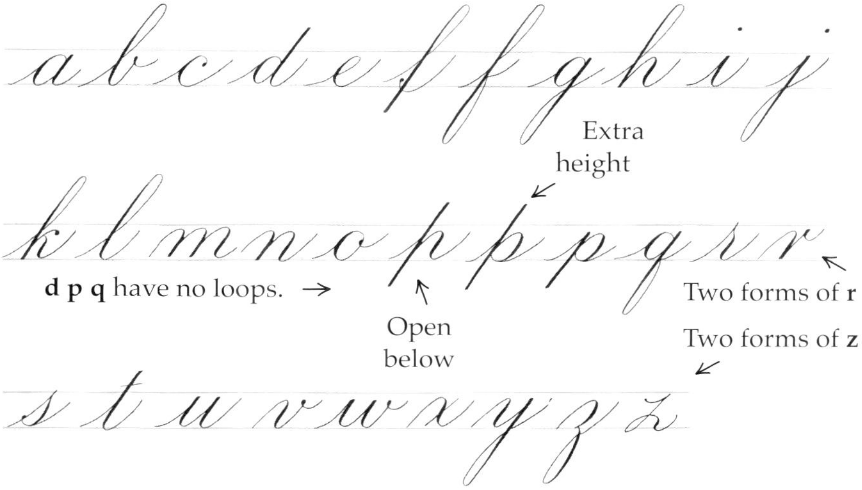

a b c d e f f g h i j

Extra
height

k l m n o p p p q r r

d p q have no loops. →

Open
below

Two forms of r

Two forms of z

s t u v w x y z z

CAPITALS

Capitals, like ascenders, are about twice the height of small letters.

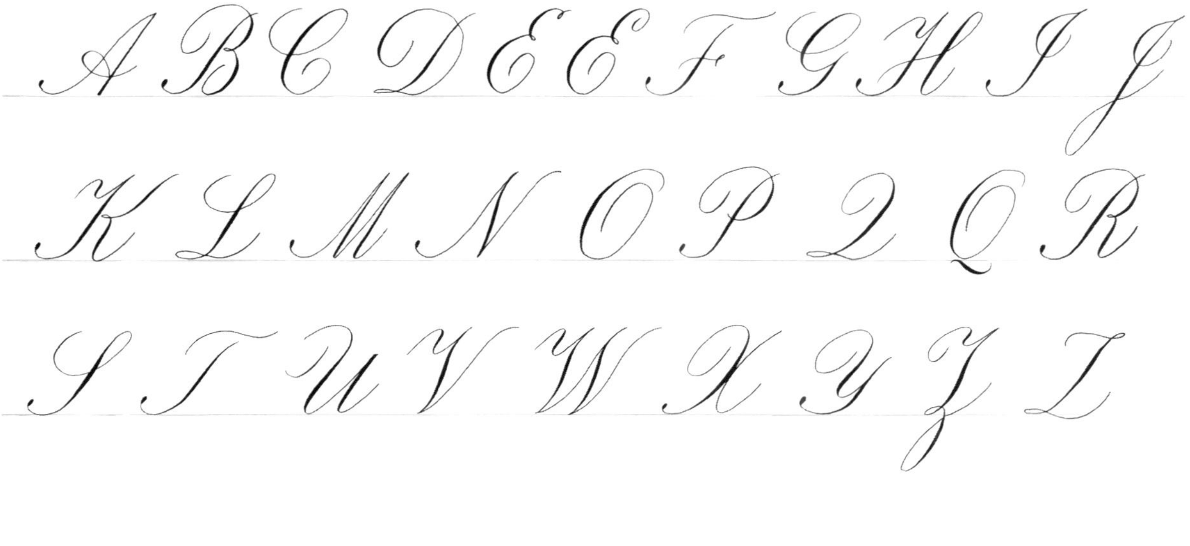

A B C D E F G H I J

K L M N O P 2 Q R

S T U V W X Y Z I

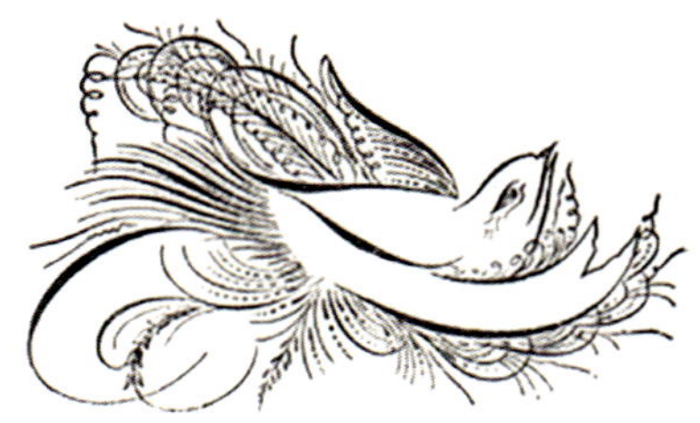

"[I am] . . . seeking
to modify the forms
that have become
Americanized and
render them
still more
Americanized."
~ *Platt Rogers
Spencer*

INDEPENDENCE FROM ENGLAND IN 1776 had let Americans claim their own ways to write, read, govern, and think. Then after the Civil War, the expanding nation would absorb a huge wave of immigration and enjoy a period of post-Civil War prosperity. Inventions proliferated, and the world of business thrived, requiring many more office workers. As handwriting evolved to keep up, imported copperplate was reshaped into native Spencerian. Stiff metal dip pens had replaced more flexible quills in the 1820s. By 1870, fountain pens were available with newly patented gold iridium nibs, rubber ink reservoirs, and free-flowing bottled ink.

Better penmanship promised to open the door to job security, social mobility, and personal satisfaction, with the assurance that "A neat handwriting is a letter of recommendation." Students flocked to evening classes given by itinerant writing masters, sometimes bringing their own inkwells and desk lamps; or they bought instruction books and practiced at home, toiling to master the scripts they hoped would be their ticket to prosperity. Those with extra talent explored the art of making spectacular pictures with pen flourishes.

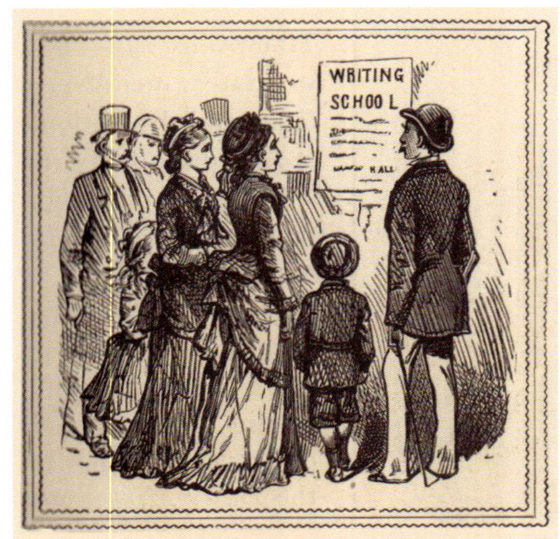

Writing schools epitomized the idea of free-market solutions for social problems; in an expanding economy, teachers could respond freely to the need for workers with clerical skills. Master penman Platt Rogers Spencer, the best known, simply gave the public what it wanted—a homegrown, name-brand script—and spread it in an enterprising way that was itself very American. And though his "simplified" script may look complicated to modern readers, it was welcomed with relief in its own era. It embodied the national character: populist, practical, and *good for business.*

*Flourished bird, above, and Writing School poster,
both from* Gaskell's Compendium of Forms.

Spencerian

Many Spencerian small letters look like copperplate, but have fewer thick strokes and more thin lines.

Capitals have just one thick stroke; small letters are likely to have none.

Purists adhere to the 52.5° slant specified by Spencer.

Narrow letter body.

This script is a natural fit for left-handers; right-handers need to rotate the paper or use an adaptor to reverse the angle.

WARM-UPS   Repeat twenty-five times

SMALL LETTERS

Two forms of **F**

Extra height

Open below

Two forms of **T**

CAPITALS

Large, embellished capitals often tower over the small letters.

A TYPICAL AMERICAN PENMANSHIP CLASS opens Horatio Alger's 1872 rags-to-riches novel, *Brave and Bold*, with a scene that captures the spirit of an era:

"The main schoolroom in the Millville Academy was brilliantly lighted, and the various desks were occupied by boys and girls of different ages from ten to eighteen, all busily writing under the general direction of Professor George W. Granville, Instructor in Plain and Ornamental Penmanship. Professor Granville, as he styled himself, was a traveling teacher, and generally had two or three evening schools in progress in different places at the same time. He was really a very good penman, and in a course of twelve lessons, for which he charged the very moderate price of a dollar, not, of course, including stationery, he contrived to impart considerable instruction, and such pupils as chose to learn were likely to profit by his instructions. There were a hundred pupils on his list . . . and there had been no disturbance during the course of lessons."

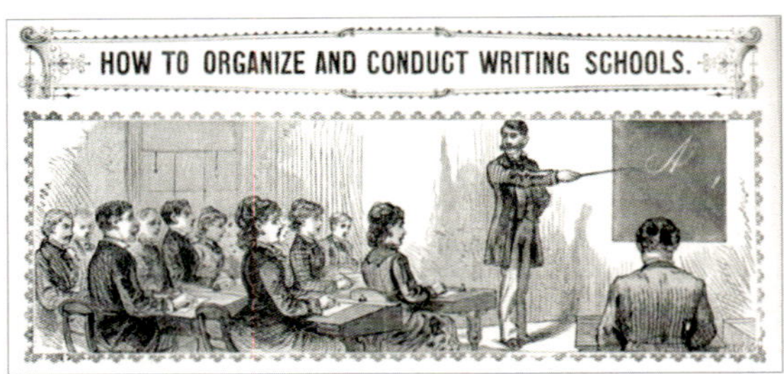

From *Gaskell's Compendium of Forms.*

In spite of such rigorous instruction, everyone's handwriting still turned out a little different, and each signature was very different, representing their unique personality. It might even be more familiar to distant friends and family than their face or voice. A signature also had consequences as well as meaning. A love letter, for instance could not be used in court as evidence of breach of promise if it was signed only with an initial. Checks had to be written and signed in ink. A businessman's signature committed his whole company to an agreement. A bill became law only when the president signed it.

Signatures have always had emotional and legal power, but in America they played an extra role; collector's item. Getting the signatures of friends and family became a widespread passion in the US in the century following 1860. Students inscribed each other's albums with mottos, jokes, wishes, and homemade poetry, and often added dates and places to their entries. The signatures in each person's book had an intense personal meaning that is now mostly lost, but thousands of these books survive to show how many different ways there were to write standard script.

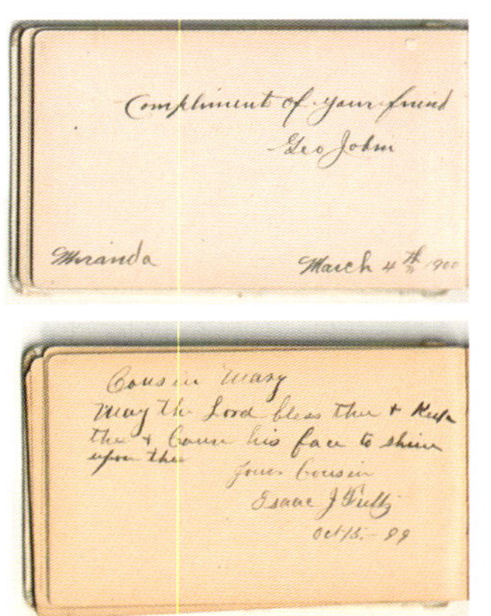

Albums from 1888 and 1899

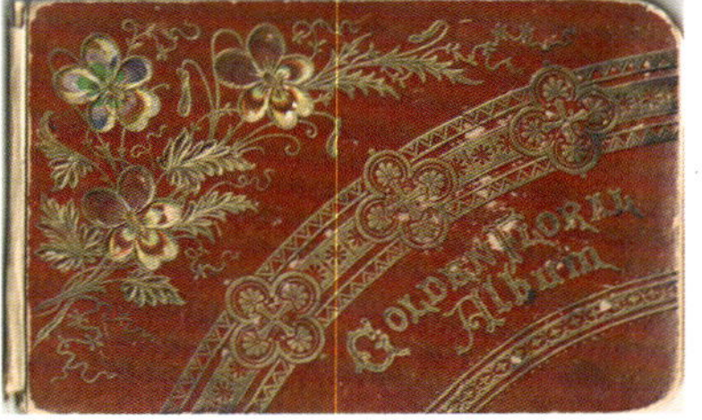

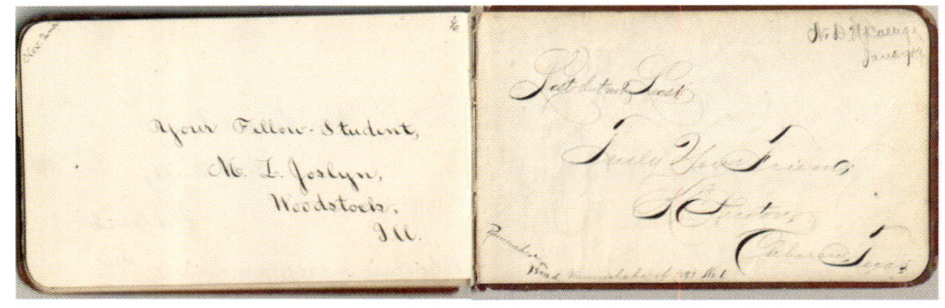

A FEW AVID COLLECTORS went beyond sentimental keepsakes to pursue the signatures of famous people they knew of but did not actually know. Owning the signature of a sports star, celebrity, or politician gave the ordinary American a feeling of connection. But these magic talismans also turned out to have dollar value that outweighed their sentimental value. Sports fans, especially, who were thrilled to get their favorite player's autograph often couldn't resist putting a price on it, which in turn made stars less generous about giving autographs.

Eventually, autograph collecting has become less about sentiment and more about money. People still build collections by hunting down historical autographs such as US presidents or movie stars. But the profiteers, the forgers, and the invention of the autopen have undermined the hobby's human connection.

By the 1950s the craze for signing things had spread into other media. A plaster cast on a broken leg might carry the names of a dozen well-wishers. School teams autographed each other's T-shirts. Graduating seniors carried their yearbooks around to get signatures on their classmates' pictures. Enterprising toy companies invented the "autograph hound," a stuffed dog made of sturdy white cotton fabric, with a pen attached and sometimes wearing a graduation mortarboard.

PERSONAL SIGNATURES CARRIED EXTRA WEIGHT in American commerce, where owners often put their own signatures on their products to inspire trust. Many logos of today's global corporations started out as their founder's signature.

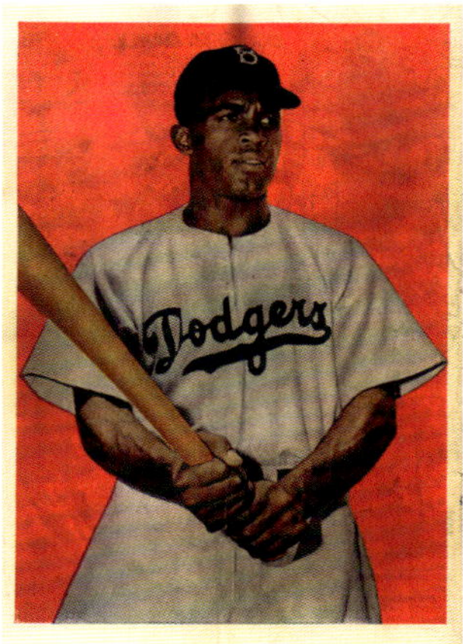

↑ *Many sports logos still in use today began as imitations of a swashed signature.*

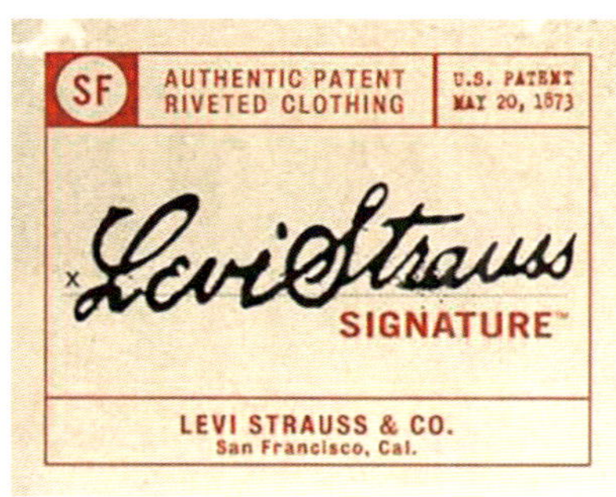

↑ *Levi Strauss made the first of America's iconic blue jeans, which are now generically called "Levis."*

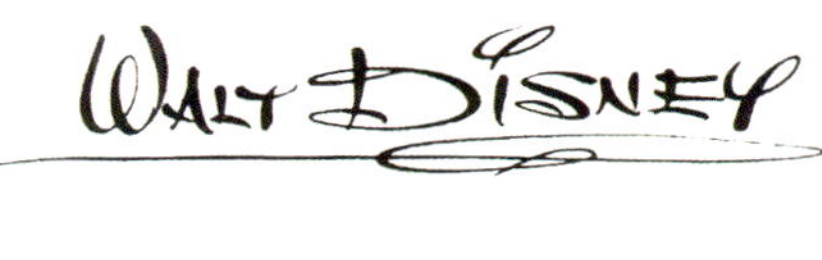

↑ *Over the decades, Walt Disney's name became what some call "the most famous signature in the world" and certainly one of the most collected. Above, a Walt Disney signature and the Disney company logo.*

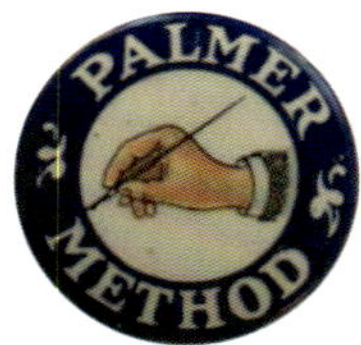

"Unfortunately, such innovations as did occur in the teaching of penmanship had been 'introduced by those whose prime interest in the matter was commercial rather than professional.'"
~ *Franklin Freeman*, Teaching of Handwriting, 1914

On the back of this ⅞" lapel button is printed, "The winner has satisfactorily mastered the first 25 drills in The Palmer Method Journal."

AFTER FINDING even the simplifications of Spencerian script too hard for him, Austin Palmer set out in the 1890s to reform how Americans learned to write. The result was a bare-bones alphabet, burdened with random left-overs from earlier styles. His claim that "no attempt is made to make the penmanship more beautiful than is consistent with utility," was all too true. He made no major improvements to letter design; instead, his true genius lay in marketing his "plain and rapid " writing method.

Palmer began by teaching business handwriting through a string of academies for job seekers. Next he adapted his materials to children in public school classrooms, where his key innovation was the offer of tuition-free summer classes to train grade-school teachers and administrators. Each Palmer student was obliged to buy copyrighted Palmer workbooks, pencils, and practice paper. Teachers could send in their pupils' work to compete for prizes, such as lapel pins and commendation letters, that kept students motivated. Alumni events, newsletters, and refresher courses kept teachers loyal to the Palmer Method, embedding it in the curriculum for almost half a century. By 1920, fully three-quarters of all schoolchildren in the United States were using it, and by Austin Palmer's death in 1927 (with an estate equivalent to $14,000,000 today), an estimated twenty-five million Americans, or one in four citizens, had learned to write using the Palmer Method.

Commercial success, however, kept the script from evolving naturally. While many students and parents, and eventually teachers too, came to loathe it, once it got entrenched in a school district it was hard to pry loose. But not impossible; by mid-century the Palmer Method was challenged by rival systems.

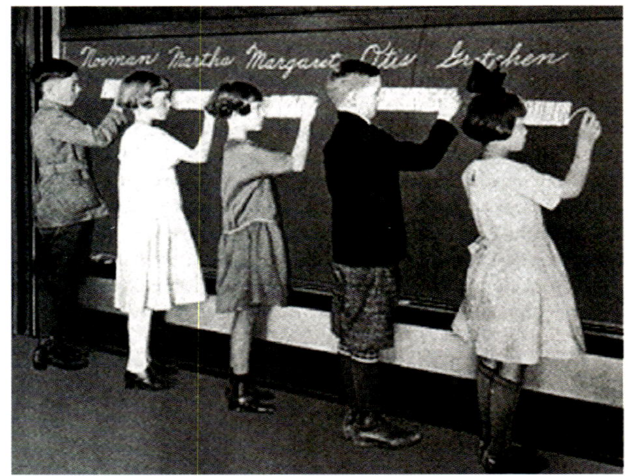

Children practicing Palmer Method handwriting, c 1912.

ABOUT PALMER METHOD

Once people began to write with a rigid stylus, chalk, pencil, fountain pen, or ballpoint, the graceful thicks and thins of scripts turned into monolines. Children were taught to move their whole arm, a natural motion while standing at a chalkboard but not suited to desk writing. As they grew older, a series of ruled practice pads taught them to write smaller letters.

Palmer kept the legacy of quirky and archaic letterforms, especially for capital **F G I Q** and lowercase **r s t**. A few were simplified in later decades.

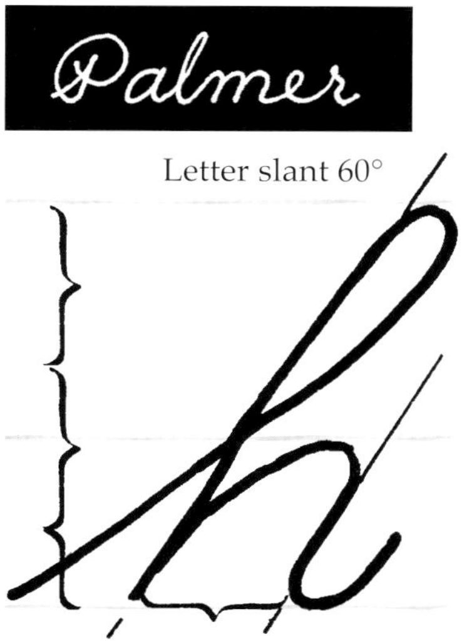

Ascenders = 2½ times as tall as letter bodies.

Palmer

Letter slant 60°

Letter body width is ¾ its height.

WARM-UPS

Repeat twenty-five times

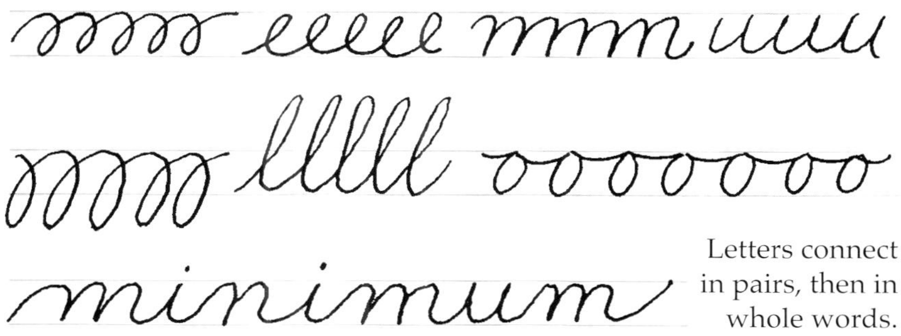

Letters connect in pairs, then in whole words. A few don't connect at all.

SMALL LETTERS

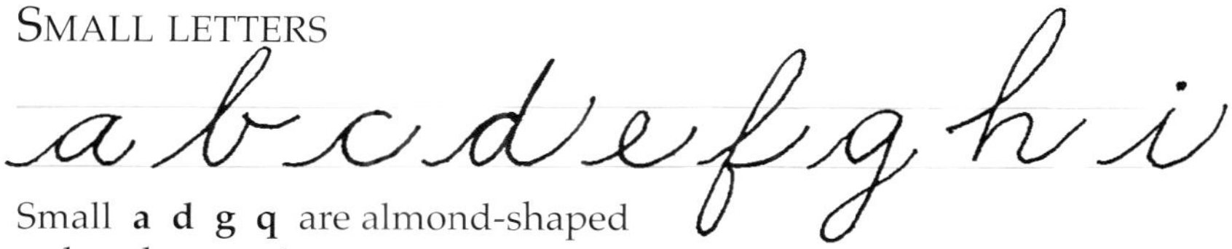

a b c d e f g h i

Small **a d g q** are almond-shaped rather than oval.

p extends up.

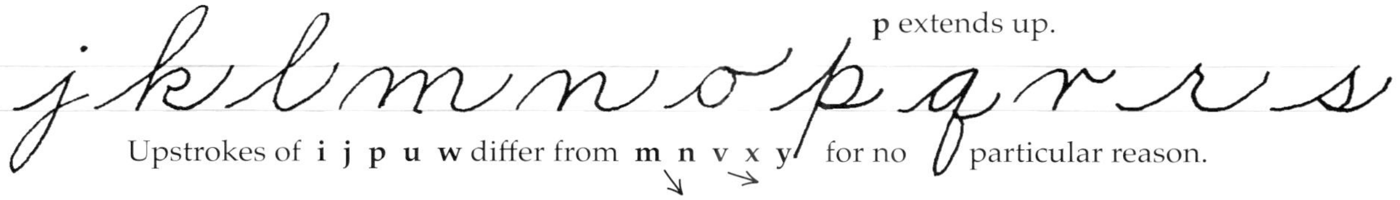

j k l m n o p q r s

Upstrokes of **i j p u w** differ from **m n v x y** for no particular reason.

↑ Dot **i j** and cross **t x**, → after the word is done.

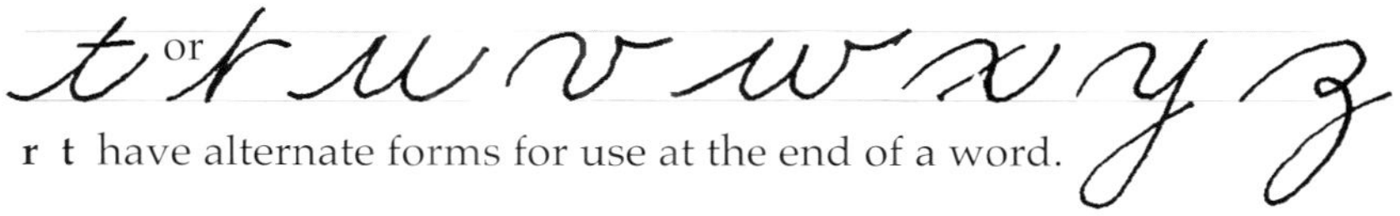

t or *t u v w x y z*

r t have alternate forms for use at the end of a word.

CAPITAL STROKES

Most capitals begin or end with one of these three strokes:

BOWL   LOOP   UPSTROKE

Concave

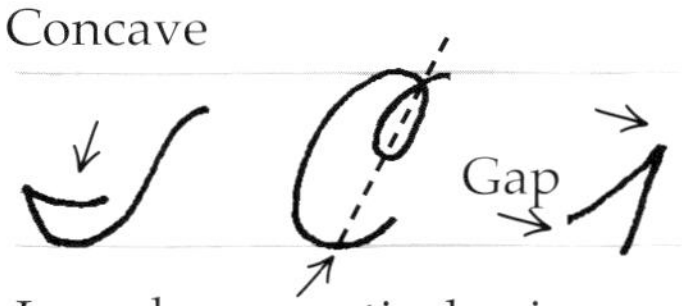

Loop has a vertical axis.

CAPITALS

Palmer specified that each capital (except **H K X**) should be written in one single stroke. The dots below show where each capital begins. Many of these capitals, from a 1917 drill book, are still taught today.

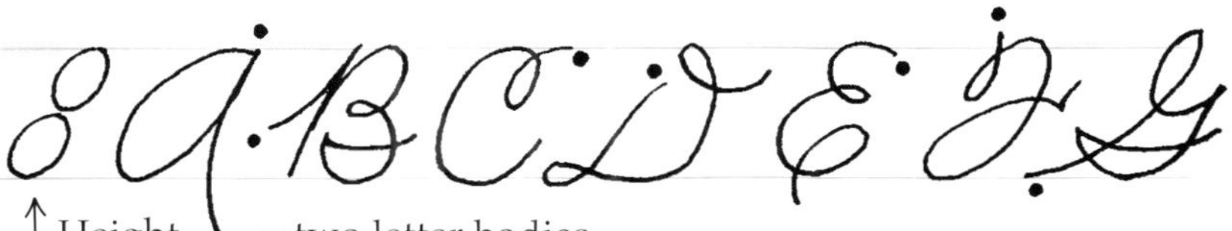

↑ Height = two letter bodies.

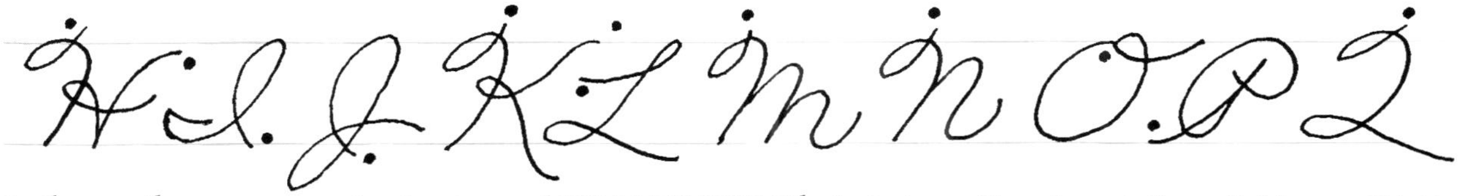

In theory, the sloping tops of **H M N U V W Y** help to transition from tall capital to small letter.

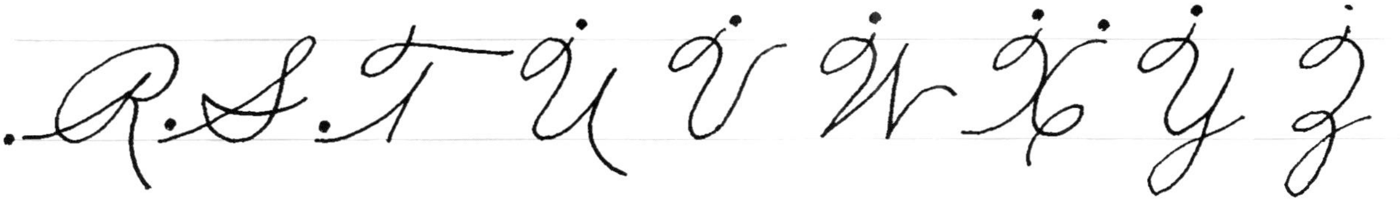

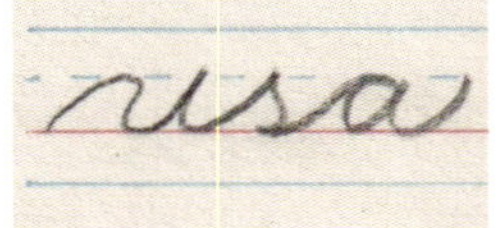

"What looked good in theory was not always workable in practice."

~ *Tamara Plakins Thornton* in *Handwriting in America*

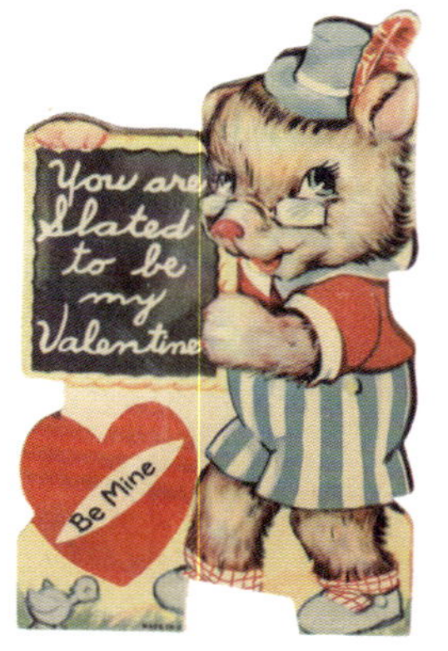

↑ *Mid-century children gave valentines to their classmates.*

THE QUEST FOR BETTER HANDWRITING, and for methods to teach it, continued after World War II. Although Palmer had promoted penmanship as a manly skill in the workplace, simply sitting still was harder for grade-school boys than for girls, leading them to dismiss good writing as girlish. And—just the wrong idea!—extra handwriting drills were often inflicted as after-school punishment. Left-handers were demonized, and children with reading or writing disabilities were not diagnosed and accommodated, but were sternly told to try harder. As a Canadian student of the 1940s remembered, "It seems we were never taught, only graded." Much-needed reform came, slowly, only after about 1950.

American educators began to have doubts about how and when—and even whether—they should teach handwriting. They had to admit that learning to write connected script did not help children who were learning to read printed Roman type. While scientific research began to help children overcome writing problems, it offered less conclusive insight into the typical child. Public opinion (and *everyone* had an opinion) could not unite around a better way to teach handwriting.

Because America did not have a national policy for teaching children to write, each school district pursued its own solution, with local school boards often battling their state legislature for control. Parents and teachers, though seldom in complete agreement, gradually turned to rival systems such as Zaner and D'Nealian that taught first-graders to "print" large separated letters and then two years later introduced them to slanted and connected small cursive. They always insisted that they were simplifying the letters. In truth, these systems still offered very few new ideas about letterforms, being similar to much of Palmer and even to some of Spencerian. Small wonder then, that so many children had trouble making the move to cursive.

THE CONNECTION QUESTION

Educators could not agree if cursive letters should be taught *with* their connecting strokes attached or *without* them.

↗

Connecting the letters lets them flow without lifting the pen, giving most words a graceful unity. But connecting some letters, such as **r t**, *reduced* → *legibility. Students had to learn alternate forms, or just lift the pen.*

Connections aren't essential to the letter; here → *they start each word without really being needed.*

Capitals, ascenders, and descenders = twice the height of small letters.

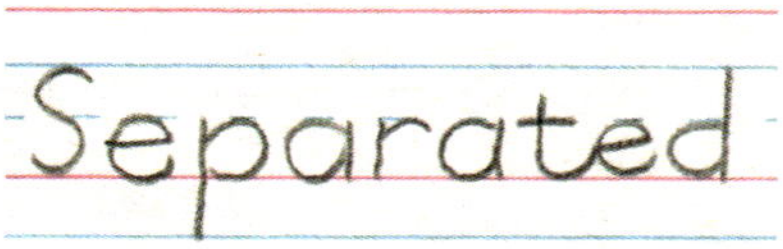

Separated

Also "Manuscript" or "Ball and stick" or "Printing." In England, "Circle and stick."

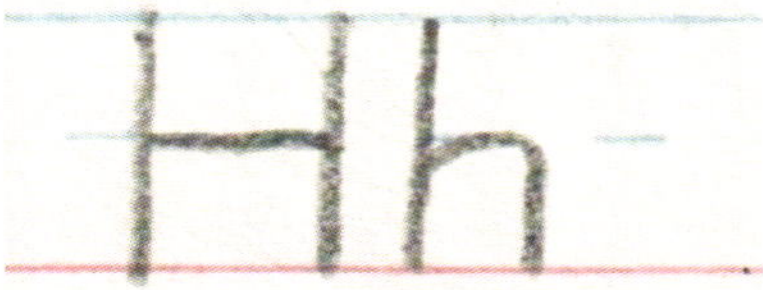

Children began learning with a fat pencil in large guidelines on newsprint paper. They moved on to writing with a thinner pen in smaller guidelines on smoother paper, and then with no guidelines.

Cursive

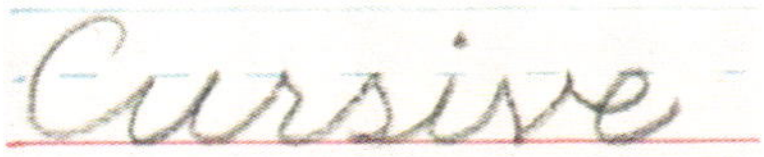

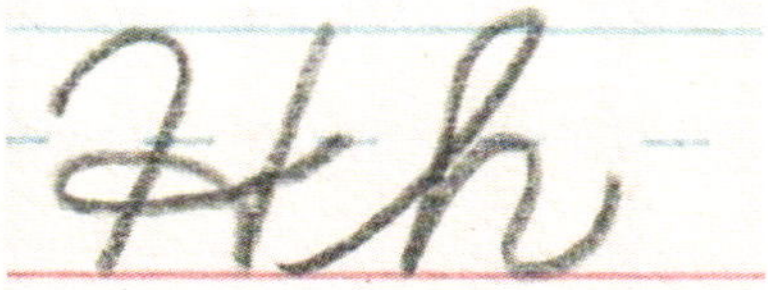

Letters slant 5° to 10° off vertical.

BASIC STROKES

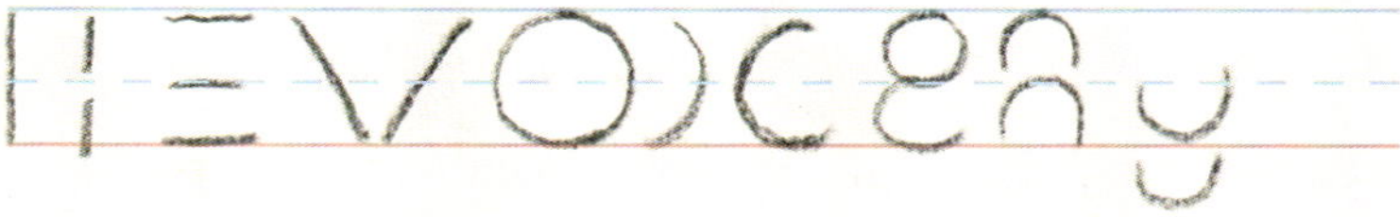

CAPITALS

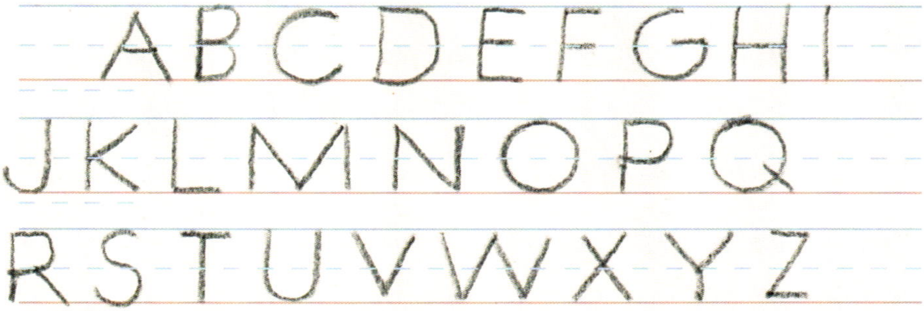

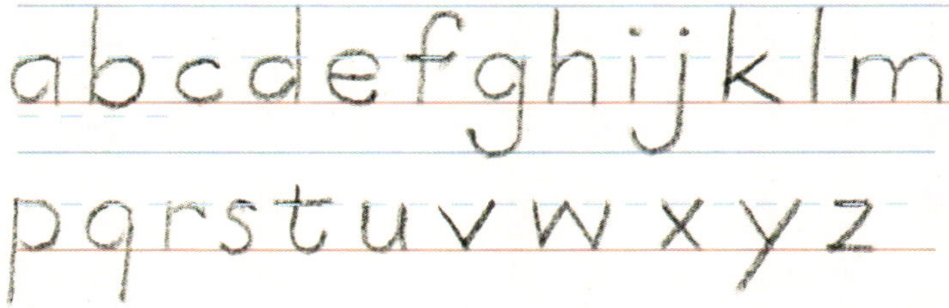

A B C D E F G H I
J K L M N O P Q
R S T U V W X Y Z

a b c d e f g h i j k l m n o
p q r s t u v w x y z

SMALL LETTERS

SMALL LETTERS

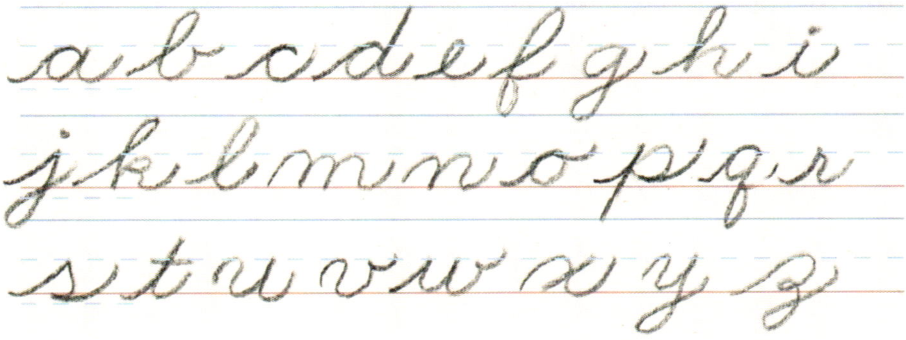

The capitals and small letters shown here are a blend from several cursive writing systems of 1950 - 2000. Since 2000, more of the older capitals have finally been updated.

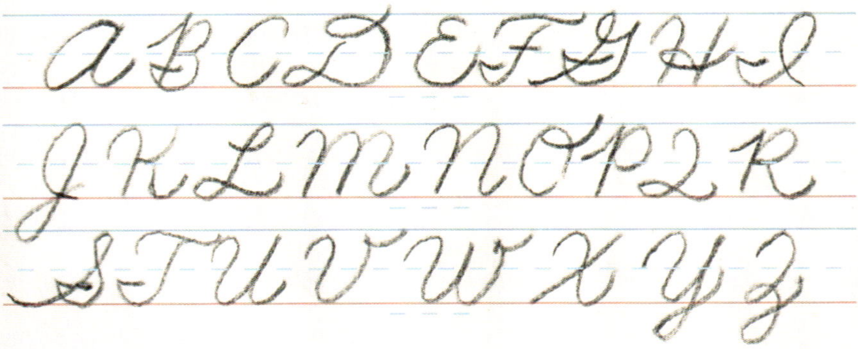

CAPITALS

Even the most simplified capitals still held onto old-fashioned forms and extra strokes:

G I Q kept their arbitrary forms.
D H L O kept their extra loops.
V W kept their exit strokes.
B F G I S T kept their upstrokes.

usa

THE DECLINE OF HANDWRITING slowed briefly in the 1970s when Americans began to discover the beauties of Italic calligraphy. It was not only easier to write and nicer to look at, but children could learn individual letters first and then connect them later, without having to start over with different letter shapes. People who had flunked cursive found a haven in Italic. (Italic, in fact, had originated in the fifteenth century as a style for effortless handwriting.) It was also visually familiar as a common type style and similar enough to Roman letterforms for easy reading. It was practical, legible, attractive, logical, and easy to learn.

ITALIC LEVELS RANGE FROM BEGINNER TO EXPERT
Add just a few swashes and don't let them curve too much.

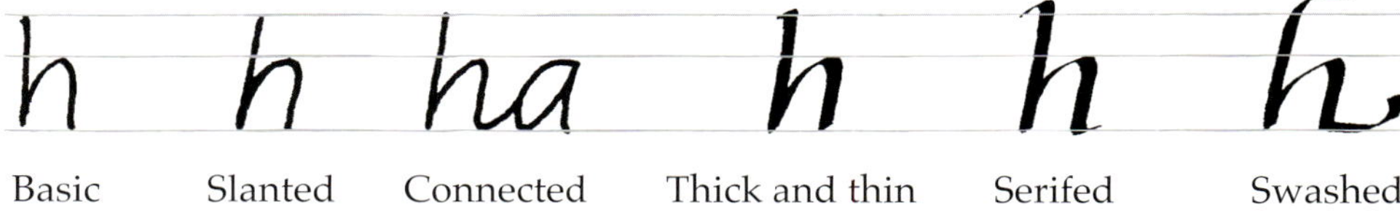

Basic   Slanted   Connected   Thick and thin   Serifed   Swashed

Italic was accessible to people of many different skill levels and ages, for many different purposes. A beginner could write the letters with a pencil and learn their rules, then write them with a pen, and then upgrade to a broad-edged pen, all without relearning them. Later, at larger size, with more expertise, and without so many joins, the letters could blossom into formal calligraphy. And on special occasions they could be dressed up with swashes.

One of the earliest American advocates for Italic was Lloyd Reynolds, the mid-century professor at Reed College, Oregon, who nurtured a generation of teachers, scholars, and enthusiasts. He said, "It seemed perfectly obvious—the only logical approach is the historical one." Reformers Inga Dubay and Barbara Getty streamlined formal Italic lettering to simple handwriting, designing graduated workbooks that spread it to primary schools of the west coast, parochial schools, homeschoolers, and hobbyists everywhere.

This revival, however, could not reverse the general decline; Italic came too late to rescue America's handwriting or to evolve into something that could.

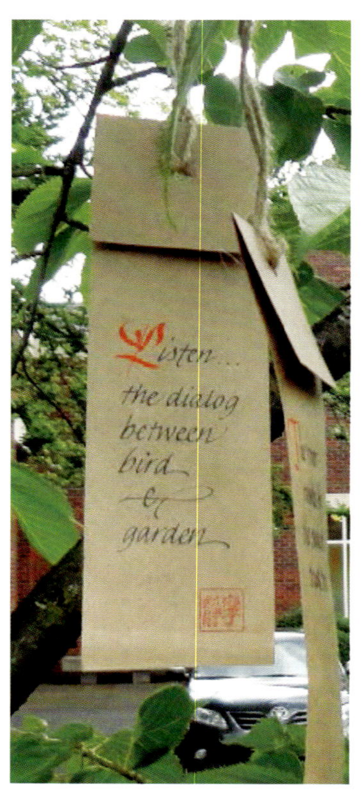

Lloyd Reynolds started a tradition he called Weathergrams, by writing lines of poetry in Italic on strips of kraft paper and hanging them outside to weather away.

Italic

Capitals, ascenders, and descenders are about 1¾ times the letter body height.

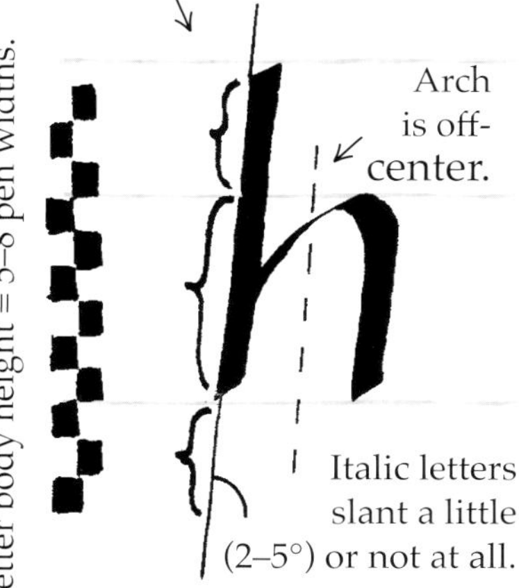

Arch is off-center.

Italic letters slant a little (2–5°) or not at all.

Letter body height = 5–8 pen widths.

Many of the small letters look just like each other if turned upside-down:

u n   h y   b q g
d p   Similar: f j

BASIC STROKES

The 45° pen angle required by a broad pen is easier for right-handers.

A thin-line pen allows both right- and left-handers to write with their usual hand position.

SMALL LETTERS IN FAMILY GROUPS

Instead of copying by rote, small letters should be sorted into groups based on body shape, and practiced together to reinforce their kinship.

A-BODY

a c d g q u y   ONE MAIN STROKE   f i j l t

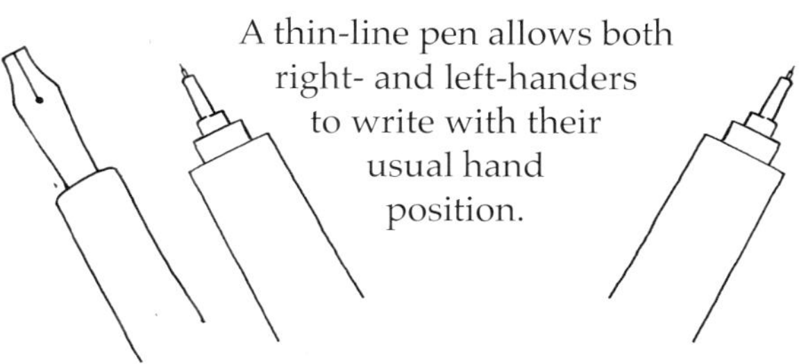

B-BODY

b h k m n p r

DIAGONAL

v w x z   ROUND   e o s   .

Swashes and dots decorate Italic.

ABOUT CONNECTING

The half-dozen letters that start at upper left and finish at lower right, like m u, are easy to connect. Those that start or end in other corners will need practice, or may not connect at all. (The Italic chapter in *Learn Calligraphy*, by Margaret Shepherd, offers a detailed chart of the best join for every possible letter pair.)

CAPITALS

Basic Italic capitals are useful for writing whole words because they are free of extra strokes. Compare to cursive. →   QUIZ   vs   Quiz

A B C D E F G H I J K L M N

Half the Italic capitals look the same as their small letters **C O S V W X Z**, or are very similar: **I J K P U Y**.

O P Q R S T U V W X Y Z

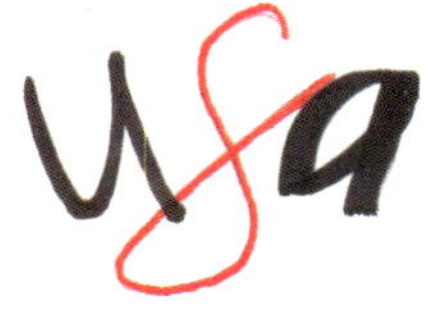

"of the people,
by the people, for
the people"
~ *Abraham Lincoln*,
Gettysburg Address

BY THE TIME AMERICANS HAD BETTER CHOICES about handwriting, they had a lot less need to write by hand at all. Even while Italic offered a workable alternative, the use of pen on paper was dwindling fast. (Emailing and texting would later reduce it to near zero.) Already by mid-century, white-collar jobs required typing, not penmanship; social life revolved around telephones, not writing desks; and a new inverse snobbery had turned an unreadable signature into a sign of genius. American life was moving forward, while handwriting trailed behind.

After 2010, grade schools began to spend more time on keyboard skills and less on any system of handwriting instruction, leaving students to figure out for themselves how to connect separated letters.

Every national writing style changes to reflect the character of its people. It seems that America's penmanship is becoming what Platt Rogers Spencer called "still more American," because people are learning new ideas from each other rather than waiting for someone in charge to teach them. Millions of these individual solutions to the handwriting challenge will help to steer it in new and useful directions. The result will truly be "by the people," a grassroots alphabet created by a nation of do-it-yourselfers.

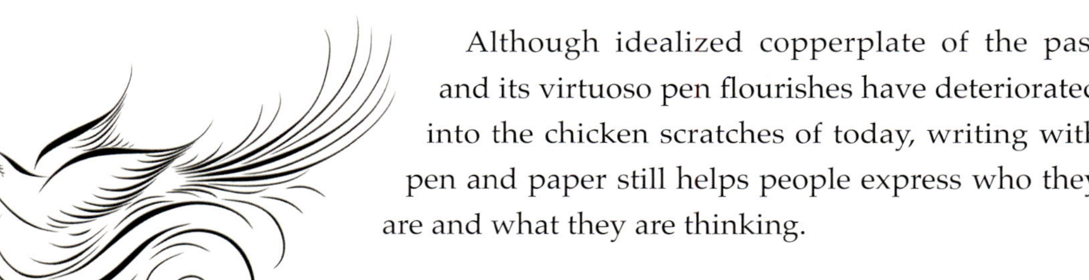

Although idealized copperplate of the past and its virtuoso pen flourishes have deteriorated into the chicken scratches of today, writing with pen and paper still helps people express who they are and what they are thinking.

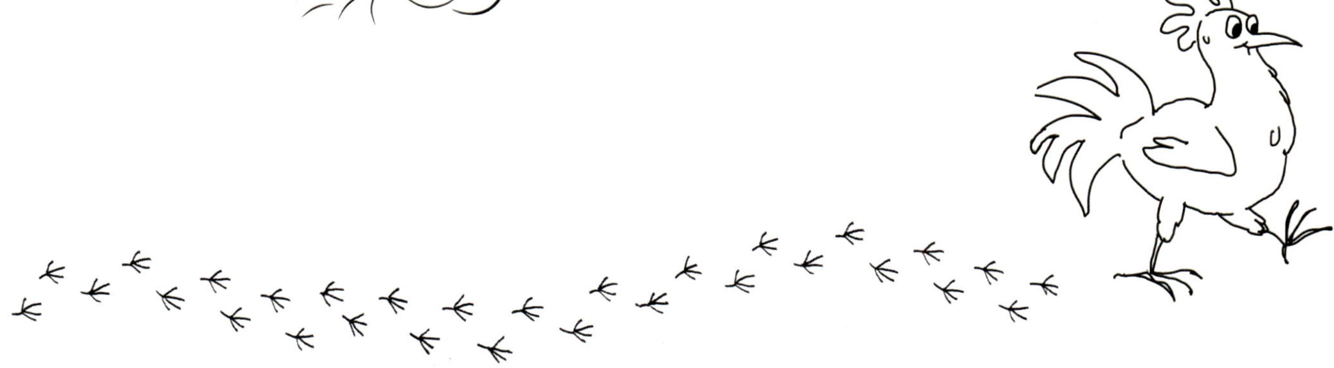

ad hoc

Resourceful Americans who are determined to communicate will help shape the new national handwriting; crowd sourcing may well be the key to its future. The samples below, from people of different ages, goals, and abilities, suggest ways to write creatively and readably. They have shaped their writing to communicate—beautifully or just adequately. Their choices may suggest new experiments.

People who mail handwritten letters often inspire their readers to send handwritten letters to them.

FIRST AID FOR YOUR HANDWRITING will make it easier to read, write, and look at--and more useful for whatever comes next. Some of the simple repairs listed here can help repair even the worst scrawl.

1. **Choose a better pen:** Each upgrade, from ballpoint to rollerball to marker to fountain pen to calligraphy pen, will make your script better.

2. **Pen size matters:** The pen's width should fit the letter's size, and vice versa. Don't try to write too small.

too heavy
just right
too thin
Weight

3. **Choose the right paper:** Avoid glossy paper, newsprint, rough surfaces, and distracting backgrounds.

4. **Guidelines help:** Use paper with faint horizontal texture, or put a lined sheet under plain paper to show through.

5. **Pad the paper:** Even the worst pen will write a better line if you lay two sheets of paper under the page you write on.

6. **Letter slant:** Slanting all letters the same makes them more legible. Choose one moderate slant, or none, and stick with it. \\\\ |||| ////

7. **Don't force** every pair of letters to connect. Some link up readily, others resist, and many won't join at all.

8. **Clean up clutter:** Shorten long strokes, clear out extra loops, and trade in your antiquated capitals for modern forms.

d   d
D   D
De-clutter

9. **Posture:** Sit up straight to write. Don't crouch, slump, or lie down. Hold the pen, don't grip it. Support the elbow of your writing arm and lean gently on the other arm.

10. **Practice, practice, practice:** Write something every day. Take a minute to warm up by repeating **n** and **u**, then the word *minimum*. Practice anything important twelve times first.

consistent
irregular

forward
upright
backward
Slant

Finally, enjoy using whatever kind of handwriting you have. There are many occasions when even the worst handwriting still communicates better than the sleekest type style. Like your own voice and your own face, your own handwriting can help you to make stronger, warmer, livelier human connections in the real world, express who you are, honor the past, and stay tuned in to the future.

TEN REASONS WHY HANDWRITING STILL MATTERS

1. Research into **how children learn** shows many ways that they benefit from studying penmanship. Writing by hand creates extra pathways in the brain; it reinforces letter shapes and word meanings through muscle memory; it develops the hand-eye coordination that is vital to all visual arts. Writing by hand can also compensate for learning disabilities and developmental delays.

2. Handwriting encourages **self-expression**. When people of any age write by hand they choose different words and feel differently about them. They write more satisfying journals and memoirs.

3. Better handwriting raises **self-esteem**, both from the confidence that comes from mastering any skill and for the special role of handwriting in presentation of self.

4. Handwriting is a tool for **communication**. People choose better phrasing when they write by hand. Reading words on paper is more intense than reading them on a screen. And each person's handwriting makes them seem more present to the reader.

5. Writing by hand sends a **social signal**, impossible to fake, that these words deserve extra attention because the writer took extra trouble. Those who seek votes, favors, jobs, or donations —or better connections of any kind—know that handwriting can be the best proof of sincerity.

6. Writing by hand continues to help people **interact** with computers, beyond keyboard and mouse, gesture and voice. Even people who prefer typing for its speed admit that stroking with a pen feels better than pounding on a keyboard.

7. Handwriting offers insight into the **human mind**. There is scientific evidence that penmanship can help diagnose multiple sclerosis, Parkinson's disease, amyotrophic lateral sclerosis, and attention deficit hyperactivity disorder.

8. People who write by hand are better equipped to read the **handwriting of others**, a vital skill for studying historical documents, learning a foreign alphabet, or decoding the scrawl of their own contemporaries.

9. Writing by hand can make it easier to **learn calligraphy**, which is a prerequisite for understanding type design, graphic design, and cultural history, as well as a rewarding hobby and a serious art.

10. Penmanship opens a **window to the past**, re-connecting people with the care and craftsmanship of a bygone era. As historian and former president of Harvard University Drew Gilpin Faust wrote recently in *The Atlantic*, "The inability to read handwriting deprives society of direct access to its own past . . . including the documents and papers of our own families." Americans respond to handwriting, not just for its quaint charm in a high-tech world, but also because they have special affection for the materials of history—pens, inkwells, sealing wax, paper, and other treasures from the country's past.

↗ This thank-you from a third-grader is warm and creative, as well as properly dated, imaginatively illustrated, and nicely laid out.

HANDWRITING HEIRLOOMS

NOW THAT WRITING BY HAND is no longer a daily chore, some Americans calligraphers like to focus on enjoying the experience itself. Old-fashioned pens, paper, and ink make words more important, in the same way that candlelight, silver, and linen make dinner more elegant. For some, these antiques actually do make their script easier to write and nicer to read. For others, they add a sense of ceremony. And others simply like to collect.

Like the letters themselves, each of these eloquent objects has a story to tell about American life. Pens, especially, have inspired hundreds of enthusiasts, who find them, refurbish them, and meet others for shoptalk about them. Fountain pens were not only tools, but often used to serve as decorative jewelry and ritual gifts. They implied high status, like the expensive pen in the suit pocket of an important executive, or signified practicality, like the pencils in an engineer's pocket protector. But whether pens are museum pieces or just sentimental keepsakes—and whether they are meant to be used for writing at all—they carry special meaning for their collectors.

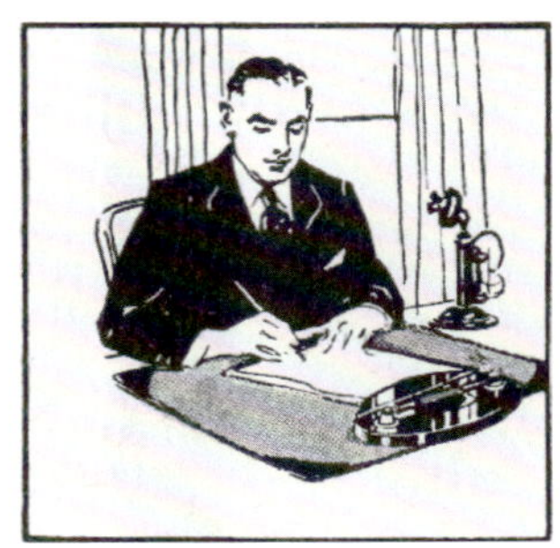

Corporate executive, 1927

↙   *People like pens with decorative bodies even though only the nib shapes the letter strokes. This "Patriot Pen" is constructed by hand from a kit, a newly popular hobby. Image courtesy of Penn State Industries.*

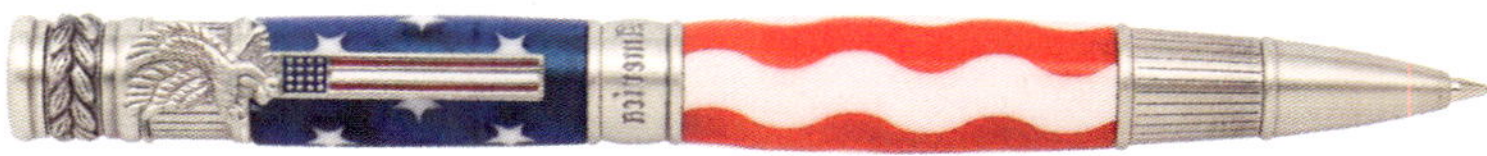

The well furnished desktop of two generations ago used to hold many such useful items, now the cherished, collectible tokens of a vanished era: an inkwell, a rocker blotter for drying wet ink, a date book, an address book, a letter opener, monogrammed stationery, a stamp dispenser or stamp folder, a stamp moistener, wafer seals, and a glass paperweight. The desk itself might be an heirloom (dedicated writers can build their own by following the Thomas Jefferson blueprints available online).

The tools for writing by hand continue to inspire writers, even if only by nudging them to write at all. A little of that inspiration rubs off on their penmanship, just as Benjamin Franklin described, so that while they know that their letters may never be excellent, "their hand is mended by the endeavor."

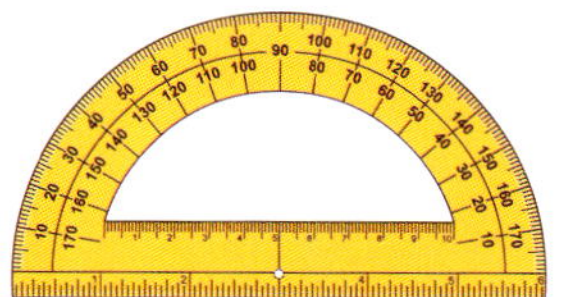

These all-purpose guidelines can be reduced or enlarged to fit individual handwriting habits and goals. Penmanship teachers measured their letter slant from the horizontal; calligraphers measure theirs from the vertical.

A variety of slanted pencil lines to add for extra guidance ↓

1. COPPERPLATE, SPENCERIAN, EARLY PALMER

Each of these historical styles had its own specific slant between 37.5° and 30°. Some instructors still insist on these exact angles. *Quill, metal dip pen, or marker.*

2. CURSIVE (UPDATED PALMER), ITALIC

These recent styles have a moderate letter slant between 5° and 20°. Rigid pen, stylus, or pencil for cursive; medium-wide broad-edge pen or marker for Italic.

3. AD HOC

Letter slant, and the choice of pen, were left to personal preference in the late twentieth century, ranging from backwards 10° to 30° and beyond. Any pen.

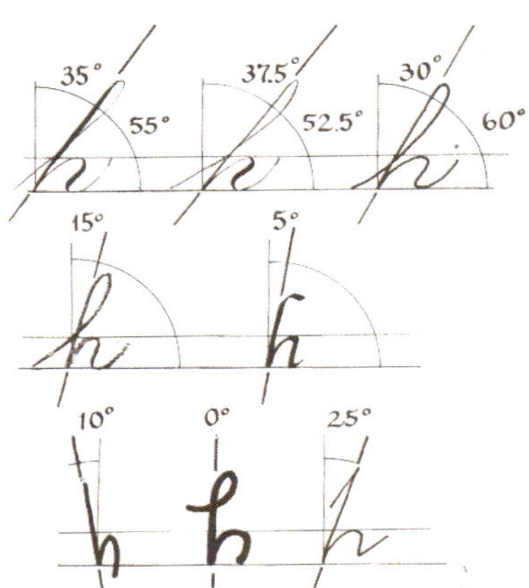

TIGHTLY SPACED GUIDELINES below allow space only for repetitive warm-up, plus short ascenders and descenders. Guidelines on the next page offer space for taller ascenders and descenders.

LETTER BODY {   }

LETTER BODY {   }

LETTER BODY {   }

LETTER BODY {   }

LETTER BODY {   }

LETTER BODY {   }

LETTER BODY {   }

LETTER BODY {   }

LETTER BODY {   }

LETTER BODY {   }

WIDELY SPACED GUIDELINES here allow room for ascenders and descenders.
Angle choices for adding slant lines are illustrated on page 57.

ASCENDER

LETTER BODY {

DESCENDER

ASCENDER

LETTER BODY {

DESCENDER

ASCENDER

LETTER BODY {

DESCENDER

ASCENDER

LETTER BODY {

DESCENDER

ASCENDER

LETTER BODY {

DESCENDER

ASCENDER

LETTER BODY {

DESCENDER

ASCENDER

LETTER BODY {

DESCENDER

ASCENDER

LETTER BODY {

DESCENDER

Dots

ALTHOUGH CALLIGRAPHY used to be narrowly defined as letters written in ink with a pen, it is much more than that. New materials, or old ones reconsidered, are helping letter artists expand the alphabet's horizons.

The kind of American lettering, for instance, that builds an image out of little bits of material has special significance and special strengths. In the recent century, this technique carried the country and the whole world, one step at a time, out of the Gutenberg era and into the digital age. Americans began with cross-stitches and quilt patches, and then moved on to light bulbs and pixels. Paradoxically, in a country famed for its rugged individualism, these letters were assembled from a lot of little bits for a shared purpose.

Making letters by arranging dots is American through and through. Such unity of equals began with the First Americans, inspired the symbolism of the Haudenosaunee belt, and is featured as the national motto on the Great Seal of the United States: *e pluribus unum*, or "Out of many, one" (see page 2).

"Happy while United."

~From a silver medal given by Sir William Johnson, at the Treaty of Niagara 1764

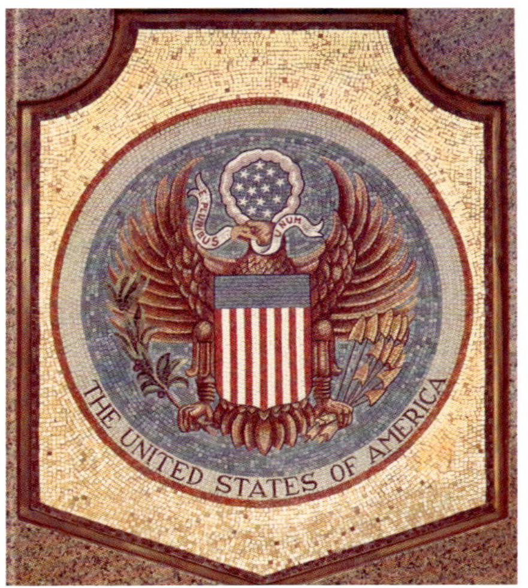

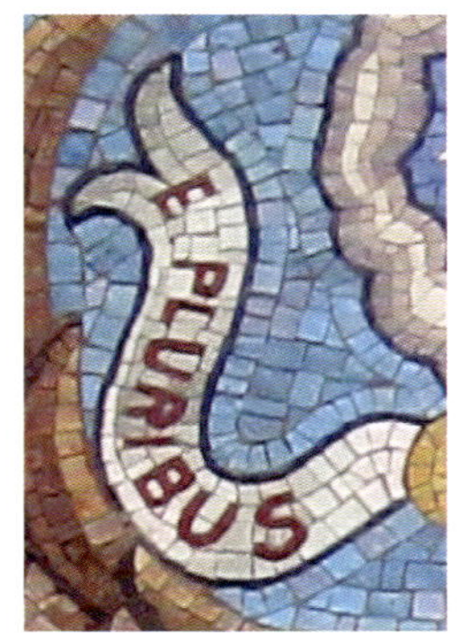

←The US Great Seal, a mosaic from the Lorenzo de Zavala State Archives and Library Building, Austin, Texas.

← Detail

↓ The Fort Niagara treaty belt of 1764 is called "The Magna Carta of the Anishinabe people" by Alan Ojiig Corbiere, Knowledge Keeper. It was given to commemorate promises that were made to and by the British, who reciprocated with a silver medal.

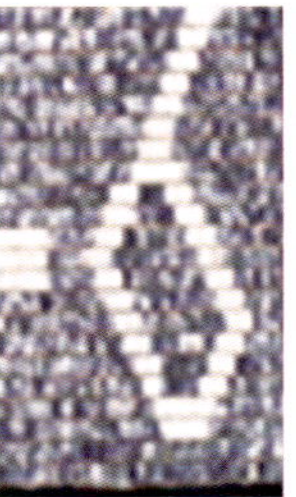

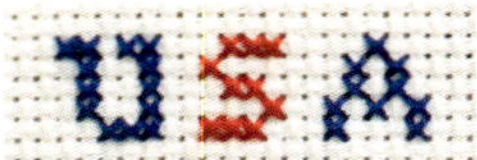

1. STITCHES

UNTIL THE 1920s, American girls as young as six years old were taught basic needlework and their ABCs by stitching a sampler. This displayed a girl's mastery of basic techniques, but also served as a reference chart for letters and ornaments she could use in future design projects.

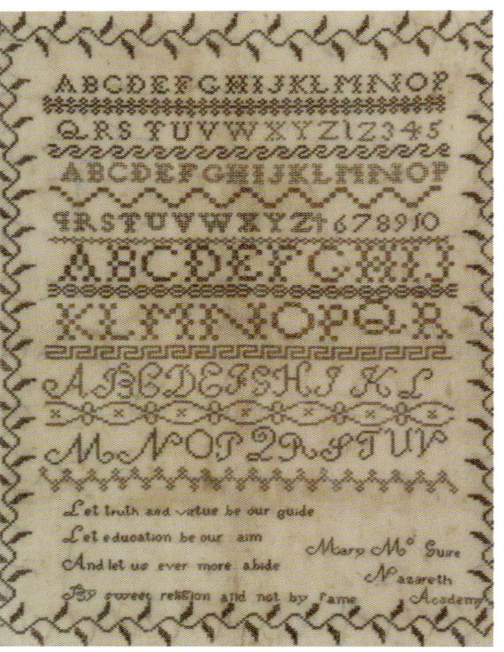

The first known American sampler was stitched by Miles Standish's daughter Loara Standish in 1643. American samplers were based at first on English designs, but soon evolved differences such as large motifs rather than tiny ones, a backing of linen instead of fine wool, and realistic decorations that showed local trees and buildings. American girls were also more willing to improvise their own letters if no original was available to copy.

↗ *This sampler by Mary McGuire, Bardstown, Kentucky, c 1836, offers a range of styles and sizes for capitals, swashed script capitals, Roman lowercase, and nine different borders.*

→ *This sampler by an unknown girl fits a motto into a small space by shrinking the ends of the last two lines. Letters **g** and **y** are raised. The long **s** was less common after 1800.*

While cross-stitch was useful for marking household linen and decorating family clothes, it was mainly seen as good for a child's self-discipline. Oliver Wendell Holmes Sr. declared, "Take your needle, my child, and work at your pattern. . . . Life is like that—one stitch at a time taken patiently and the pattern will come out all right." These laboriously produced moral lessons became family heirlooms.

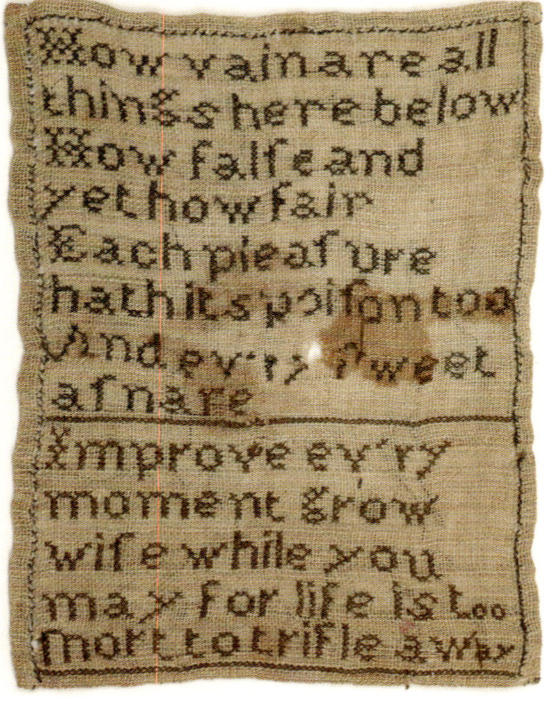

Today, collectors and curators study samplers not only for their endearing beauty but also for their roots in history. They are full of information about where and when they were made. Like many other treasures of American calligraphy—Frakturs, coverlets, many quilts, and even some gravestones—the artist's name is part of the design.

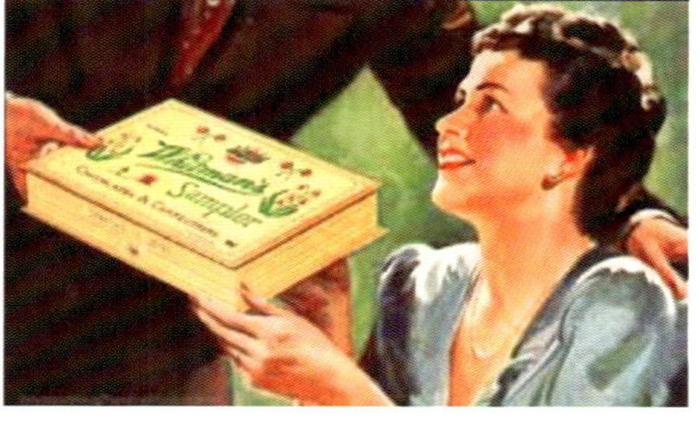

→ *In 1912, the Whitman candy assortment was introduced with an iconic cross-stitched sampler on its box. This advertisement from 1940 shows it in its frequent role as a Mother's Day gift.*

Cross-stitches were usually sewn on a coarsely woven linen backing by counting. Most beginners' letters were one inch (2.5 cm) and seven stitches high, for a resolution of 7 DPI.

The human eye has a strong urge to recognize images made out of very few bits of virtually any material. Calligraphers who learn to make letters with dots are often surprised to find how few stitches or pixels or quilt patches or mosaic tiles or bricks they need to make a readable letter.

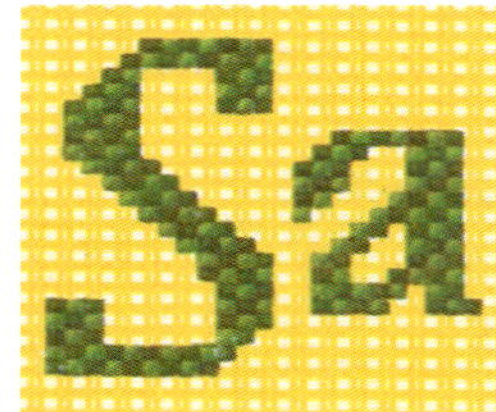

Detail from box.

Even a five-by-five grid can accommodate the whole alphabet and numerals (widening the square by two dots makes M and W easier to read). The seven-by-seven letters in beginners' samplers set the stage for decorative serifs, lowercase letterforms, and articulated corners. A ten-by-ten grid enables extra niceties like thick and thin strokes, swashes, and slanted script capitals.

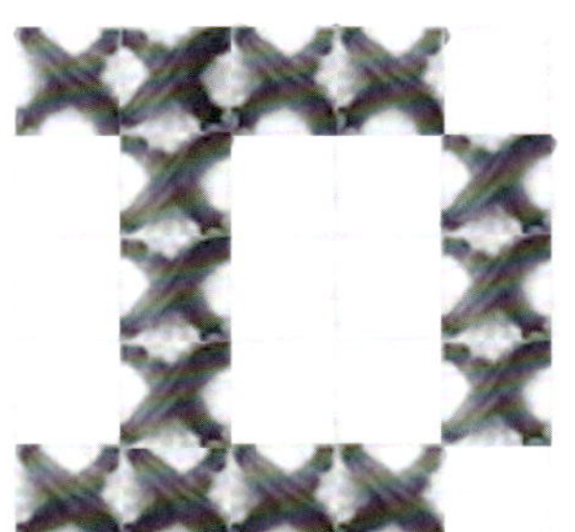 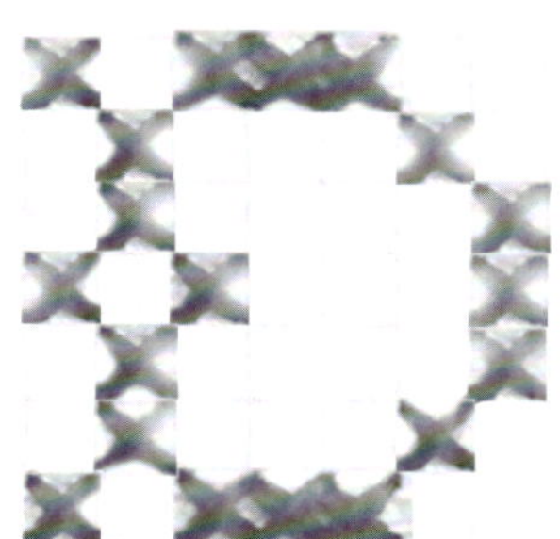 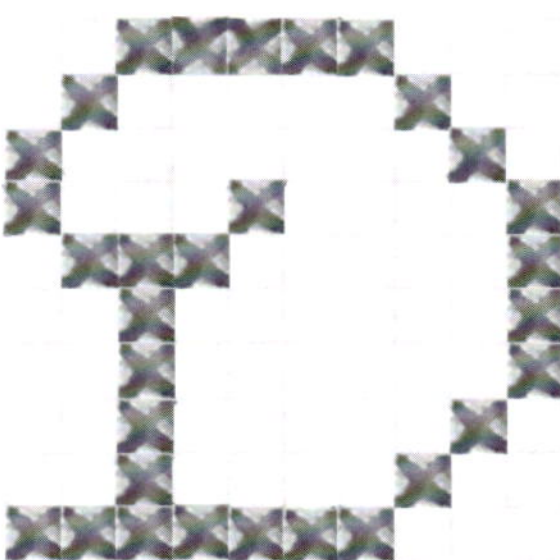

↑ *Cross-stitchers can refine their letters further by using a half-stitch, which looks like a diagonal bar \ / instead of an X. Though it is less common on samplers, other classic designs use this workaround.*
↓ *Half-stitches soften the corners and curves of cross-stitched letters.*

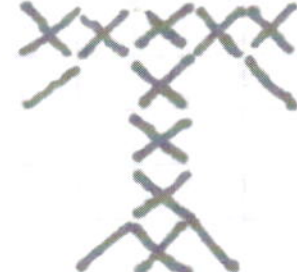 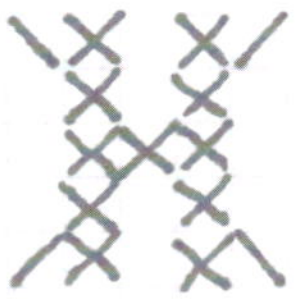 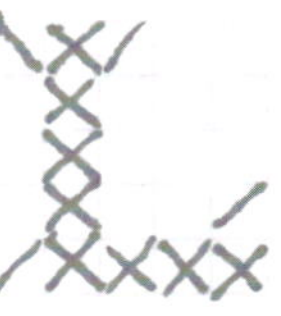 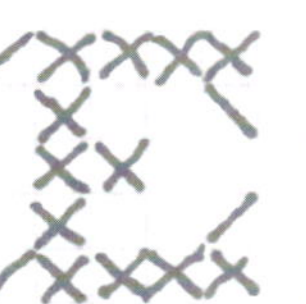 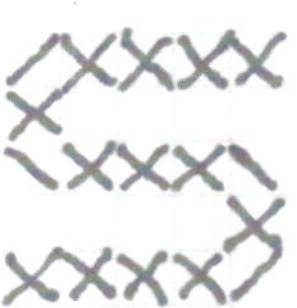 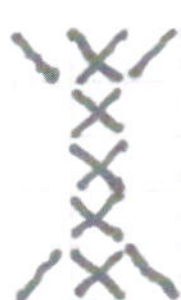

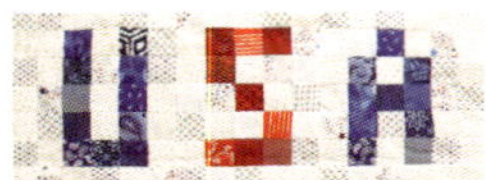

"The whole quilt
is much more
important than any
single square."
~Rohinton Mistry

2. QUILTS

ALTHOUGH MANY OF AMERICA'S EARLY SETTLERS lived far from teachers and textbooks, art supplies and tools, they took pride in turning the simplest materials into beautiful and useful heirlooms. This craft connected quilters, mainly women at first, with family, friends, and each other.

Even poor families had fabric available that was nearly free: a scrap bag of cotton cloth left from making dresses and shirts. The quilter usually trimmed them into uniform shapes, and sewed them together to make the top layer of a blanket.

A few ambitious quilters pieced together letters in geometric grids: squares, rectangles, triangles, and hexagons.

Quilting in America enabled anyone who could sew to speak an artistic language that everyone could understand. For many, designing an original quilt top brought out visual talent they did not know they had.

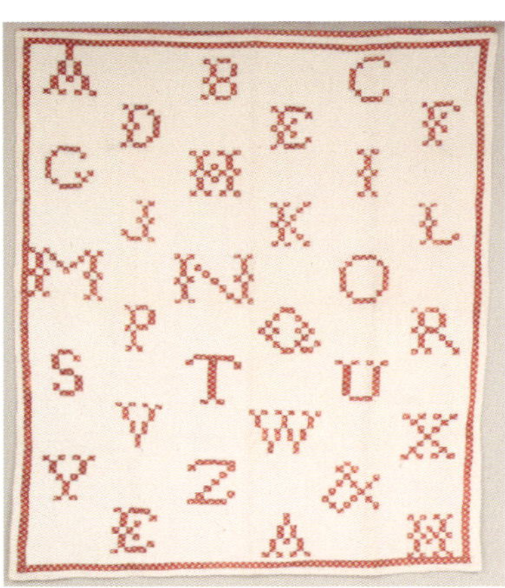

↑ *These letters were made in the 1920s on a 7 x 7 grid of squares, likely modeled on familiar letters from a cross-stitch sampler.*

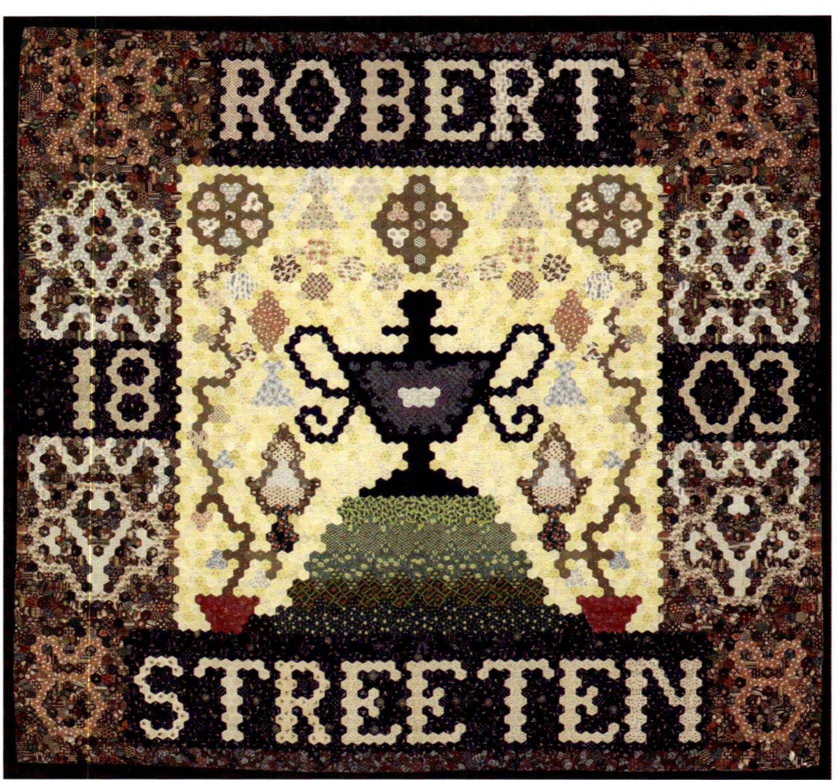

↑ *This virtuoso wall hanging was made with a letter height of nine hexagons. The urn in the center suggests that it was stitched as a memorial for Robert Streeten (1803–1874), who lived in New York.*

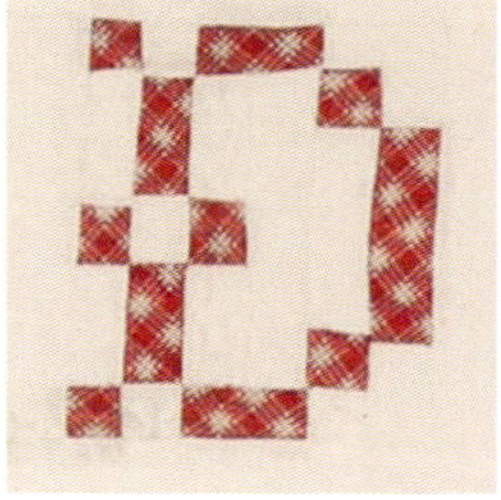

↑ *Detail. The square patches of cloth themselves were made of fabric printed to look like red cross-stitches.*

While most quilts were in nightly use on family beds, a few were proudly displayed on special quilt racks. Little girls started by making nine-patch blocks from the scraps left over from their home-sewn dresses. Women met in quilting bees to help each other join the top to the filler and backing with decorative stitches. They showed off their best work at local competitions and state fairs, picking up and spreading new techniques. Some quilters bartered their quilts to pay for supplies or sold them to make a little cash for their families. One special tradition evolved where members of a group each wrote their signature on a 6" x 6" square (15 x 15 cm) and made it permanent with embroidery stitches. The blocks were then assembled into "friendship quilts" for weddings, christenings, retirement gifts, or fund-raising raffles.

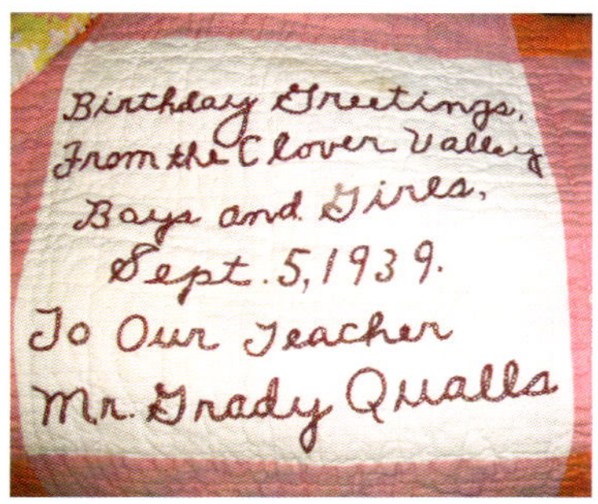

Quilts in America spread far beyond their origins. These scraps of cloth, lovingly pieced together, were used to tell the stories of enslaved Africans and America's indigenous peoples as well as those who immigrated from everywhere else in the world. Today's quilts are made by everyone—young or old, metropolitan or rustic, privileged or oppressed.

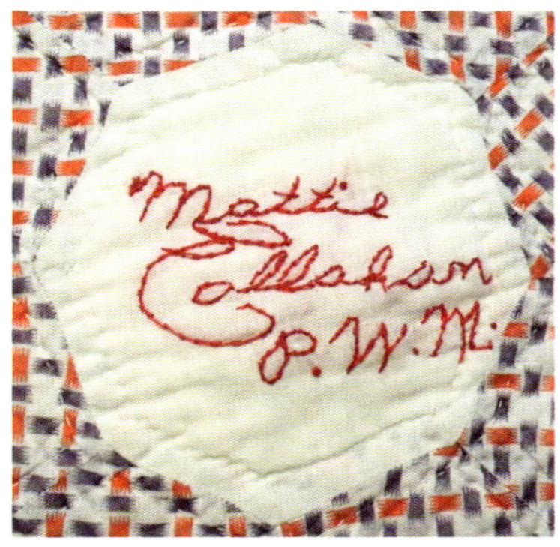

↖ This 1939 birthday quilt was signed with student names neatly written in Palmer method script, and embroidered for a favorite teacher in Clover Valley, AR.

↖ A typical friendship quilt block, stitched in Cyril, Oklahoma, in the 1930s.

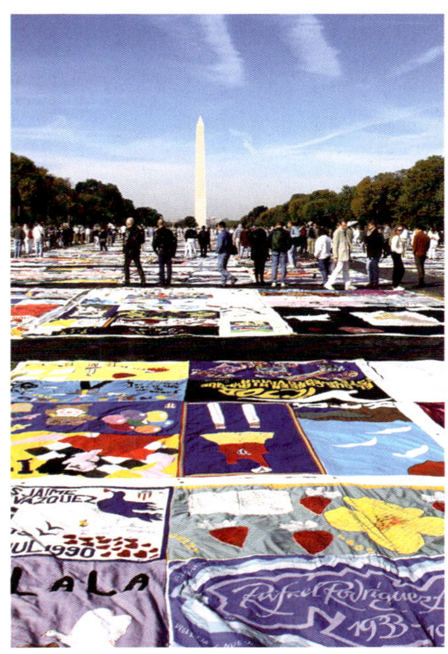

→ Friendship quilts provided the underlying metaphor when American activists initiated the AIDS Memorial Quilt. Starting in 1984, each square was pieced, painted, embroidered, or appliquéd with the name of an AIDS victim. The quilt has grown to more than 100,000 names.

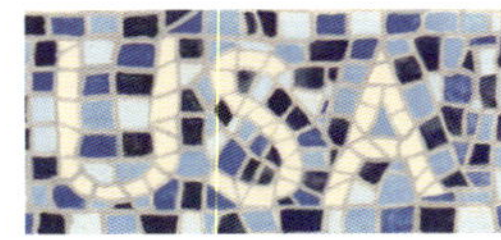

"Not a
melting pot
but a beautiful
mosaic."
~Jimmy Carter

3. Mosaics

Mosaics offer a special perspective on how to build images out of different dot shapes--not only when the letters have to fit into a grid but also when they ought to push against it. Letter artists learn which rules they have to obey and which rules they can ignore.

Brick grid

Some grids give the artist almost no flexibility. Bricks, for instance, can not be rotated, cut, or left out without weakening the structure. It is hard to smooth out their hopscotch verticals and uneven curves.

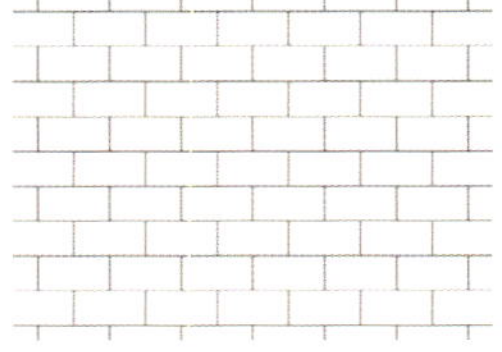

The American landscape was once dotted with smokestacks that spelled out their companies' names in contrasting brick, like the L. H. Hamel Co., Haverhill, MA. Photo by Alison Colby-Campbell. ↗

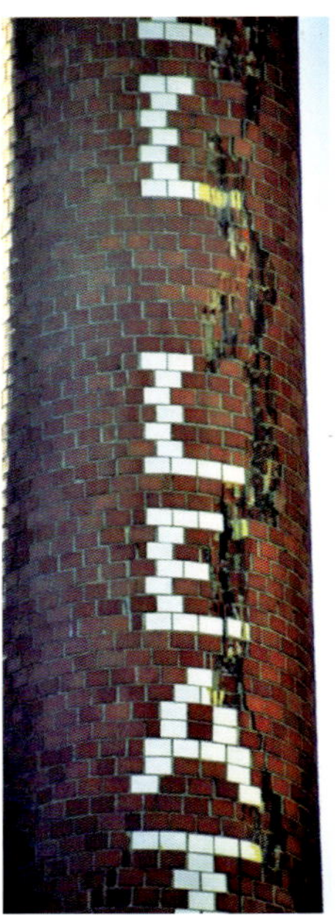

Hexagon grid

A hexagonal grid can be filled with circles, triangles, or hexagons. The 120° corners help the tiles resist chipping underfoot.

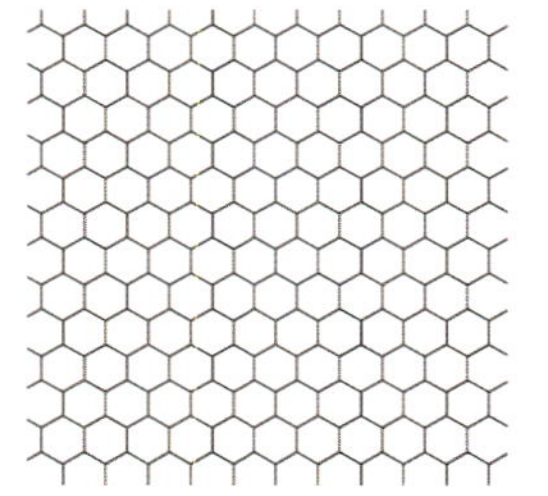 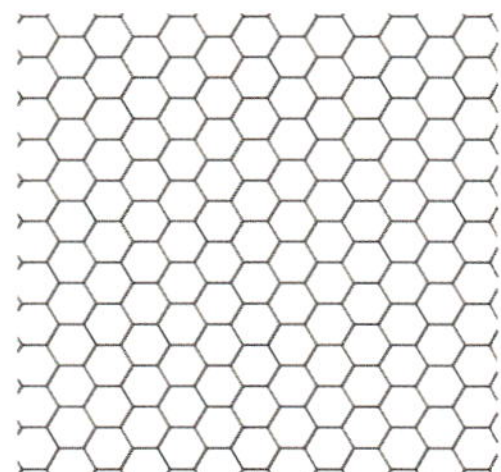

Calligraphers trying to fit letters into this grid first have to decide if the hexagons will be on their flat sides or on their points. Both orientations will make some of the curves rigid and some of the straight lines lumpy. Neither is quite ideal for standard letters.

Hexagons on their points ↖ versus hexagons on their flat edges ↖ .
Points fit slanted letters ↙, while flat edges fit slanted lines ↓ .

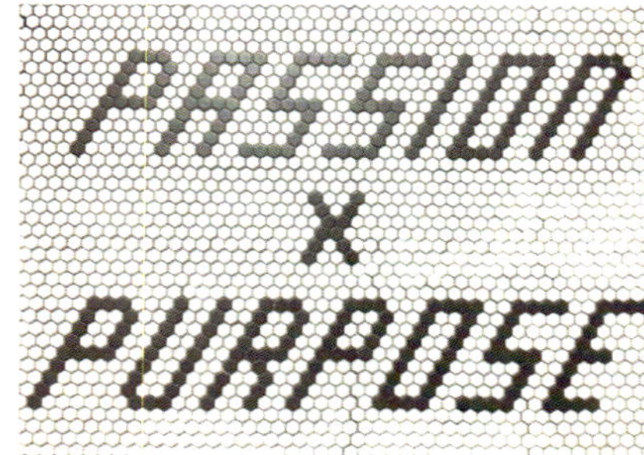

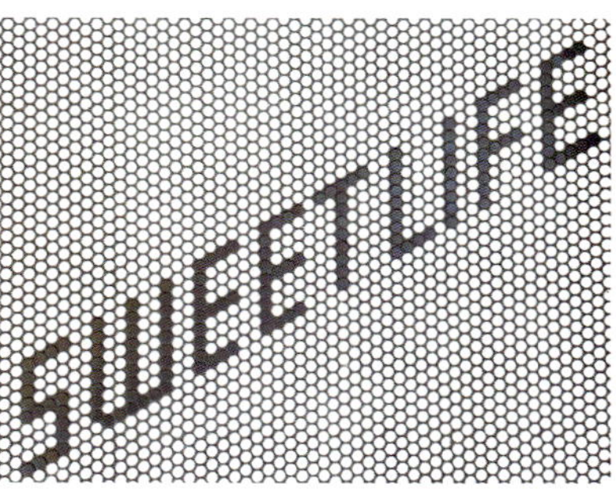

Since hexagonal grids of both orientations do not fit comfortably with curves and vertical lines, they need a different alphabet. The built-in 60° bias favors slanted letters or slanted layouts. Either way, straight strokes will dominate.

Square grid

Although mosaic letters have been around since ancient Greece, some of the world's most creative designs were made just over a hundred years ago and can be seen in the subway stations of New York City, plus a few in Boston. Careful conservation and replacement has preserved them as models of how great art can help fit round pegs into square holes.

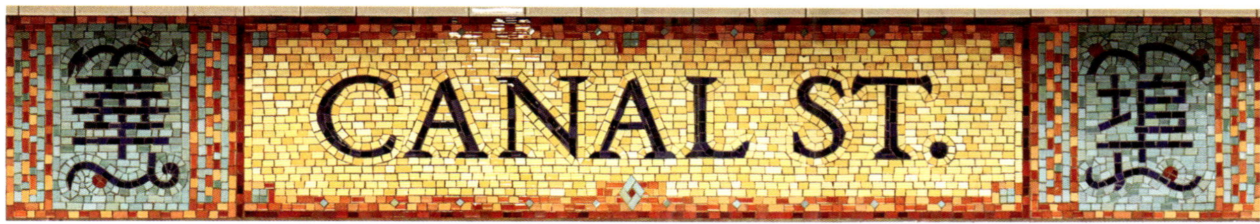

The grid is freeform in the middle, linear around the letters, and square at its edges.

Letters usually have curves and diagonals that don't fit smoothly into a square grid, and that would look jagged even at higher resolution. For centuries, mosaic artists have transformed this problem into an asset by simply overruling the grid's conformity in favor of individuality. They knew that after they cut and rotated the pieces, color would help camouflage the disruption, and they could then just fill any gaps with grout.

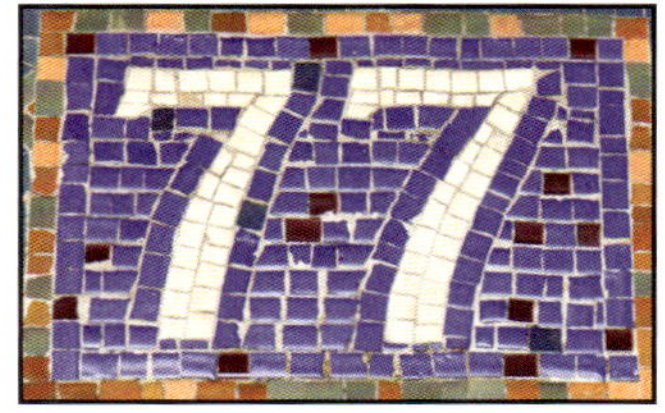

Letters and numbers like these are built up by trimming square tiles to whatever shapes will help make the characters readable and graceful. Next, one row of tiles in the background color outlines them, which then dovetails into the squarish background grid and its frame. →

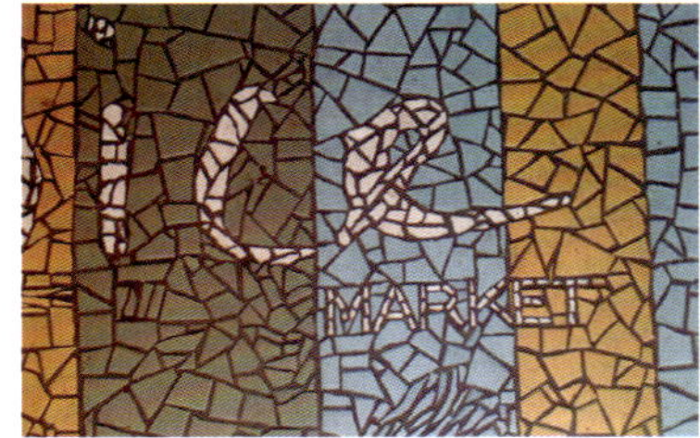

↑ *The letters here have their own boundaries, reinforced by contrasting color. Choice Market, Brooklyn, New York, c 1990*

Crazy paving

While a square grid can bend the rules to accommodate areas that don't conform, a few "crazy quilt" mosaics don't follow any grid at all. A striking, readable design can be made out of careful placement of random shapes, proving that even a crowd of oddballs can collaborate on a common goal. Letters, after all, are only human.

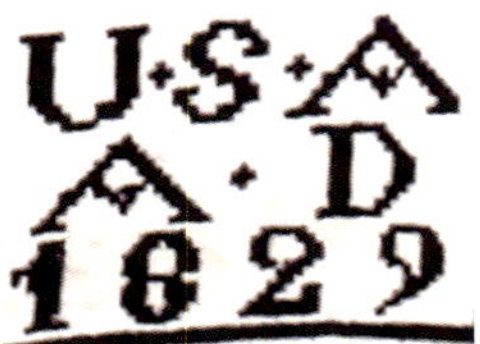

"We all have our
own life to pursue,
our own kind
of dream to be
weaving."
~Louisa May Alcott

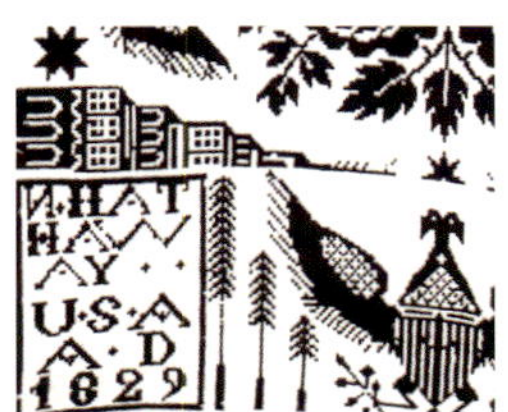

4. Weaving

The looms of the eighteenth century enabled the digital fonts of the twenty-first. All it took was holes in a stiff card.

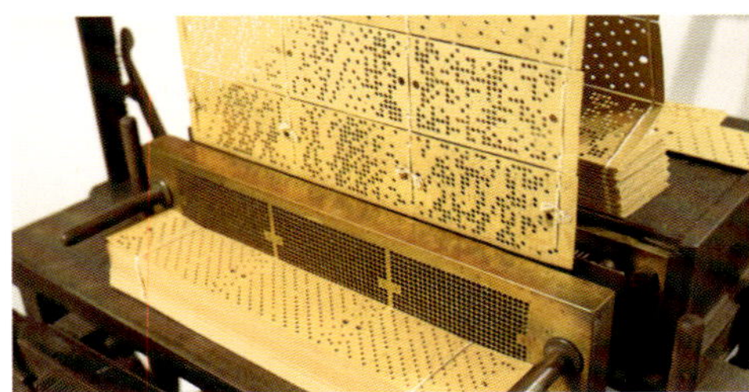

→ *Nineteenth-century jacquard punched cards were linked together in dozens, to guide looms to weave patterns.*

America's colonial households had looms where weavers developed their distinctive fabric, usually made from a warp (long threads) of linen and a weft (cross threads) of home-dyed wool, which was limited to indigo blue at first. The warp showed white when it crossed on top; the weft showed dark blue when it crossed on top—the essence of a binary system.

← *A typical repeating geometric pattern, with the weaver's initials and date.*

↙ *This weaver's name, N. Hathaway, has mostly symmetrical letters. Detail above.*

Although this fabric, nicknamed "linsey-woolsey," was too coarse to make most clothing, every family needed blankets. Soon, inventive weavers expanded the simple repeats into large designs, gradually adding stylized stars, trees, eagles, pine cones, and flowers. They made use of jacquard punched cards, an idea imported from France, linking them in sequence to lift a complex set of warp threads during each pass of the shuttle. Imported dyes made more colors possible. Weavers signed these "figured and fancy' designs with letters similar to those made by cross-stitchers or quilters on square grids.

↙ *As coverlets got more complicated, weavers signed them with their name, date, and place, and sometimes the name of the buyer, who had often provided the yarn.*

→ *Two corner blocks of a multicolored coverlet.*

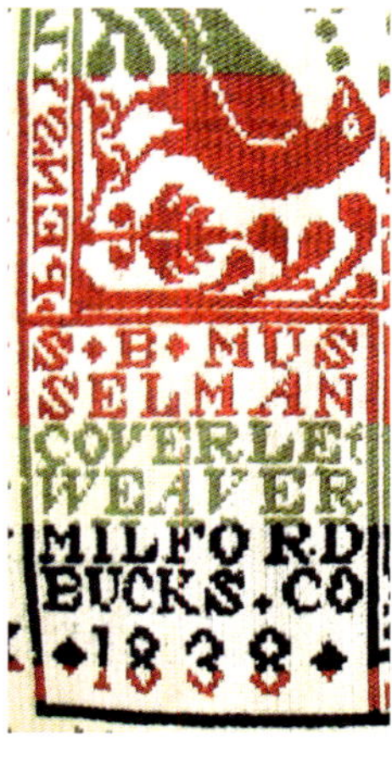

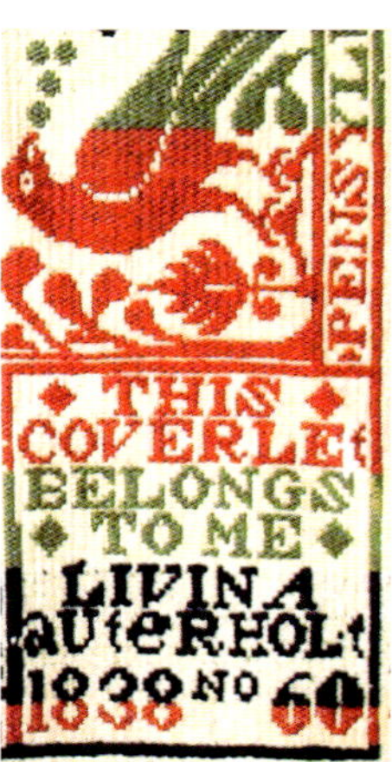

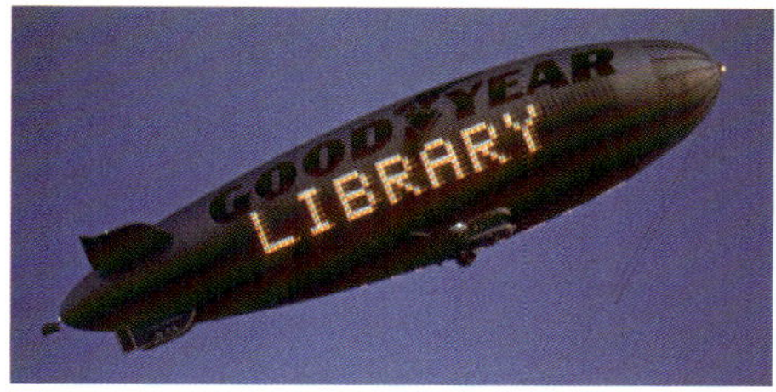

The Goodyear blimp displayed messages made with a grid of light bulbs, c 1980.

Holes in cards made it easy to weave complicated patterns and letters—easy enough that a machine could take it over. Weaving was brought into factories, along with many other American handcrafts, and its punched cards came with it. Dots embedded themselves in American life. From punched cards that controlled looms, and punched paper rolls that controlled player pianos, it was a short step to punched cards that controlled calculating machines. They were first used on a large scale to handle data from the 1890 US census by the Tabulating Machine Company, which was later acquired by International Business Machines, eventually known as IBM.

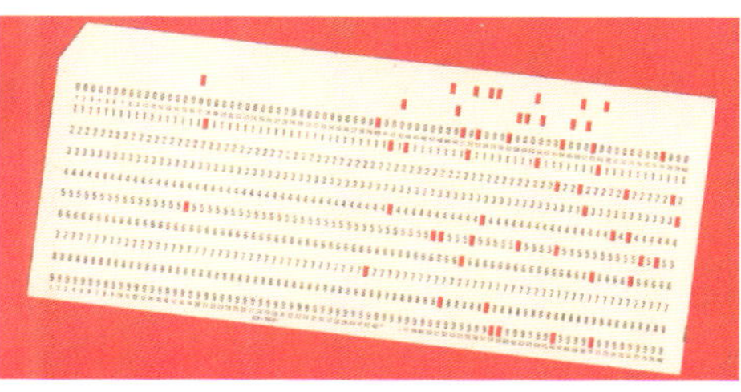

→ *A standard computer card had eighty columns of twelve rows and an angled corner. Punched with rectangular holes, cards were everywhere from 1940 to 1980: targeting bombs, registering college students, and mailing telephone bills.*

Early in the twentieth century, punched cards spread again. Engineers used them to animate letters and images in New York's Times Square, programming them to move images across grids of thousands of light bulbs. Strips of perforated paper, a continuous version of punched cards, also provided input and output: for the ticker tape machines that reported stock prices until the 1960s; for the Goodyear blimp display made of three thousand colored lightbulbs; for the teletype machines that transmitted news until the 1970s; and for the Altair computers that ran the first Microsoft operating systems in 1975. Digital letters and their standards were created in American companies, universities, and research labs, and then spread abroad.

Today, virtually all of the letters that people read are made of dots displayed in pixels on screens and dots printed out with ink on paper. Decades of progress have refined these letters, but they are still the great-great-grandchildren of American samplers, quilts, mosaics, and coverlets.

Letters were improved by higher resolution and antialiasing.

ALTHOUGH THE TRANSFORMATION of reading and writing from lines of ink to grids of dots felt like a modern revolution, it actually had deep roots in America's art and philosophy. The US Constitution spelled out ways for individual states, and individual people, to work together. While the country went through times when it seemed that solitary striving was the only way to achieve the goals that mattered, there were more eras where citizens put their trust in what they could accomplish with a group. Dots and the images they made reflected this.

Although computer type designers took a brief detour into analog displays and printers in the 1990s, digital letters made of pixels won out. Today's American alphabets are made out of many pieces, by many hands. Together they have created a new world of letters expertly built of dots.

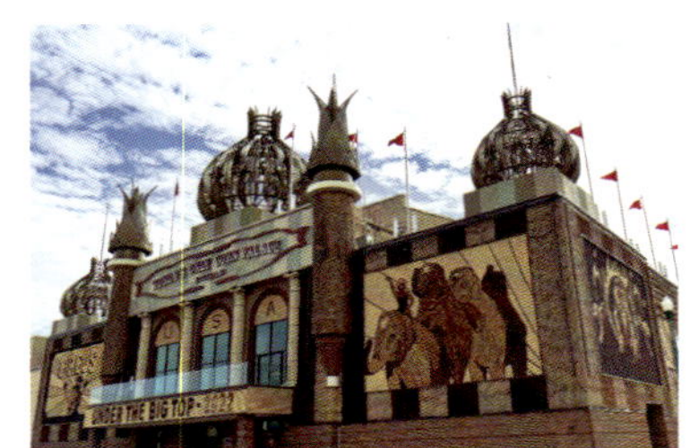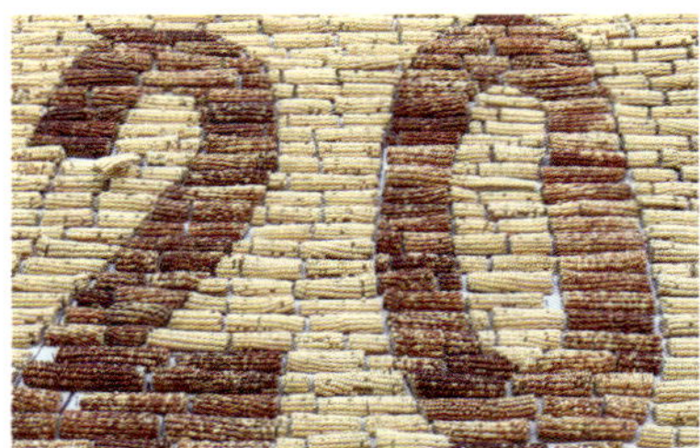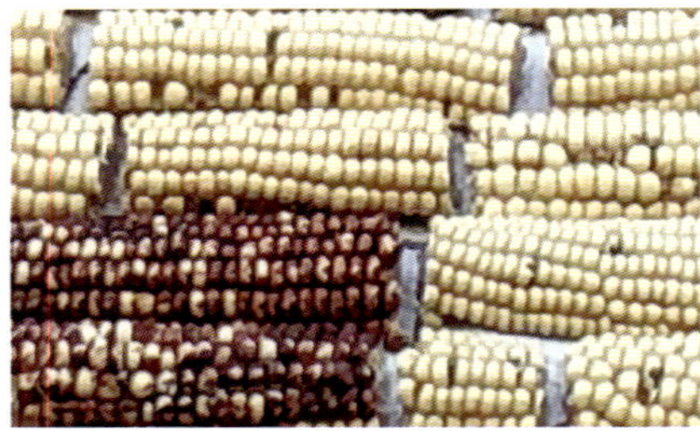

The Corn Palace in Mitchell, SD, is decorated every year with patriotic pictures and words made from ears of corn, which offer a palette of purple, russet, golden, yellow, and white. Up close, each ear of corn itself is also a mosaic of kernels.

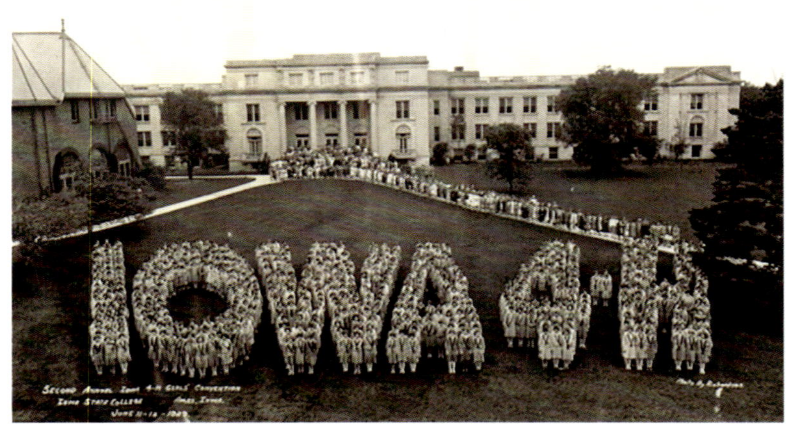

The young women of 4-H, standing together at their annual state convention in 1929, formed their logo to dramatize the power of people in groups.

These four useful grids help to visualize cross-stitched, mosaic, quilted, woven, and pixelated letters. They can be filled with x marks, squares, dots, or solid pencil.

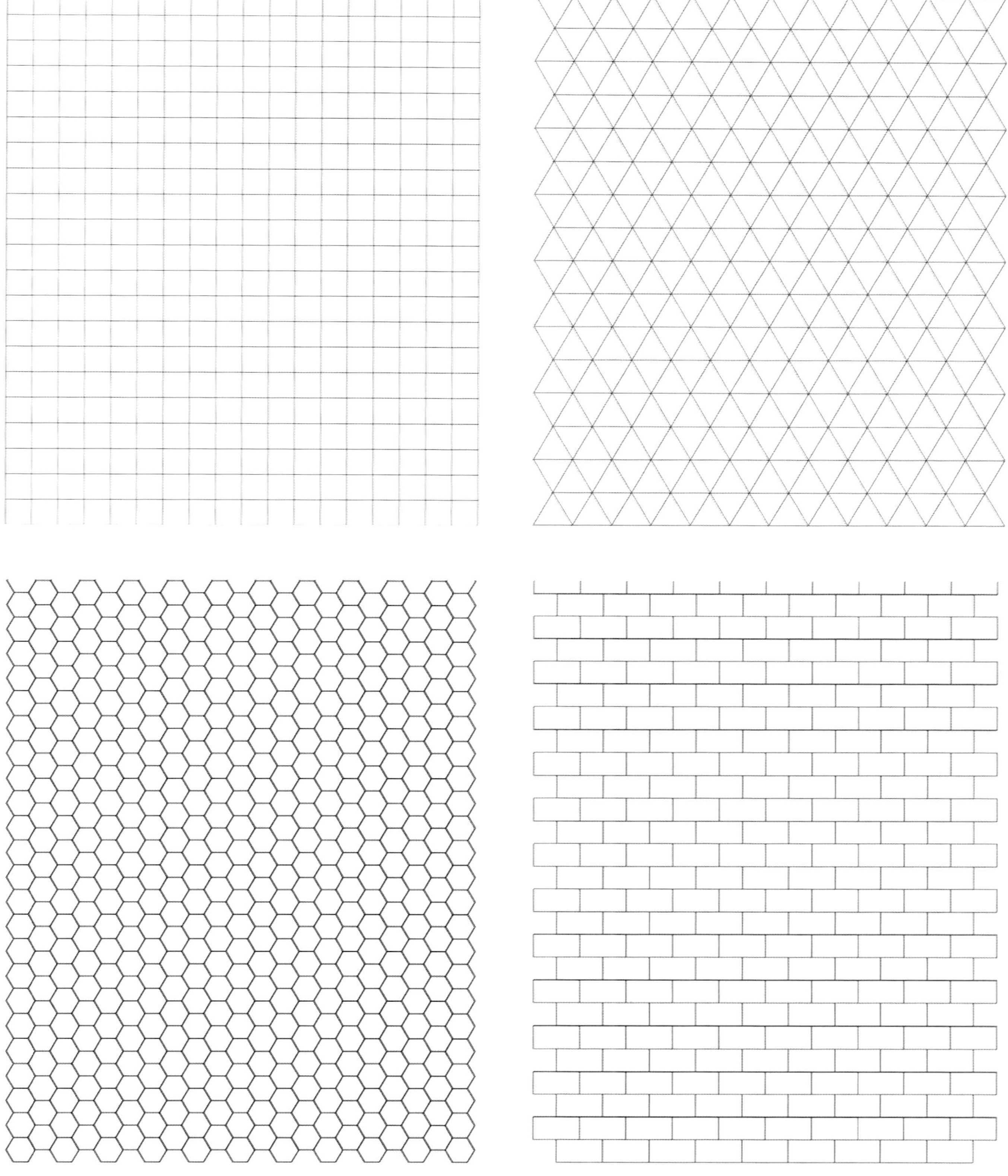

Roman Revivals

Long before the Roman capitals first crossed the Atlantic, they had already been revived in Europe half a dozen times, from fifth-century Rustica to Charlemagne's ninth-century minuscule to humanist hands of the Italian Renaissance. New regimes love to wrap themselves in the mantle of Roman capitals, not just because they are easy to read, but because for two thousand years they have symbolized a break from the compromises of the recent past and a return to older, purer, more civilized ideals.

"Each age tries to form its own conception of the past."
~ Frederick Jackson Turner

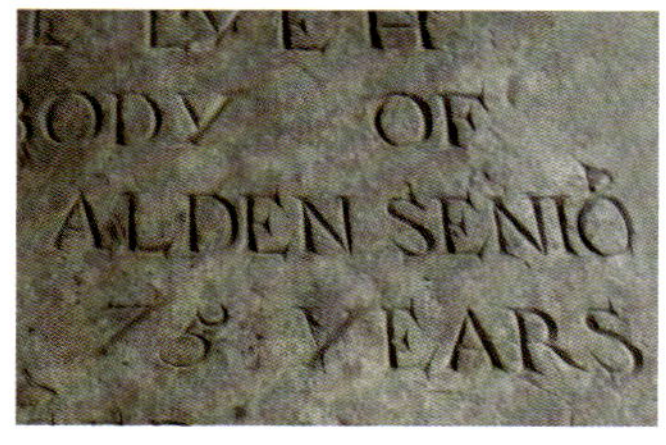

Detail from precolonial gravestone carving. Now in Old South Church, Boston.

Roman capitals arrived, thrived, and declined. The first Puritans, though untrained in carving, instinctively put Roman capitals to use for gravestones. The Bay Psalm Book, America's first printed book, 1640, was printed in Roman type. The Declaration of Independence, while written out longhand for signing in Philadelphia, was immediately set in Roman type and widely distributed as a printed broadside. Roman capitals added the voice of authority to civic buildings, gravestones, monuments, and book typography.

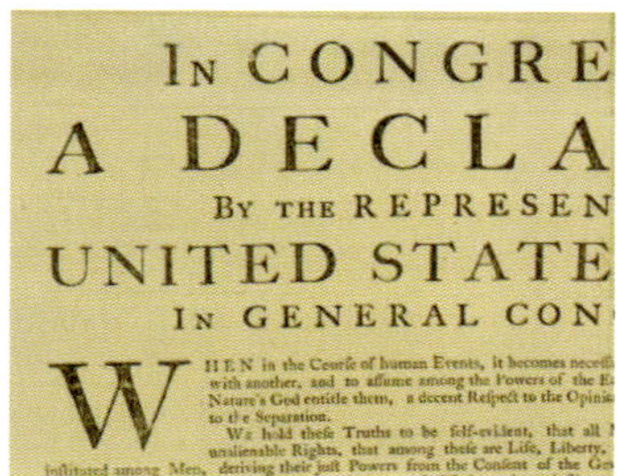

Detail from the Declaration of Independence in its typeset format for printing as a broadside.

Like everything else that was transplanted to the new United States, however, Roman capitals evolved into something new even as they were called on to preserve the past. Calligraphers gradually forgot the Roman alphabet's time-honored rules and made letters that mimicked the fashions of their own era, using the tools they had handy. Copying copies of copies, they ignored the difference between letter widths, measured the distance between letters rather than estimating the area, substituted mechanical drafting for freehand writing, and reverted to a single simplistic pen angle.

Whenever the original Roman letters deteriorated, however, an improved version of Roman would evolve to take their place. Looking back, each of these alphabets offers a window into its era and into the essence of Roman itself.

Detail from an inscription commemorating the 1789 inauguration of George Washington, c 1883, New York City.

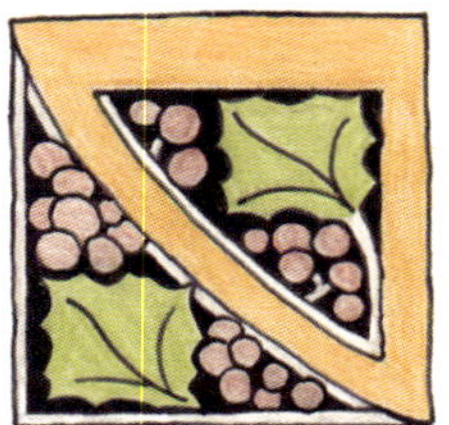

THE ARTS AND CRAFTS MOVEMENT, which began in the late nineteenth century, thawed out the frozen Roman letters. It aimed to revive hand craftsmanship, promote a humanistic aesthetic, and reunite the roles of designer and artisan. Growing out of the work and thought of English utopian William Morris, the movement took root in 1880s Boston and quickly spread all over the United States and on to Japan, where it helped fuel the Mingei crafts movement. Its advocates wanted to evoke an earlier age, before the Industrial Revolution took individual craftsmanship out of daily life and flooded society with machine-made objects. Its English founders aspired to change society and repair the cultural damage done by industrialization to traditional ways of life. In America, critics seemed to care less about how these handcrafted objects might improve the lives of the artisans who made them, and more about what they might look like in the homes of the newly prosperous middle-class people who coveted them.

"Give me success or its eternal pursuit and I'll take the pursuit."
~ Dard Hunter.

Arts and crafts book artists lovingly combined type design, paper-making, and creative bookbinding. Calligraphy also harmonized with the style of many other newly revived decorative arts: pressed copper, pottery glazed with earth pigments, hand-dyed textiles, carved and dark-stained wood, and rustic local building stone. Collectors admired the rough edges and irregularities of objects made by human hands. Artists of the arts and crafts movement decorated the interiors of suburban bungalows with their cozy hand-lettered quotations—many of them about the role of art in everyday life—framed in a nook, painted on tiles around the hearth, or gilded along the moldings.

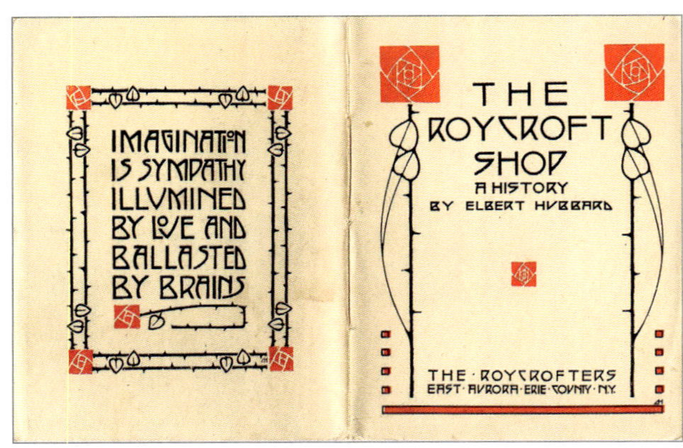

Master craftsman Dard Hunter defined some key aspects of America's arts and crafts movement. For many books, he designed and cast and set the type, hand-made the paper, printed the pages, and created the binding. He also designed frames and jewelry, and gave his name to the color "Hunter green." A typical Dard Hunter design above, from a history of his printery.

*A detail from the cover. Just like Roman carvers of two thousand years ago, Art and Crafts letter artists shrank a few letters to help with spacing. They often made the letter **O** smaller to fit it in without ruining its proportions.*

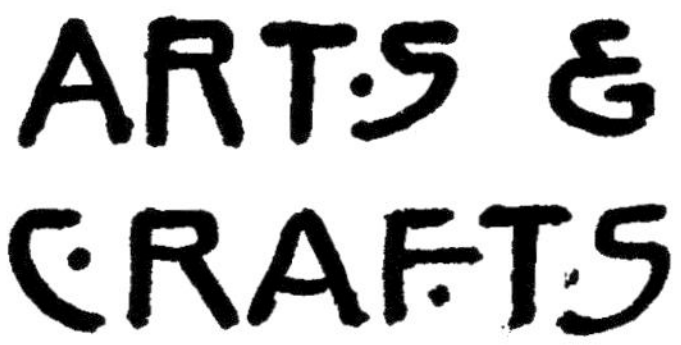

BASIC STROKES

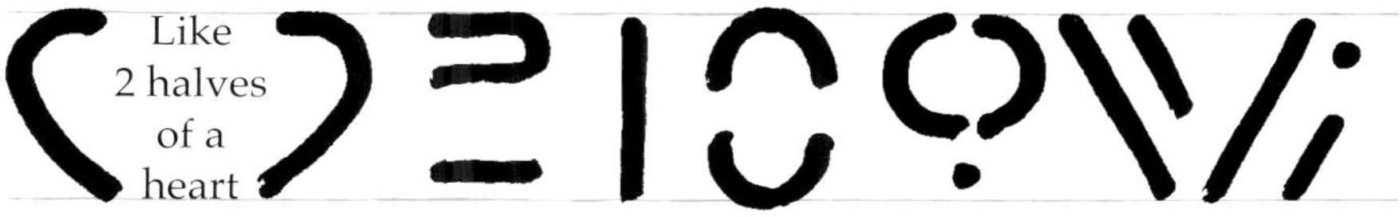

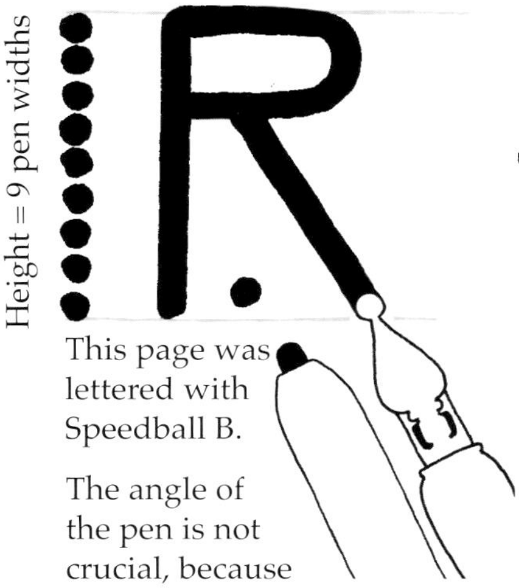

LETTER CONSTRUCTION
The top strokes of **C E F G** are shortened.

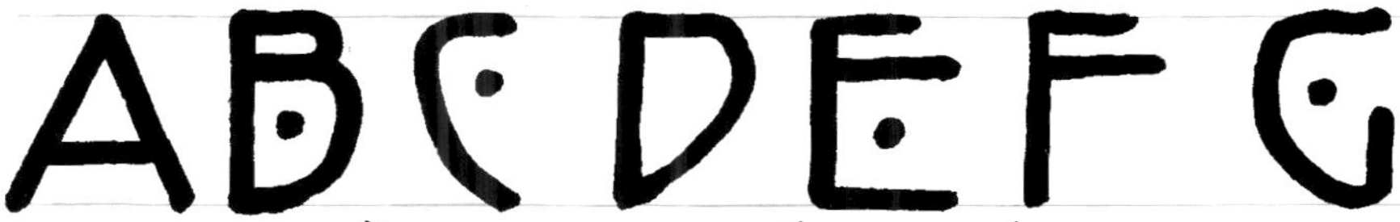

Many letters are high-waisted **B E F G H L P R X Y**.

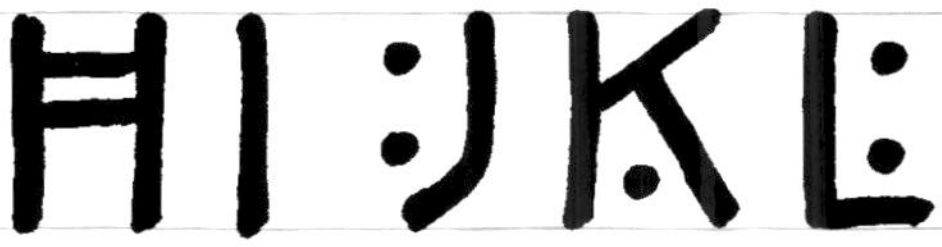

M's mid-strokes meet above center.

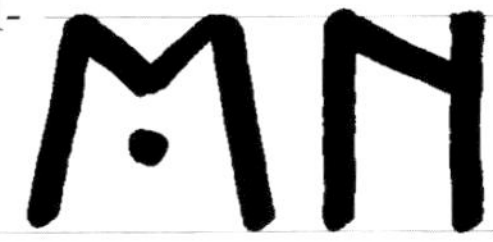

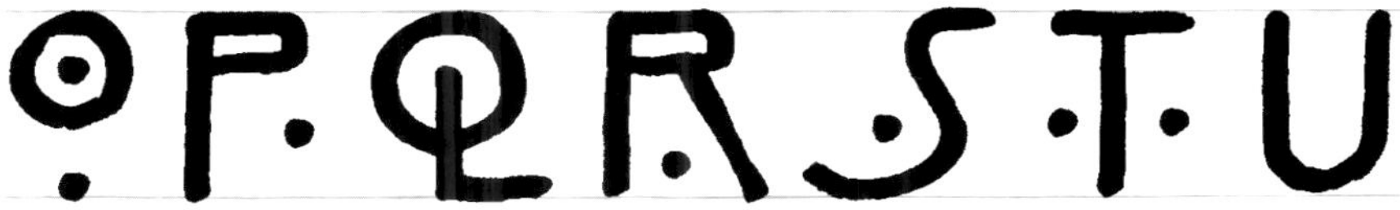

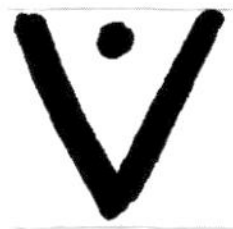

This page was lettered with Speedball B.

The angle of the pen is not crucial, because a blunt marker or a circular Speedball B nib makes unvarying lines and uniformly round dots in every hand and arm position.

Height = 9 pen widths

W's mid-strokes meet below center.

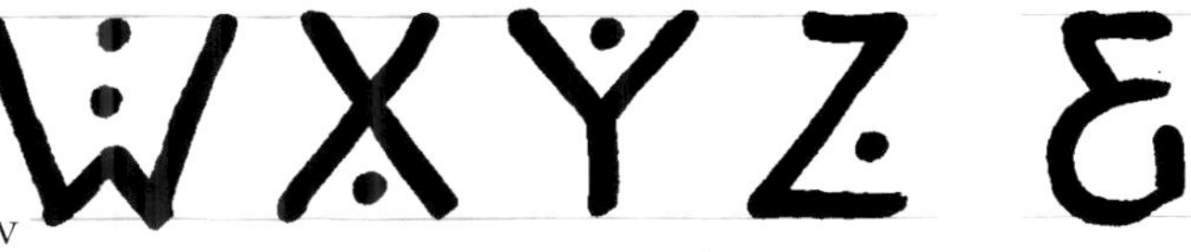

Dots add emphasis; some can be in color.

Amper-sand

LETTER CHOICES

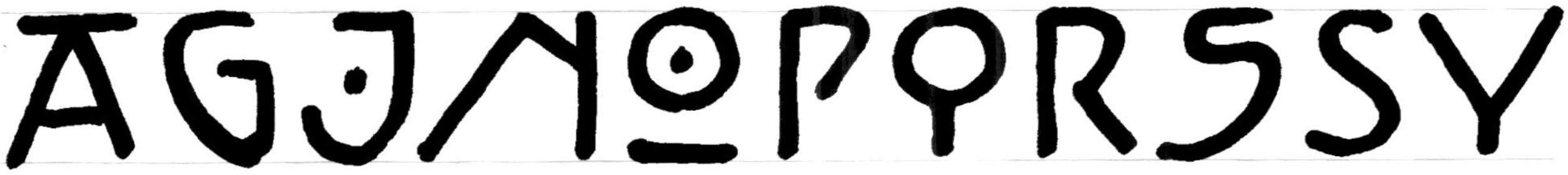

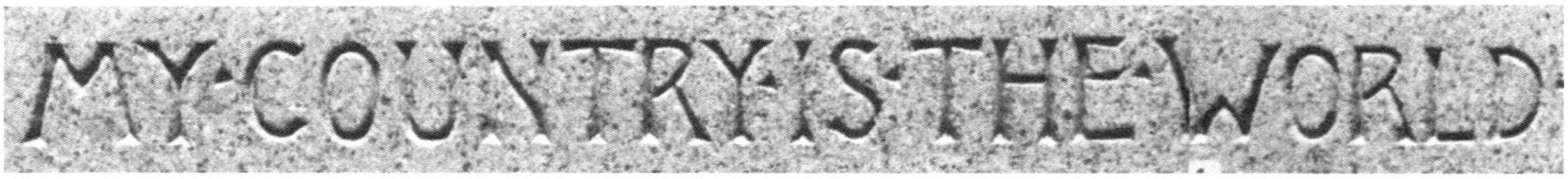

The curved wedges are the original Roman way to separate words, which eventually evolved into punctuation. The dots that are so often added to arts and crafts letters make reference to this history. From an inscription on the 1886 statue of abolitionist William Lloyd Garrison, Boston. Letters are 3" (8 cm) high.

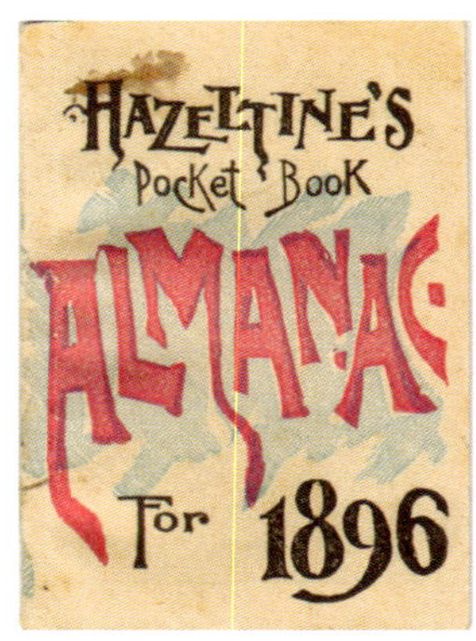

"The letters . . . give off an air of languid exhibitionism."
~ *Thomas Beer*

ART NOUVEAU CALLIGRAPHY BEGAN as a curvy version of arts and crafts (see pages 74–75). It softened further as letter artists followed the public's taste for letters that echoed the long, flowing hair, and elegant, narrow, high-waisted fashions of the era.

Art nouveau aspired to be an international art but in fact it brought out each nation's particular personality. At their best, art nouveau letters in America created lush, organic designs of great complexity. At their worst, they breathed out an effete air of boredom, depravity, and self-indulgence. Thomas Beer, in his seminal work *The Mauve Decade*, contrasted the "fribbles and light poets" of Art Nouveau with the earnest New England transcendentalists of two generations earlier. An eccentric color palette was all the rage at the end of the century, featuring pale green, lime yellow, and a new synthetic mauve dye that gave the decade its nickname.

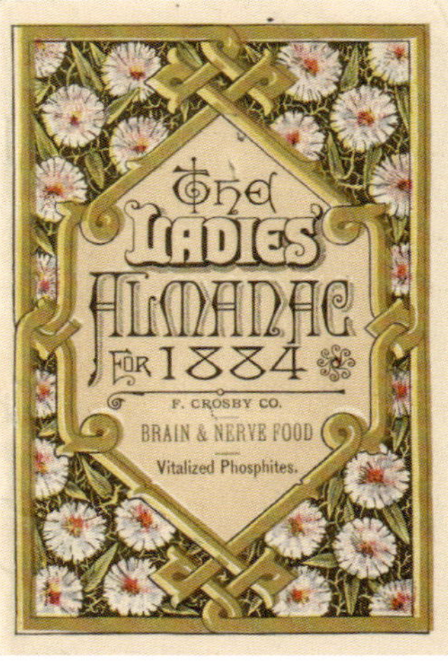

Pocket-sized almanacs were popular as promotional giveaways. 3" x 4" (8 cm x 10 cm)

Eventually art nouveau escaped the discipline of any pen and ran wild as hand-drawn forms described by even their fans as "writhing" and "sinuous" and by their critics as "tortured" and "flaccid." Artists took to drawing elaborate letters with outlines, not writing them with pen strokes.

Smaller than pocket-sized, this almanac measures 3¼" x 4" (3 cm x 4.5 cm)

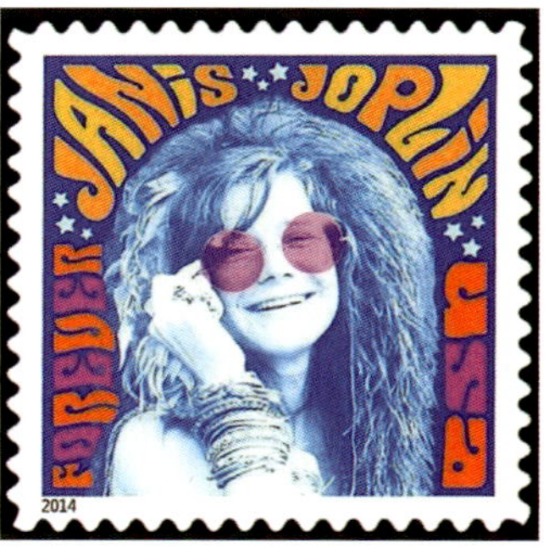

A recent commemorative stamp celebrates singer Janis Joplin in the psychedelic lettering of her era.

NEW AGAIN

ART NOUVEAU CAPITALS got their own revival in the flamboyant 1970s, with bell-bottomed letters that echoed the era's bell-bottomed clothes. Packed tightly together, their elastic shapes got weirder and weirder, requiring the calligrapher to draw them rather than write them. Color, too, tracked the prevailing mood, as it morphed from a happy hippie rainbow into the weird Day-Glo tones of a bad acid trip.

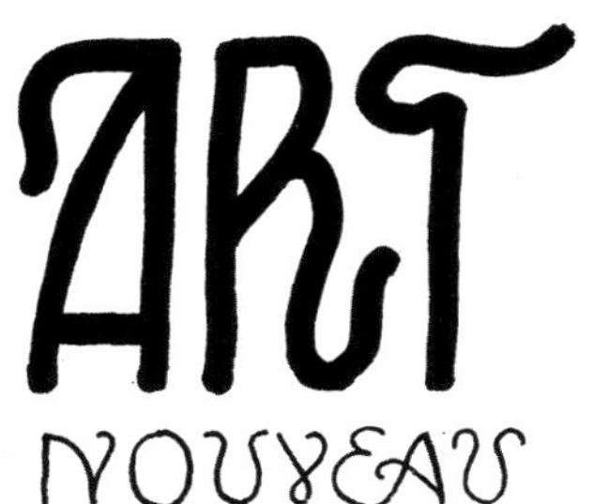

BASIC STROKES

Many verticals are slightly bowed.   Gravity seems to make the curves sag.

CONSTRUCTION OF LETTERS

A B C D E F G H I J

B P R share similar strokes and joins (circled areas).

K L M N O P Q R

M = inverted W

S T U V W X Y Z

Letter width is half its height.

Height = 12–15 pen widths

A blunt marker or Speedball B nib.

Pen angle is not crucial.

LETTER CHOICES

A B C E G J L M

Some of the horizontal strokes in **A E F H W M** can be doubled.

A few flowing curves can grow into optional tendrils and leaves.

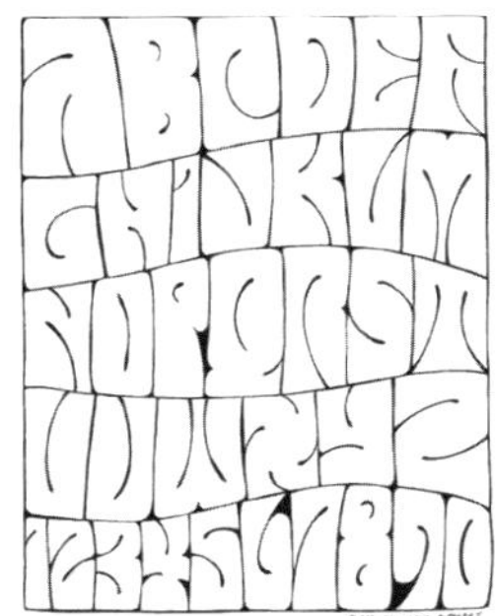

Type by Wes Wilson

NEW AGAIN IN THE 1970s

THESE LETTERS SPRAWLED so much that the spaces inside and between them, rather than the strokes themselves, were written with a thin line. To get started; the basic art nouveau letters crowd together; they sway in unison on undulating guidelines; for extra flavor, they can be filled in with clashing colors.

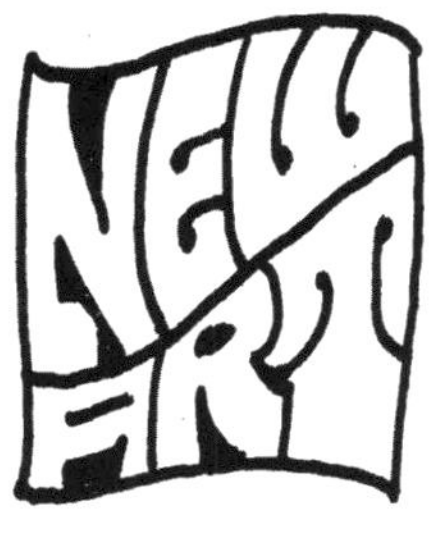

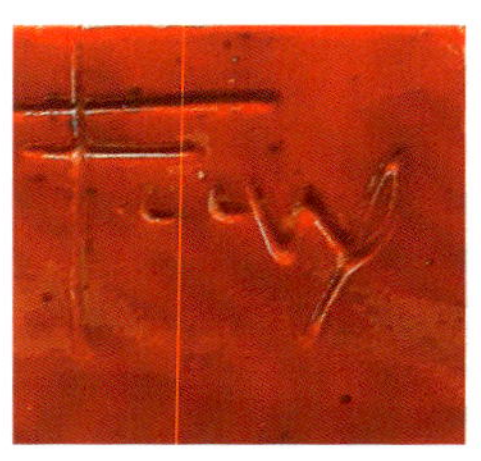

USA

*Wright liked to "sign"
his buildings with his
initials scrawled on a
glazed tile, anchored by
a large abstract F. This
square, in a striking color
he named "Aztec Red,"
embedded his graphic
identity in drawings,
stationery, magazine
covers, and posters. It also
makes visual reference
to the signature stamps
of Japanese painting and
calligraphy.*

PRAIRIE LETTERS FORMED a visual bridge from the arts and crafts movement and Art Nouveau to something plainer, overtly American.

Rooted in the Midwest, Frank Lloyd Wright's "think simple" philosophy spread from architecture to the related arts, shaping the design of furniture, ceramics, textiles, landscaping, metal craft, and lettering during much of the twentieth century. During his life, Wright soaked up every major development, starting with special wooden blocks in his childhood, borrowing heavily from the designs of his employees as well as his employers, and culminating in his nineties with the innovative poured-concrete spiral of the Guggenheim Museum. Like many of America's best thinkers, he found ways to illuminate the country's national identity while spotlighting its regional styles. Over the decades, he gathered visual ideas from Southwestern deserts, Indian motifs, and prairie vistas, as well as pre-Columbian monuments and Japanese houses. In turn, his eclectic ideas shaped American design for decades.

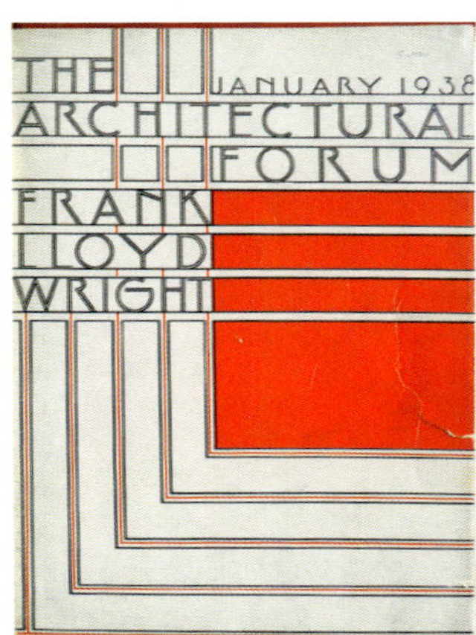

Typical Prairie page layouts usually included vertical and horizontal lines, geometric blocks, and tight vertical spacing.

Frank Lloyd Wright advocated design rooted in the American landscape and emancipated from European cityscapes. He labeled his stripped-down, functional, Utopian-style "Usonian," an acronym for United States of North America. Continuing the mission of the arts and crafts movement, Wright dreamed of a future where Americans could live better lives surrounded by good-looking, affordable design. He specified hand-loomed textiles and hand-fired tiles for his buildings and even developed his own shade of red glaze. Over the decades, his design institute, Taliesin West in Arizona, transformed hundreds of students into disciples.

Wright insisted that every detail of a built environment, from cabinet hinges to table settings, should be the architect's responsibility. He created numerals, letters, and even logos for many of his buildings. His signage echoes the coiled floor plan of the Guggenheim Museum in New York City; his Southwest signage has a Mayan flavor; and his Prairie letters make Roman letters look both carefully thought out and casual and friendly. This personal graphic style was instantly recognizable for its inventive letterforms, the grid of lines, and his signature red square.

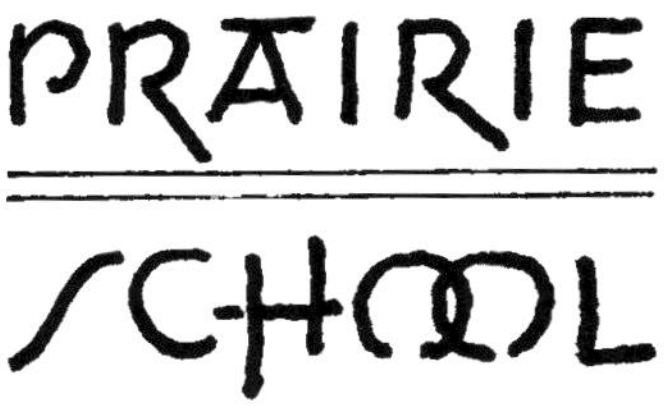

PRAIRIE
SCHOOL

Architects of the recent past used to label their drawings with Roman capitals in pencil or ink, for later duplication in blue or brown. They modified these letters to echo their building's style.

BASIC STROKES

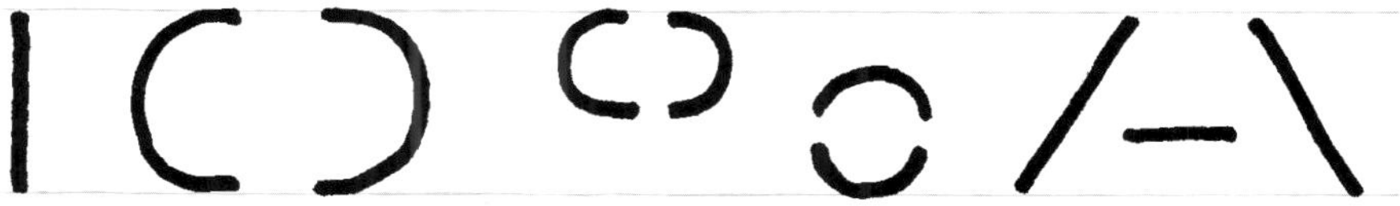

LETTER CONSTRUCTION

Though based on Roman capitals, most of these letters have quirks that warm and humanize them: gaps at the corners or midpoints; midpoints that are in fact above or below the center; and strokes that are too long or too short for the guidelines.

A B C D E F

G

Subtly different heights give this letter **H** energy.

H I

J curve bends slightly.

J K

L

M's diagonals meet above center.

M N O P

Q R

S is top-heavy.

S T U

V W

X inter-sects below center.

X Y Z

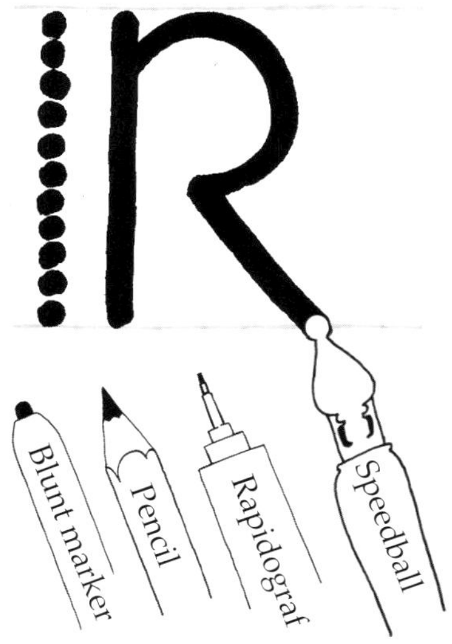

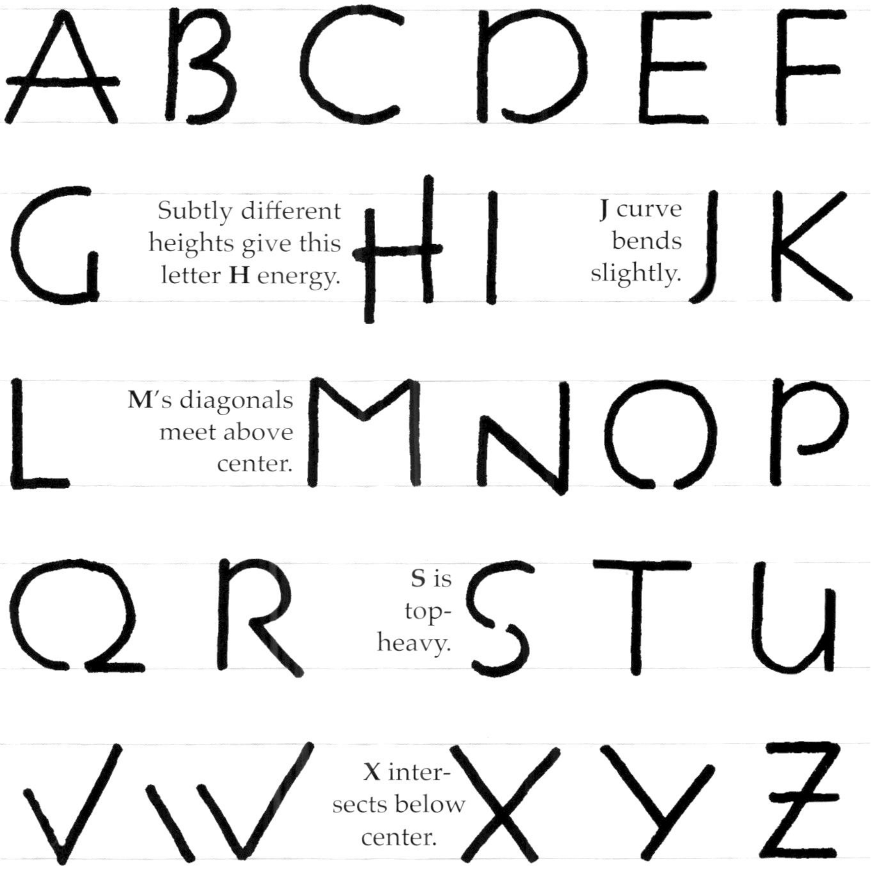

W omits a minor stroke. **Z** adds a minor stroke.

NUMERALS

1 2 3 4 5 6 7 8 9 0

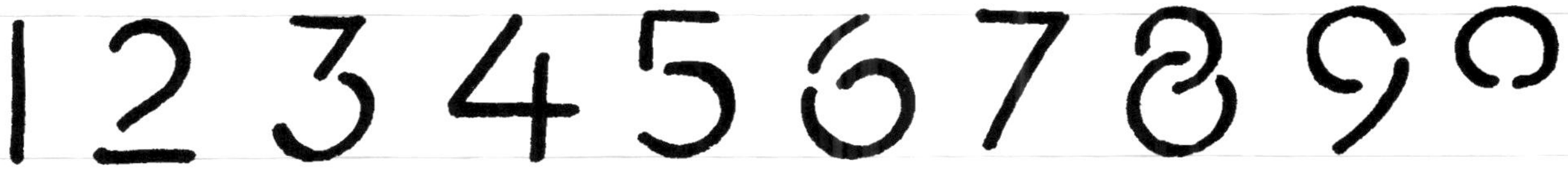

LETTER OPTIONS
The calligrapher can modify the basic alphabet with variant forms like these.

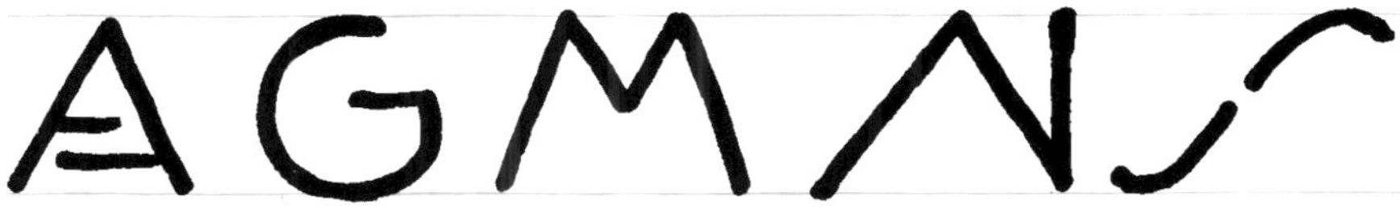

A G M M S

U/A

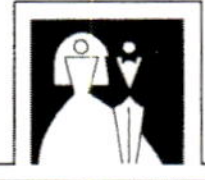

Mr. and Mrs. Frederick N. Hughesie
have the honour of announcing
the marriage of their daughter
Carolyn Heather
and
Winston Ander Smith
on Friday, the ninth of January
nineteen hundred and ninety
Riverside Church
New York, New York

*Today, art deco still
adds elegance to the
hand-lettered items that
formal weddings call for:
invitations, envelopes,
place cards, monograms,
and seating charts.
Graphic courtesy of
Shelley Payette*

ART DECO RULED THE 1920s, a decade when designers glorified the hard-edged sleekness of machine-made objects. In contrast with previous American letters, it embodied the tuxedo not the hand-woven smock, the cocktail lounge not the workshop, the metropolis not the prairie, and the skyscraper not the cottage. The dandy on the cover of *The New Yorker* magazine symbolized the attitude, raising his monocle annually in February under the original masthead of stylized, stylish Roman letters.

Calligraphers too fell in love with the novelty of art deco. Their letters echoed the dramatic contrasts, parallel bands, and chrome-plated surfaces that unified this style across the fields of architecture, furnishings, industrial design, and graphic art. They added this stylish flavor to all their lettering, but especially to their Roman capitals.

Three details distinguish art deco from the original Roman alphabet:

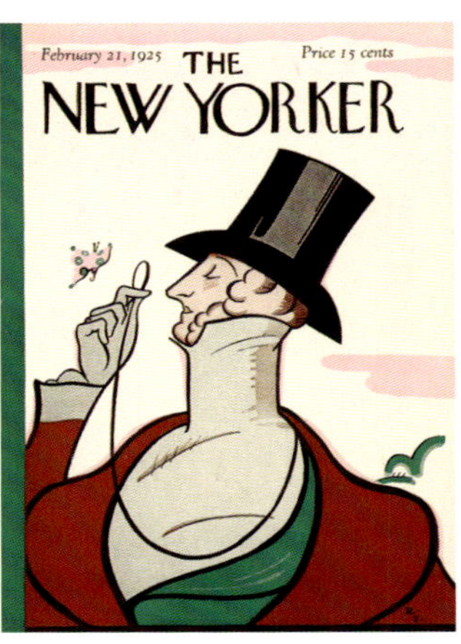

Eustace Tilley and The New Yorker *cover are virtually unchanged since 1925.*

LINE CONTRAST	DISPLACED CENTERS	PRECISION
Roman moderation vs	*Near-center Roman vs*	*Organic Roman vs*
ROMAN	**EHBGA**	**HANDS**
extreme contrast	*Art deco far up or down*	*Mechanical art deco*
ROMAN	**EHBGA**	**TOOLS**
Contrast of thicks and thins was heightened by pen angles of 0° or 90° or 45°.	Strokes slightly below or above center were raised or lowered, pushing their subtleties to extremes.	Letters were shaped by geometry, not the human hand and eye. Ornament looked machine-drawn too.

For years, Art Deco letters radiated the savvy air of those who know it all. This brash confidence lasted all through the "Roaring Twenties," epitomized by the cool chic of fashion magazines and the urbane polish of literary journals. Then late in 1929, the country's worst economic crash pulled the plug on prosperity, and people woke up to a diminished view of America, one with its own Roman revival of Roman letters.

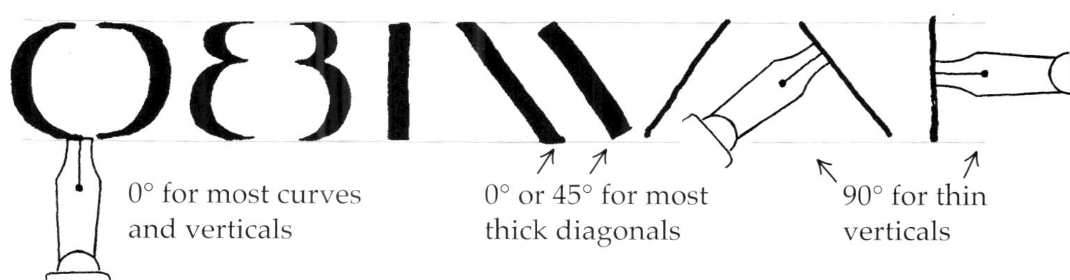

BASIC STROKES

0° for most curves and verticals

0° or 45° for most thick diagonals

90° for thin verticals

CONSTRUCTION OF LETTERS

ABCDEFGHIJ

Most intersections and horizontals are ⅓ to ¼ from the top or bottom guideline, seldom in the middle.

K needs three pen angles; **A M N Q R U Y** need two.

KLMNOPQR

T can be wider or narrower.

Dotted lines mark optional strokes.

∫TUVWXYZ

Useful detail in **A N V W**: thin lines join thick ones at the *outside* of the corner.

LETTER CHOICES

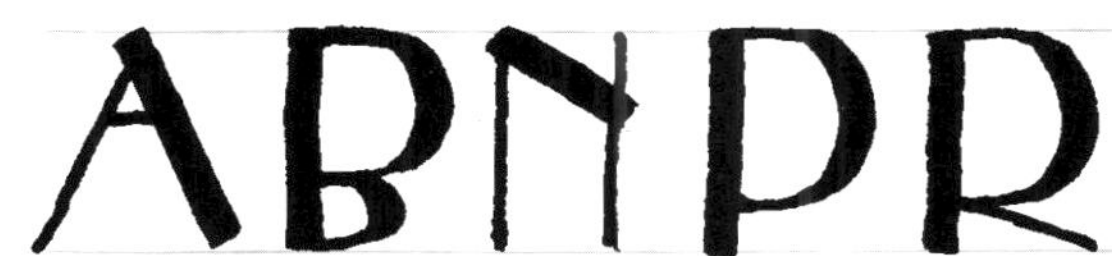

Letters can be made wider or narrower, with their centers raised or lowered.

MAKE DECO DECORATIONS WITH PEN STROKES

A few parallel bands flanking a text box add extra Art Deco flavor.

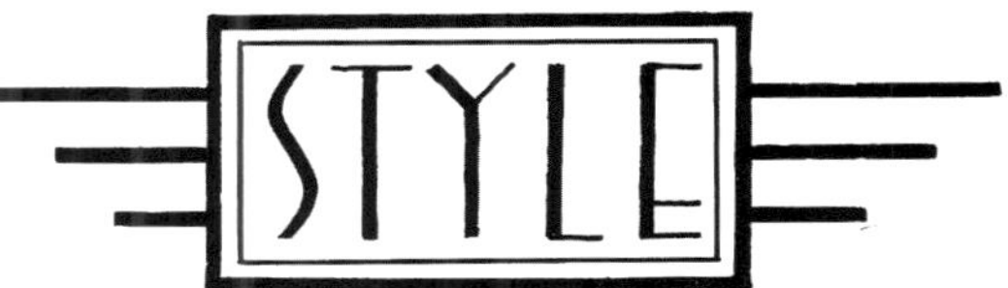

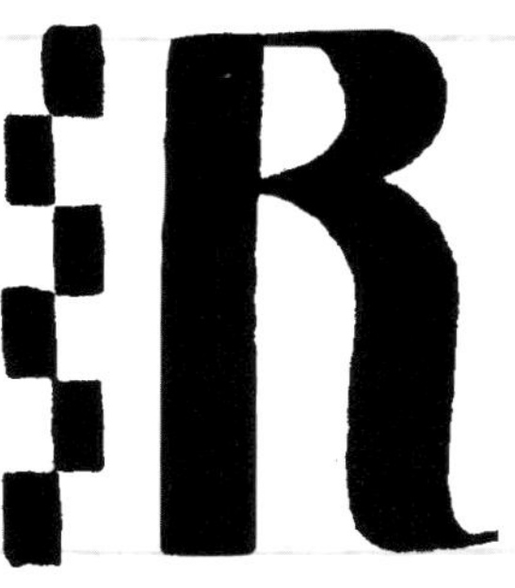

Height = 6 pen widths.

A 0° pen angle makes the most contrast between thick and thin strokes.

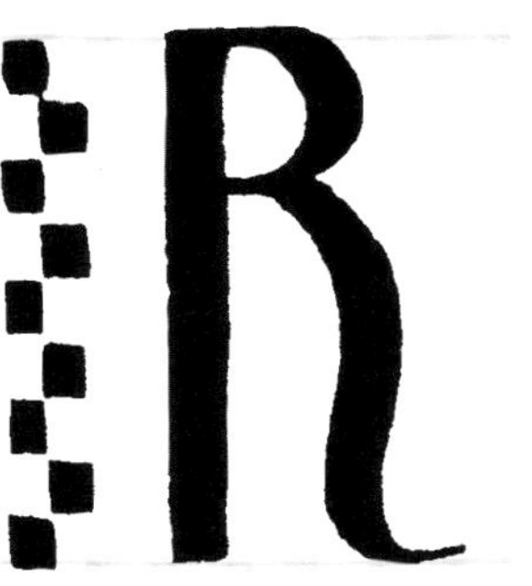

For *The New Yorker* style (facing page), the height is 9 pen widths.

Decorative corners can be made by turning the pen 90° and stacking the strokes.

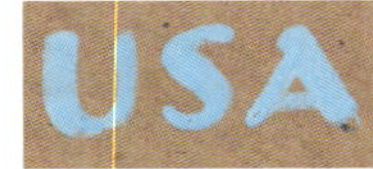

"National parks are the best idea we ever had. Absolutely American, absolutely democratic, they reflect us at our best."
~ *Wallace Stegner, Pulitzer Prize winner and early environmentalist*

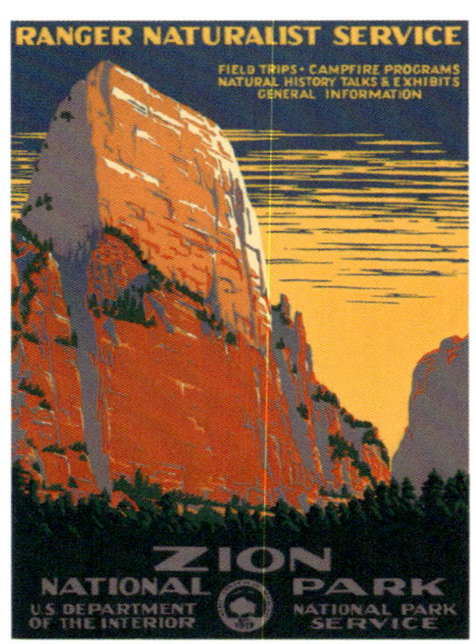

NEW DEAL LETTERS were modest and practical, in contrast to the glamorous and worldly art deco letters they replaced. In economic hard times, big-city letters no longer spoke to the kind of ordinary people who ate supper at home and vacationed at national parks. Humbler ways to write the Roman alphabet grew from this American landscape.

Invented in America, national parks began around 1850, were established at the federal level in 1912, received extra funding during the New Deal, and by the mid-twentieth century had grown to be a key part of the country's self-image. It should come as no surprise that national parks inspired an alphabet of their own and based it on Roman capitals.

RANGER NATURALIST SERVICE

↙ *During the Depression, US relief programs put unemployed artists to work on a now-classic poster series promoting America's natural beauty, with captions lettered in the era's favorite alphabet (detail above).*

The structure of New Deal shares many virtues with the original carved Roman alphabet: moderate proportions, thick and thin lines, and weather resistance:

PROPORTIONS: Although short and stocky, the letters still maintain the original Roman letter families based on their width in relation to their height.

E Narrow

N Medium

Q Wide

M Very wide

LC Roman   **LC** New Deal

CONTRAST: Thick and thin strokes are in the same places as in traditional Roman capitals but have $^2/_3$ less contrast. Thins are about as heavy as thicks.

DURABILITY: New Deal letters were visually robust, but physically sturdy too. In park signs, they were routed out of wood and the grooves were painted sky blue or white on a rich brown to keep them readable.

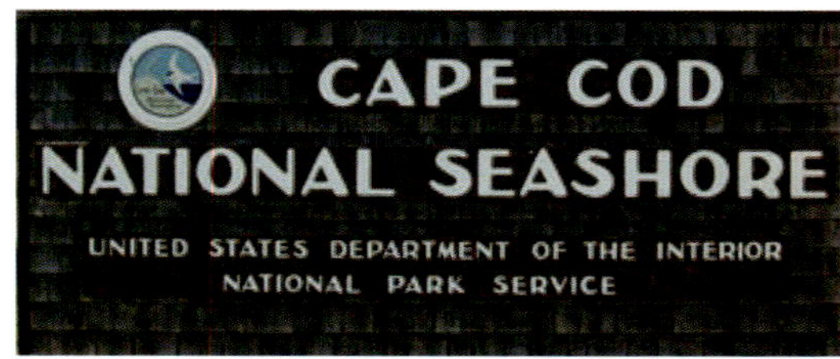

NEW DEAL

Only the Speedball D pen nib can render this style properly; it provides moderate contrast of thick and thin, and rounded stroke ends.

Height = 4 pen widths

BASIC STROKES AND PEN ANGLES

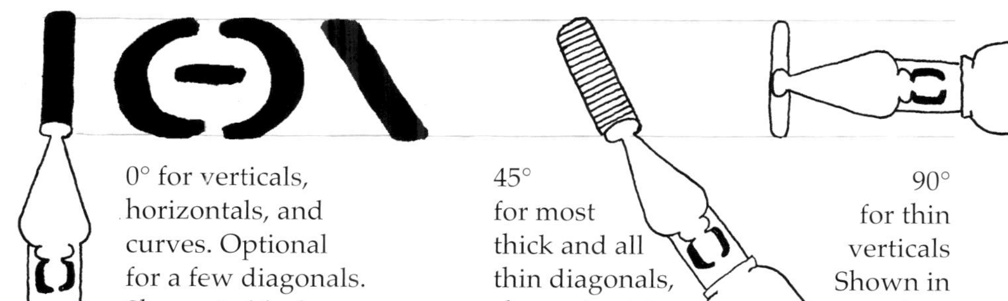

0° for verticals, horizontals, and curves. Optional for a few diagonals. Shown in black.

45° for most thick and all thin diagonals, shown in stripes.

90° for thin verticals Shown in outline.

Diagonal options on **A:**
0°   45°

CONSTRUCTION OF LETTERS

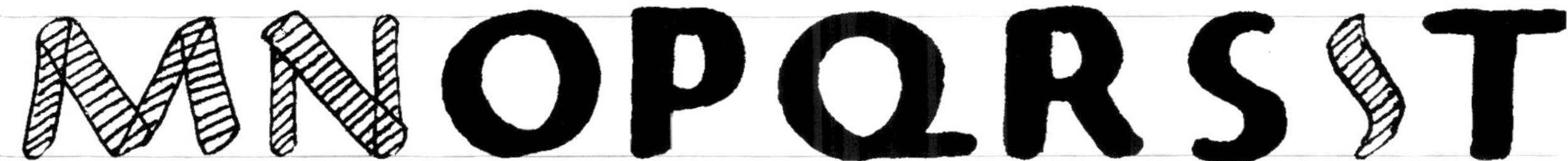

A B C D E F

G H I J K L

The **J** does not need to curve back up.

Optional 0°on last stroke of **K.**

M N O P Q R S T

Optional 45° for center stroke of **S.**

The pen angle changes from 0° to 90° to make the thinner second stroke of **U**, a refinement based on Roman capitals.

U V W X Y Z

The vertical stroke of **Y** and all strokes of **Z** use a 0° pen angle.

Letters can slant about 5°.

Adding white highlights can create the illusion of raised, shiny letters.

Different widths of pen make letters heavier or lighter.

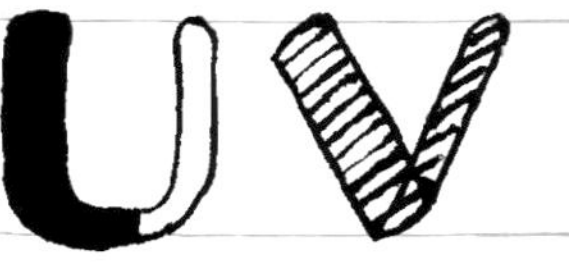

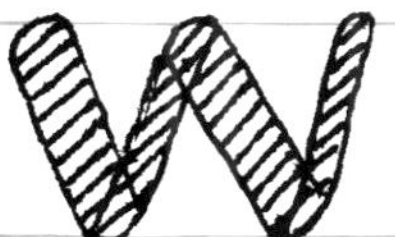
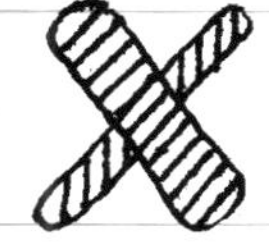

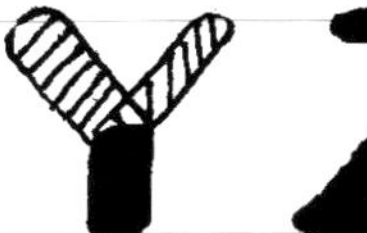

Usa

PLUMP, STURDY COOPER LETTERS, like New Deal, were shaped by the unique Speedball D nib. The typeface is best known today in its heavy version, named for its designer Oswald Cooper, but it was useful at many sizes and weights, to all kinds of letter artists, across every graphic medium. Type designers produced dozens of versions. Signcard artists liked its heft and clarity. Calligraphers enjoyed its simplicity and novelty. Its pudgy serifs were particularly appealing—attention-grabbing, friendly, and legible at the same time. Although the letters looked simplistic, they drew their basic architecture from Roman capitals and small letters, making them easy for calligraphers to learn and recognize. Cooper's versatility made it popular in the expanding new fields of packaging, advertising, and logo design.

Cooper Black persisted into the era of Letraset® and Instantype®, when a novice without any training at all could rub letters onto poster board, machine panels, and store windows.

Widespread popularity doesn't guarantee eternal life, however. In the second half of the twentieth century, Cooper Black eventually, inevitably went out of style. But even that became one of its strengths; its decline has become part of its personality—the humble, hardy, hard-working survivor that is impervious to the ups and downs of fashion. As type critic Bethany Heck says, "It's a beautifully crafted design that's just waiting for the next adventurous designer to teach an old dog new tricks."

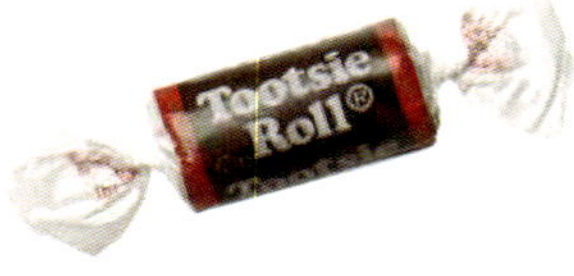

The Cooper Black letters in Tootsie Roll's logo have pudgy little serifs the shape of Tootsie Rolls™. It was a popular letter style for many other classic American candy wrappers such as Baby Ruth.

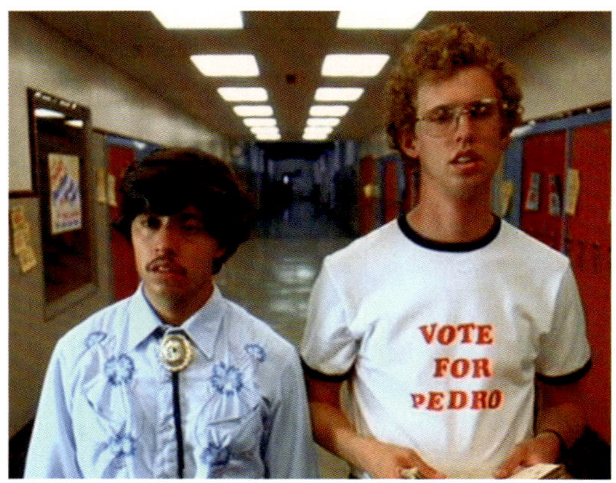

The nerdy hero of the 2004 movie Napoleon Dynamite *wears a T-shirt with an iron-on slogan in Cooper Black that suggests how uncool he is. Alert viewers will pick up on the visual message; this letter style is so out it's in.*

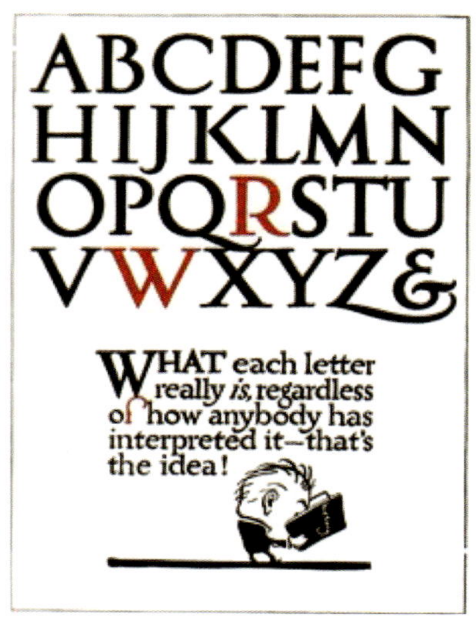

Letters by F. G. Cooper from the 1916 edition of Lettering *by Thomas Wood Stevens, published by the Prang Company. Image courtesy of Randall Hasson, specialist in Speedball D calligraphy.*

COOPER

Only the Speedball D pen nib can render this style properly, with its rounded stroke ends and its moderate contrast of thick and thin.

Ascender height = 5 pen widths, a little taller than the capital.

Capital height = 4½ pen widths.

BASIC STROKES AND PEN ANGLES

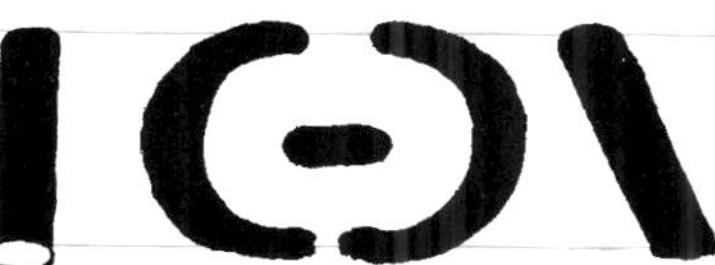

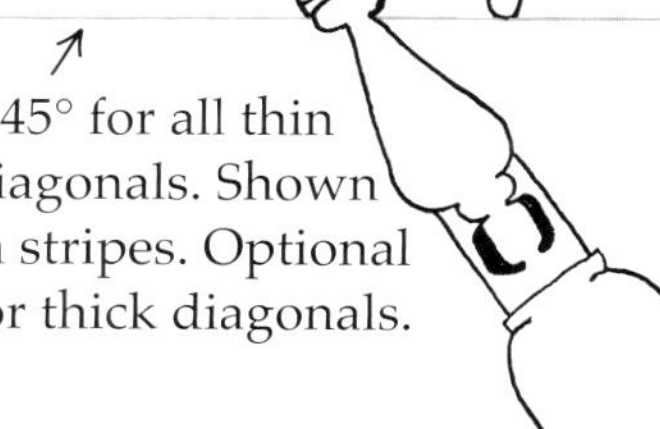

0° for verticals, curves, horizontals. Diagonals at 0° will connect better to their serifs. Shown in solid black.

45° for all thin diagonals. Shown in stripes. Optional for thick diagonals.

Height of letter body = 3 - 3½ pen widths.

Descender height = 4 - 5 pen widths.

SERIFS

Serifs should extend half a pen width beyond both sides of verticals.

On the top of an ascender, serifs should extend only to the left.

R l l e q

CONSTRUCTION OF CAPITAL LETTERS

ABCDEFGIIIJ

KLMNOPQR

STUVWXYZ

U has one thick stroke at 0° and one thin stroke at 90°.

Diagonal strokes in **A K M N V W X Y** connect with their serifs more easily if both are at 0°.

CONSTRUCTION OF SMALL LETTERS

abcdefghijklm

2½–3 pen widths for very hefty letters. Serifs are easier on thinner letters (3–4 widths).

nopqrstuvwxyz

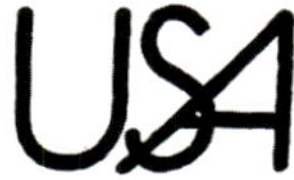

"It's extremely easy to use
Avant Garde badly."

~ John D. Barry

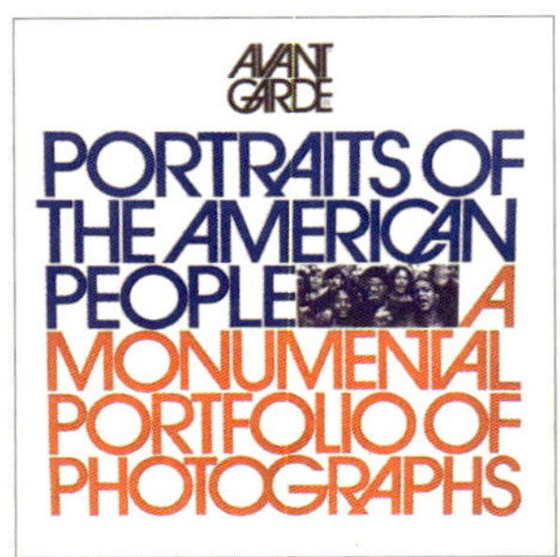

*This book cover shows
Avant Garde's paired
letters used with restraint.*

AVANT GARDE (FRENCH FOR "OUT IN FRONT") debuted as a magazine logo and proved so popular that a whole typeface soon followed. In step with the tumultuous late 1960s, this stripped-down version of Roman had repeated upsurging diagonals and tight letter spacing.

Although its goal was to be at the cutting edge, Avant Garde made use of the two-thousand-year-old calligraphic custom of joining pairs of Roman letters. pairs of these letters were meant to be sprinkled sparingly throughout a basic alphabet of stripped-down letters. Unfortunately, most graphic artists headed straight for those eye-catching ligatures and overdosed on them. Like so many other good ideas in the arts of that noisy, anarchic era, Avant Garde struck a pose, but soon became a caricature of itself.

Avant Garde enjoyed a decade of popularity but fell victim to its own distinctiveness. Its creator, Herb Lubalin, insisted that his typeface was misunderstood, misused, and overused. But even his kindest critics called it "the paisley of typefaces" and "the world's most abused typeface." New York typographer Ed Benguiat declared, in a backhanded compliment, that "the only place Avant Garde looks good is in the words Avant Garde."

Calligraphers nevertheless will enjoy a chance to pair up letters in truly innovative ways.

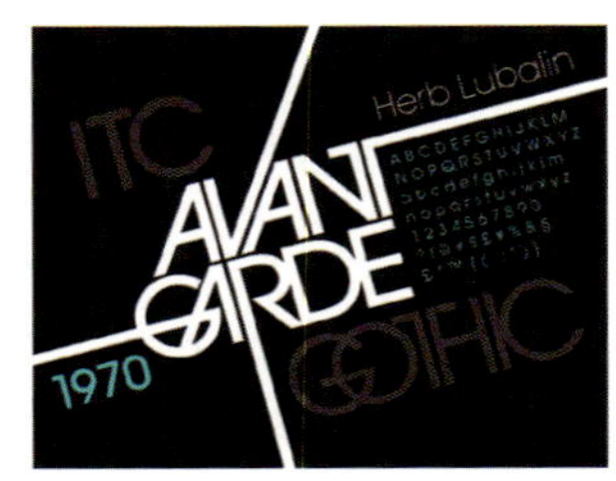

*By extending a few letter
strokes, graphic designer
Tina Shao dramatizes the
structure of Avant Garde.*

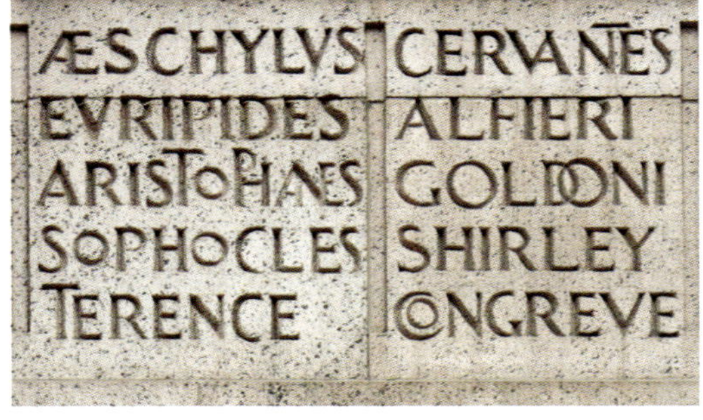

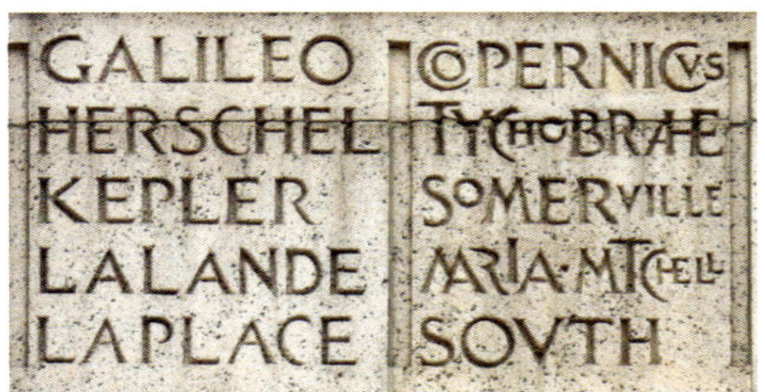

*Ingenious overlapping, in Roman letters carved
on the Boston Public Library, c 1890.*

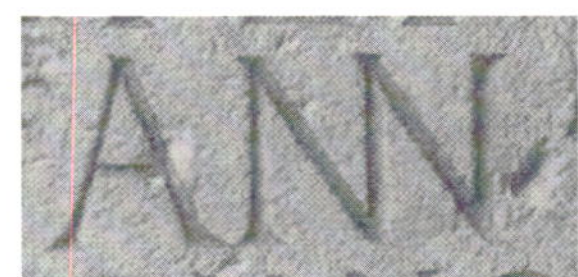

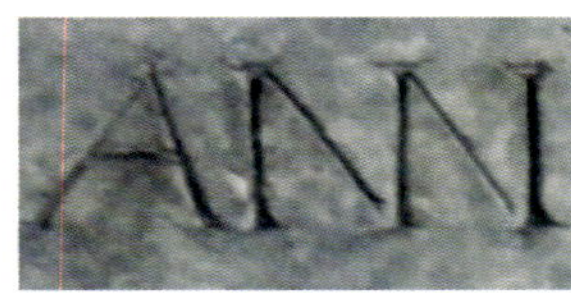

*Letters that join, shrink, or
overlap are a time-honored
Roman tradition. The letters
above, paired up the same
way, date from the first
century, and from 1676.*

AVANT GARDE

Speedball B nib
or blunt marker.

Height = 12 pen widths.

BASIC STROKES

Various diagonals
from 45° to 75°

LETTER CONSTRUCTION

True center

ABCDEFG
HIJKLMNO

↑This **M** is not
an upside down **W**

PQRSTUVW XYZ

LETTER CHOICES THAT HELP LETTERS FIT TOGETHER

AA MM VV WW Y

↖ This **M** *is* an upside-down **W**. ↗

LIGATURES: A SAMPLING

Extend   Intersect   Share   Shelter

CA CO   Nest   FA FR GA HT VA LL

LA NT RR RA SS ST TH UT

Parallel strokes are one pen width apart.

Overlap   Touch

VARIATION I: LIGHTWEIGHT

Height = 14+
pen widths.

AVANT

VARIATION II: HEAVYWEIGHT

Height = 6
pen widths.

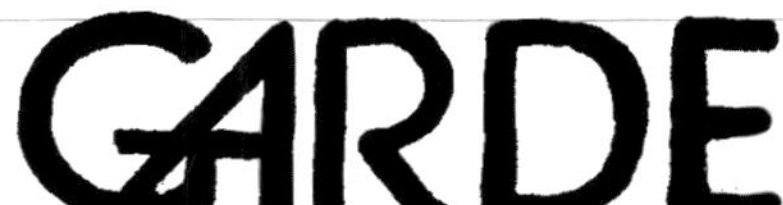
GARDE

USA

THE NEXT REVIVAL OF ROMAN CAPITALS in America coincided with a boom in calligraphy's popularity. By 1978 even the solemn *Wall Street Journal* had pronounced the trend "hotter than macrame." While most new enthusiasts were content to copy old Gothic and Italic manuscript styles using set pen angles, serious calligraphers took a fresh look at the original Roman capitals, using scholar Edward Catich's photographs, rubbings, and his analysis of the definitive Trajan column inscription from 113 CE—and some of them thought they saw something new. The familiar thicks and thins came under renewed critical scrutiny, challenging twenty centuries of conventional wisdom. A few adventurous American calligraphers, inspired by the calligraphic typefaces of Arthur Baker, felt that any deviations from strict geometry could only have come from changing the pen angle while the pen was moving. They modified their techniques, invented new pens to experiment with, and followed Roman letters down a new path.

The effects could be subtle or spectacular. In skilled hands, at larger sizes, pen-turning gave the calligrapher control over every part of the letter, in real time. It also opened up new possibilities; devotees crafted their own pens to make eye-catching striped and multicolor letters, while others were inspired to make designs so abstract that they were not even meant to be read.

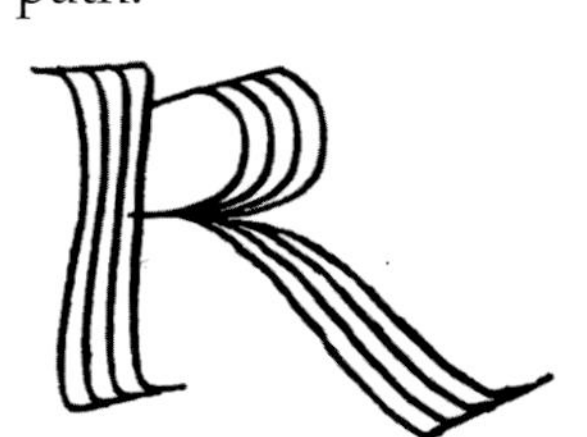

Written with a music staff pen.

While pen turning gave rise to its own revival of Roman, it kicked off dramatic new Gothic and Italic styles as well. The past looked different now. The rules that had specified one unchanging angle for each alphabet— something beginners learn in their first lessons—no longer seemed set in stone. As Jackie Svaren pointed out, "Almost all of the historical alphabets require some manipulation of the pen angle."

Forty years later, pen turning is now accepted as just one more useful technique for exploring the alphabet. Some new pen or technique of the future will trigger the next revival of the inexhaustible Roman alphabet.

Although this alphabet looks flexible, it must be written with a rigid pen— Pilot Parallel, or chisel-tipped (but not wedge-shaped) marker. For letters larger than 3" (8 cm), use a foam paint brush or Ultrasuede poster pen. Good practice requires large motions, many variations, and a lot of paper.

Hold the pen like this . . .   . . . not like this.

TURNING

Nicknamed "Bone Script" for its enlarged stroke ends.

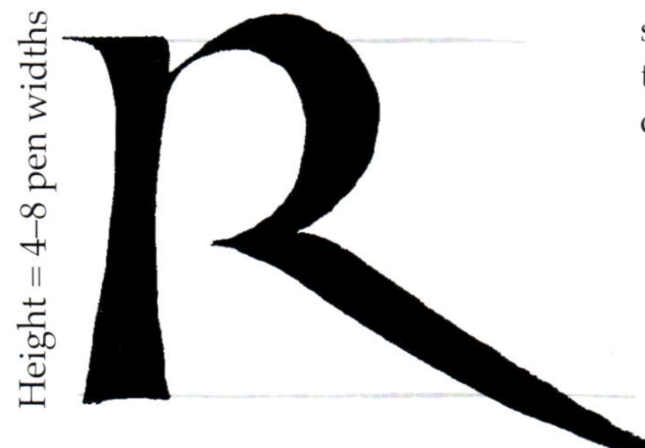

Height = 4–8 pen widths

BASIC STROKES

In a typical vertical stroke, after the pen turns, it can end at its original angle . . .

. . . or it can finish at a different pen angle.

Turning the pen can widen a curve or diminish it.

Practicing larger letters than shown here will teach beginners to move their arm rather than their fingers.

A SELECTION OF ALPHABET LETTERS

Small lines next to the stroke show its pen angle at that moment.

VARIATIONS:

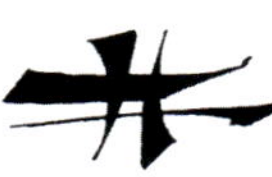

Repeated abstract strokes create patterns, and are good practice too.

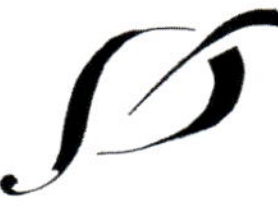

Turned pen strokes make simple pictures.

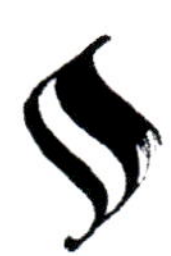

A notched pen makes stripes that add drama.

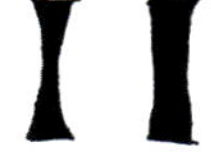

Contrast between thick and thin can be dramatic or subtle.

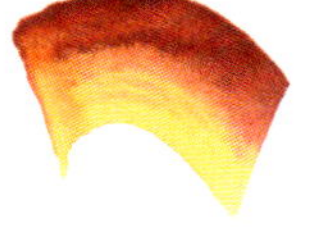

Two colors of ink can blend in the pen nib.

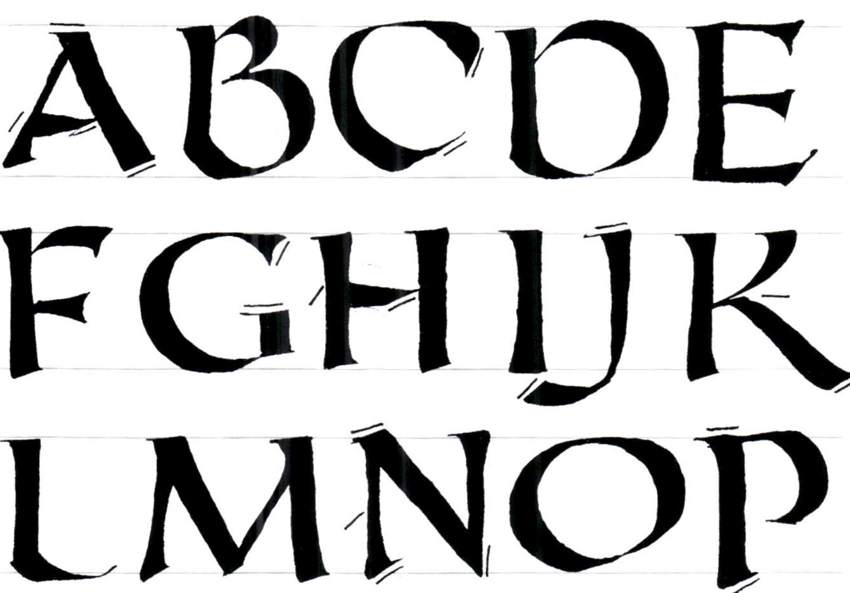

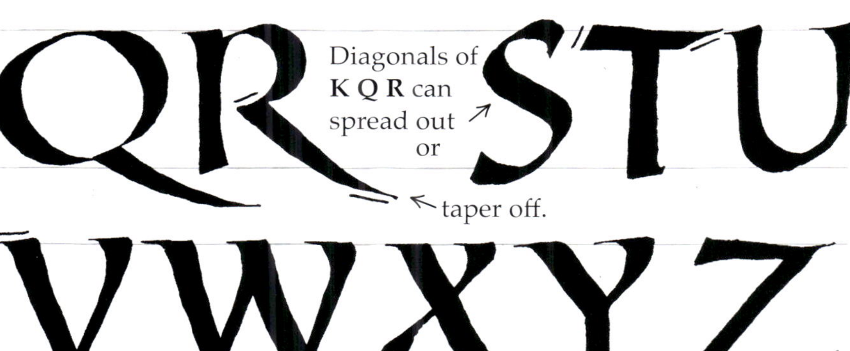

ROMAN REVIVALS HAVE A LOT TO TEACH, not just about the letterforms themselves but also about the forces that have shaped them in specifically American ways. Although like Western philosophy, architecture, and political thought, these capitals were born in Greece and Rome and grew up in the Old World, they went on to become the tool for New World discovery and exploration. Their revivals over the centuries mirror the American experience.

To revive is to revise, however; letters never look, or are looked at, quite the same way once a new generation brings them back for its own purposes. Roman calligraphy's strength rests on its long and resilient response to the challenge of being revived. Each new interpretation highlights a different facet: its elegance, modesty, dignity, architectural structure, moderation, stylishness, flexibility, and even its soft spot for fads. Many calligraphers are surprised to learn that what they thought were essential characteristics can be optional if other strong Roman features are present, such as traditional letter proportions, thicks and thins, and spacing. Classical Roman style survives in the intention and the context as well as in the details of execution, and it often bends its own rules to accomplish this.

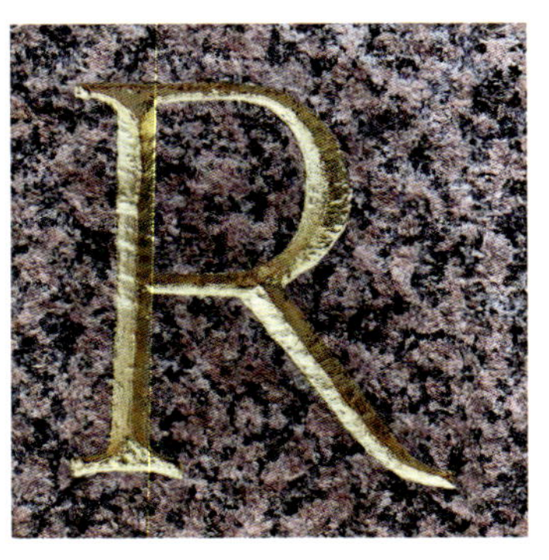

This timeless Roman capital is cut from granite and coated with gold leaf.

Steve Jobs, inventor and visionary founder of Apple, recalled his own immersion in calligraphy at Reed College, "It was beautiful. Historical. Artistically subtle in a way that science can't capture," and credited calligraphy with his company's signature elegance of design. Studying calligraphy is important, and starting with Roman is worth the effort. Every beginning calligrapher who learns its basics and explores its variations could have something unique to contribute to its future shape. Because how we read and write underpins our national identity, pen and ink will help every new American generation to reinterpret the Roman alphabet with their own unique insights.

By turns grandiose, aloof, chic, homespun, hip, or whimsical, the Roman alphabet expresses the American experience. It takes us on a guided tour of the past so we can make a map for revivals of the future.

DECO TURNED NEW DEAL COOPER ART NOUVEAU ARTS AND CRAFTS PRAIRIE AVANT GARDE

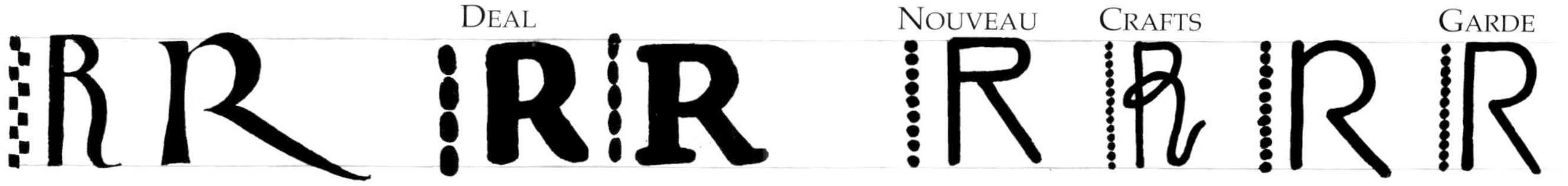

Broad-edge pen or marker *Speedball D* *Blunt marker or Speedball B*

CAPITALS

CAPITALS

CAPITALS

CAPITALS

CAPITALS

CAPITALS

CAPITALS

FRAKTUR

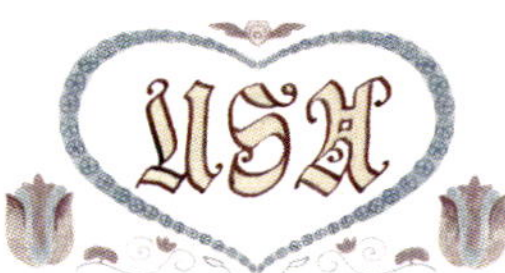

FRAKTUR CALLIGRAPHY, which used to be dismissed as a minor decorative craft, is now considered a major treasure of American folk art. It was originally used by amateurs who lived in close-knit rural towns, to celebrate the milestones of family life, both secular and religious. Treasured in private, it gradually reached the public. Fraktur today is highly prized by collectors, preserved by museums, intensely studied by historians, and lovingly imitated by calligraphers.

Although Fraktur script originated in the late-medieval lettering of Northern Europe, it took root so readily in the United States that it now seems native to North America. German-speaking immigrants (called "Pennsylvania Dutch" when the German word for German—Deutsch—was misinterpreted) outnumbered English speakers in much of eighteenth-century Pennsylvania, eastern Ohio, and southern Ontario, Canada. They not only held on to their own dialect but also kept the "fractured" letters they wrote it in. By making the most of limited materials and humble occasions, they kept the memory of the Old World alive while they invented an American identity for themselves in the New. And as they adapted the distinctive Fraktur page layout, decoration, and lettering to celebrate events in their own lives, these artists transformed ordinary documents into heirlooms.

The German word "Fraktur" (fracture) describes the angular strokes that form the letters. It became a catchall term for any design on paper in this style, such as certificates of birth, baptism, and marriage, student merit awards, genealogies, house blessings, bookplates, and even valentines and formal courtship letters. America's first Christmas card, in fact, was a small one-of-a-kind Fraktur design created around 1800 by a Moravian artist, seventy years before the first commercial card was printed.

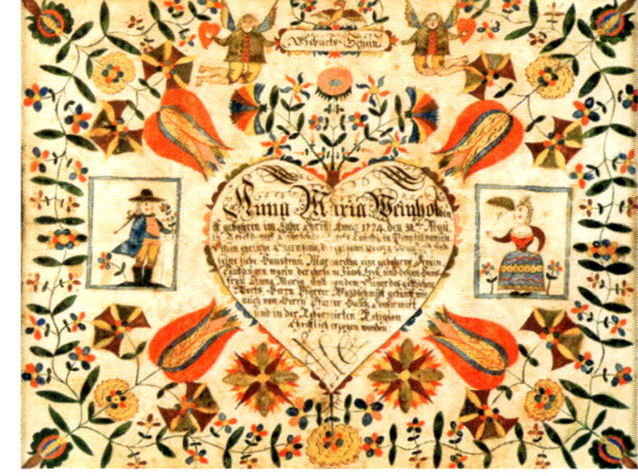

A birth and baptismal certificate from 1784, with typical Fraktur design and colors. Courtesy of the Philadelphia Museum of Art.

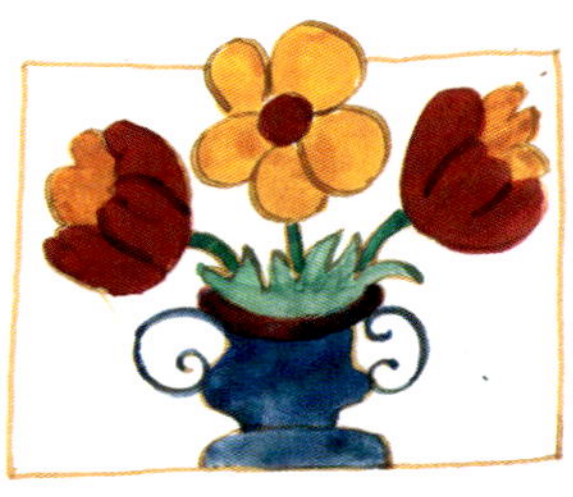

A TYPICAL FRAKTUR PAGE combines small, medium, and large lettering with swashes, elaborate capitals, floral borders, and lavish decorations. The lines of lettering often form the shape of an arch, a labyrinth, or a heart. Careful planning and a limited palette of blue and orange kept these richly textured designs from looking cluttered.

FRAKTUR TEXT LETTERS

There is no single, uniform Fraktur alphabet. Letter styles varied from town to town, since rural isolation reinforced the regional differences that settlers had brought from their home towns in Germany. (For instance, Ontario alone had four distinct styles in four tiny settlements.) And many of the characters had several forms, while other characters mutated over the decades and then dropped out. Still, Fraktur letters shared three fundamental features:

HYBRID LETTERS: Although some calligraphers preferred the geometrically precise parallel strokes of blackletter Gothic, a more typical—and more easily readable—style of Fraktur text letters combined a straight stroke on the left with a curved stroke on the right. Just a few letters might have curved strokes on both sides.

FRACTURES: Letters were broken at their corners, where the strokes curved outward and got thin before they connected at an acute angle. Or they might fail to join each other, leaving a gap that made them literally fractured.

SEMI-VARIABLE LINE: While a few calligraphers made letters with geometric precision, most let the strokes flow. In addition, broad-edged quill pens were flexible enough that extra downward pressure could make the Fraktur stroke wider. (Metal dip pens, available since the 1840s, could also be flexed, though to a lesser extent.) This added subtle visual grace to the text letters and allowed for pulling the ink with the corner of the nib.

CHOICES

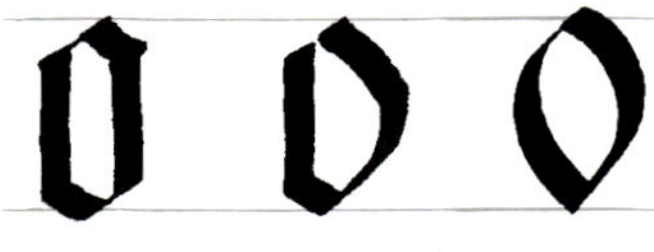

Blackletter   Half-   Double
Gothic   round   curve

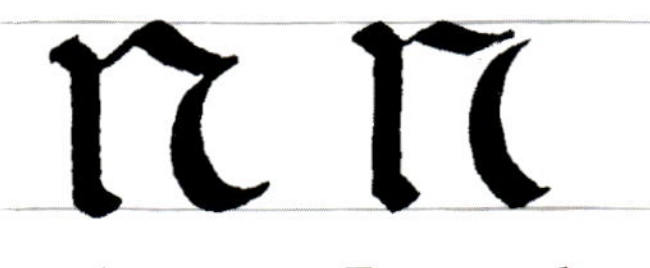

Acute   Fractured
corner   corner

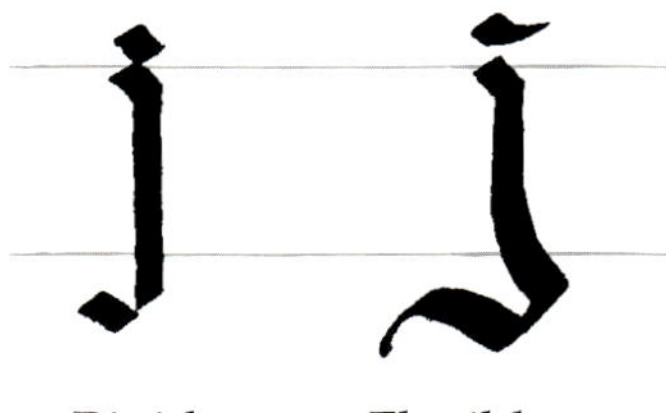

Rigid   Flexible
strokes   strokes

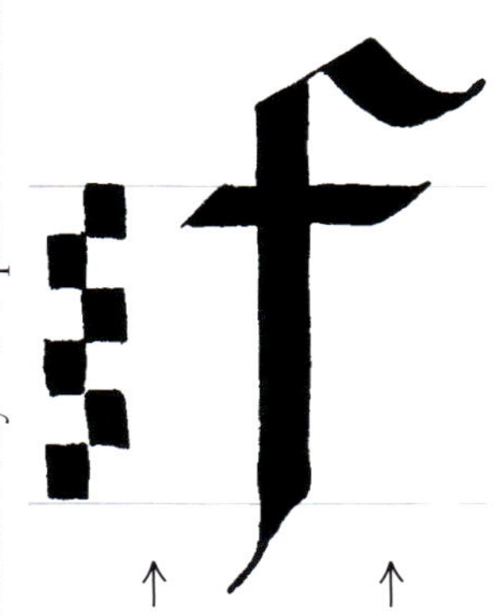

Fraktur

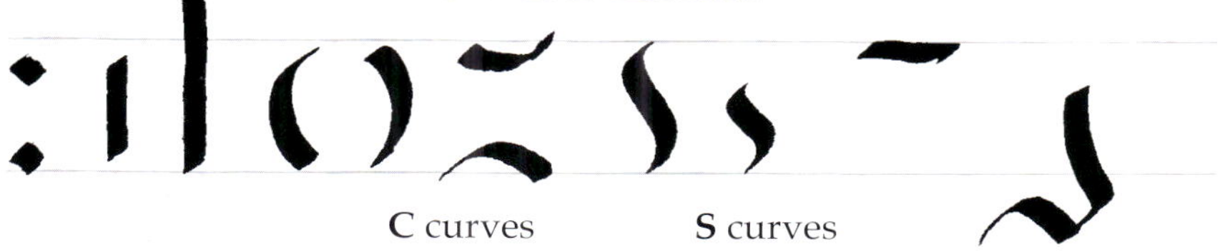

Height of ascenders and descenders varied from two to six pen widths.

Letter body = 5–7 pen widths tall.

The letter's body was about ⅗ as wide as its height.

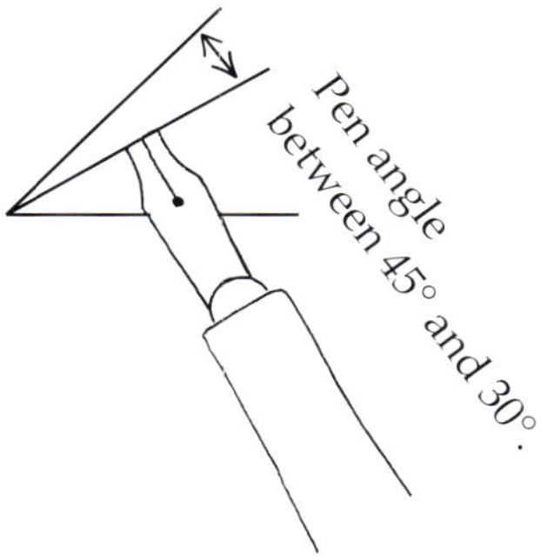

Pen angle between 45° and 30°.

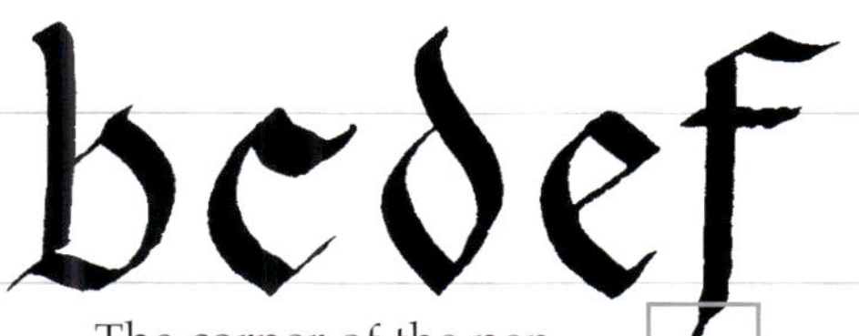

FRAKTUR TEXT LETTERS with modern versions for **A G K N P R S**.

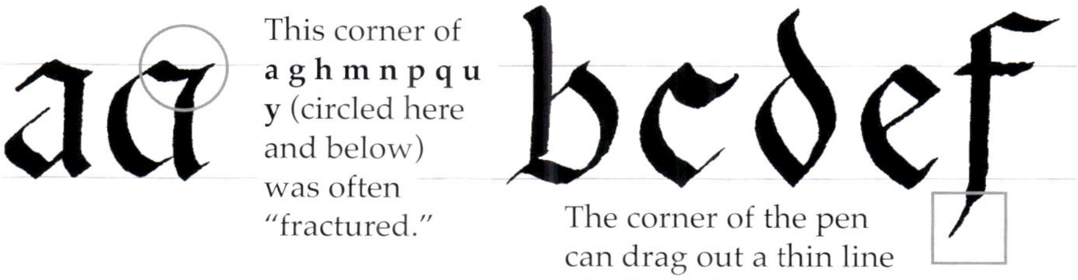

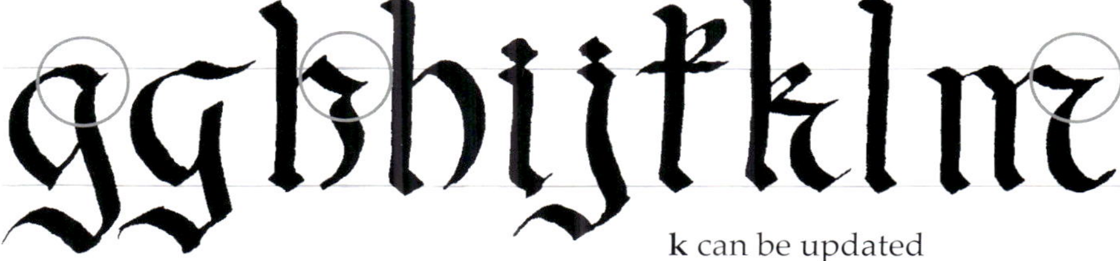

This corner of **a g h m n p q u y** (circled here and below) was often "fractured."

The corner of the pen can drag out a thin line of ink, on **f p q** and long **s**.

k can be updated for modern eyes.

Archaic form of **r**

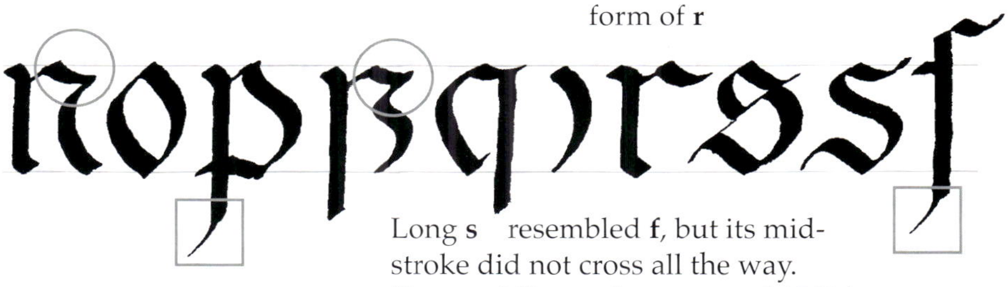

Long **s** resembled **f**, but its midstroke did not cross all the way. (Long **s** fell out of use around 1840.)

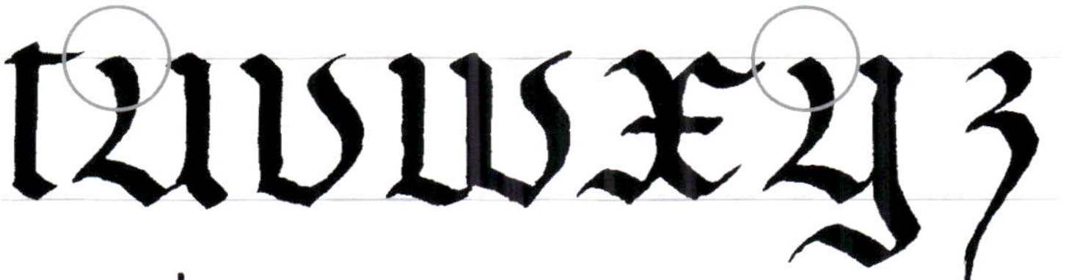

A separate line of lettering was sometimes slanted back 5° to 10° to add emphasis. (A forward slant was less typical of Fraktur.)

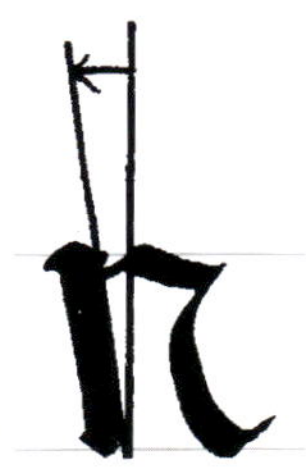

Each calligrapher's choice of curves will be slightly different.

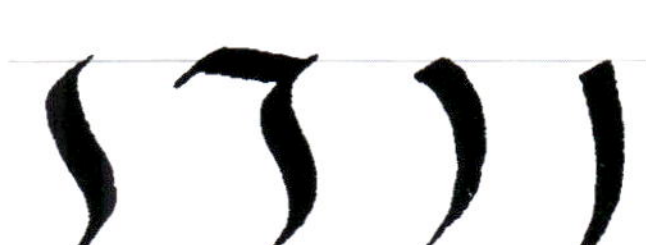

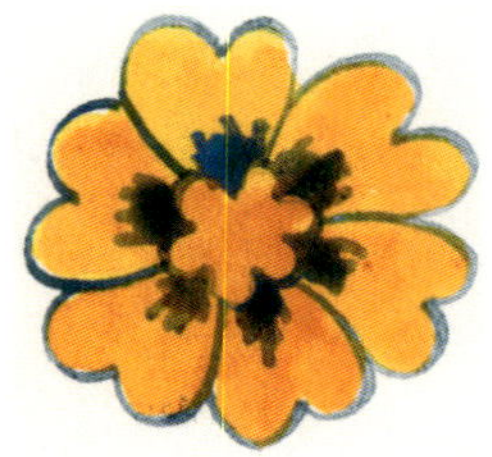

There were two main ways to write the pen capitals that were so very plentiful in written German*: embed them in the block of text, or leave a space for them and come back later (see page 97). Small, simple capitals were written with the same pen, using the same ink, at the same time, and at the same scale as the text letters. They were made of three or four individual pen strokes, to which the writer might add a decorative extra stroke.

*All German nouns are capitalized, a custom dropped from English two hundred years ago.

The alphabet chart below is based on a Fraktur "Vorschrift," a page of model letters to copy. Capitals are to be a little shorter than ascenders.

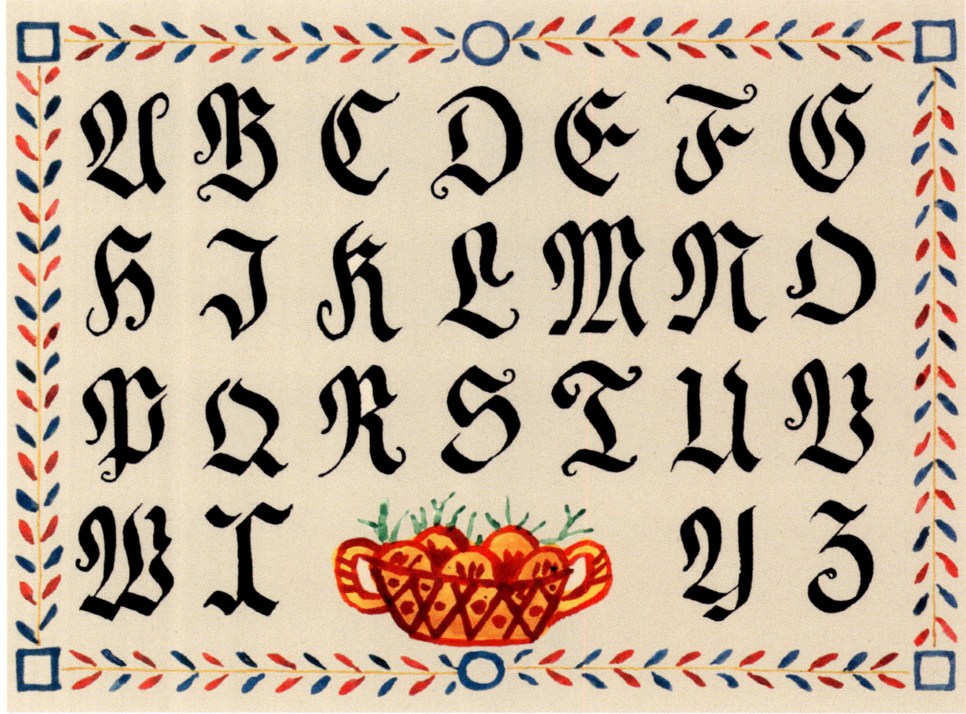

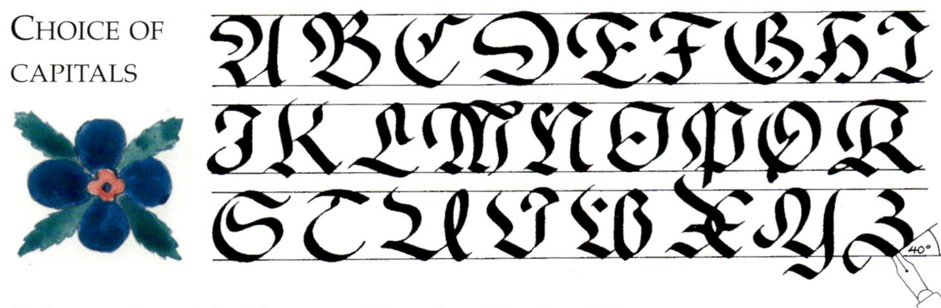

Choice of capitals

Fraktur style varied with every calligrapher. Here is a different alphabet of pen capitals, simplified but still swashed and decorative. (From Calligraphy Alphabets Made Easy, *by Margaret Shepherd.)*

FRAKTUR CALLIGRAPHERS LEFT SPACES in their page layout so that the most important capitals could be inserted after the text was done. They enlarged them, painted them with colors, or reinforced them with repeated flourishes. They added lines, curlicues, dots, or flowers. They filled the space around and inside the letters, and then went on to create even more space inside the letter stroke itself.

Some Fraktur artists used *all* these decorative techniques together on the same page, or even in the same letter.

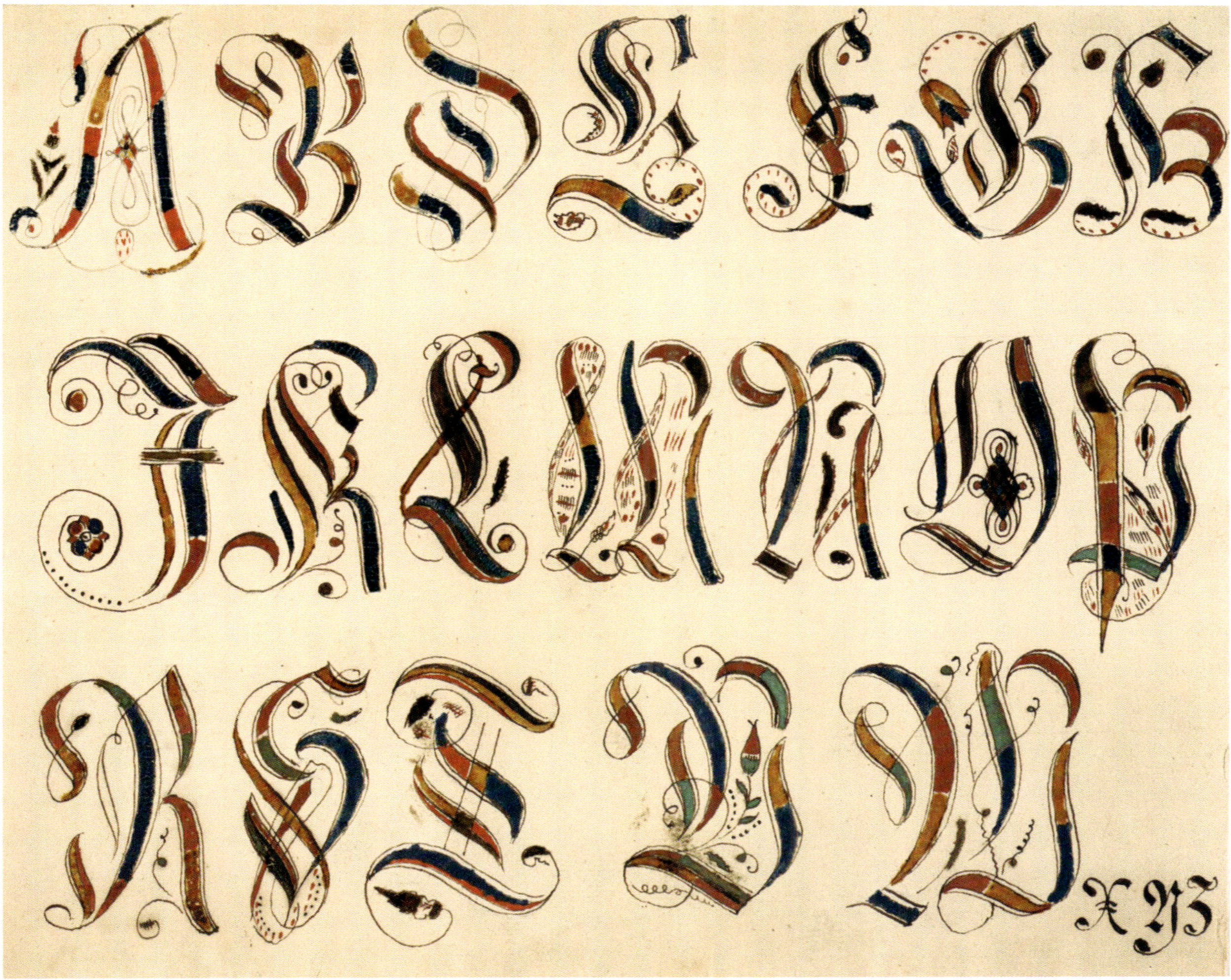

These capitals use color and penwork to add richness.
From the Free Library of Philadelphia.

OUTLINED STROKES

After decorating the spaces inside and around the letters, calligraphers went on to create more spaces inside the strokes. The alphabet below shows text letters written with a two-pointed nib. The facing page shows larger letters outlined by hand.

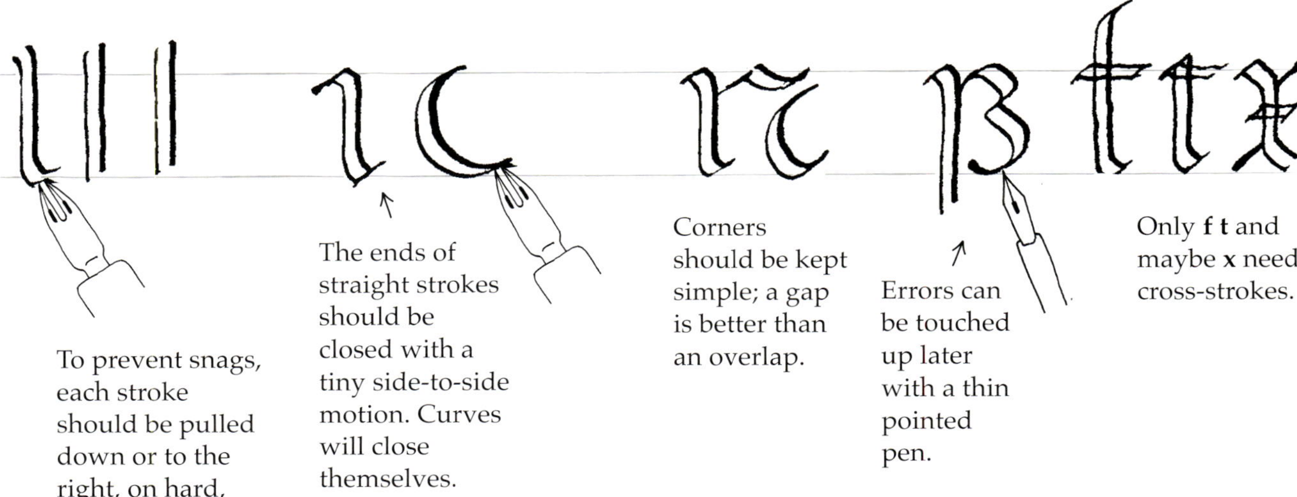

To prevent snags, each stroke should be pulled down or to the right, on hard, smooth paper.

The ends of straight strokes should be closed with a tiny side-to-side motion. Curves will close themselves.

Corners should be kept simple; a gap is better than an overlap.

Errors can be touched up later with a thin pointed pen.

Only **f t** and maybe **x** need cross-strokes.

FRAKTUR CALLIGRAPHERS found ways to dress up even the smallest split letters.

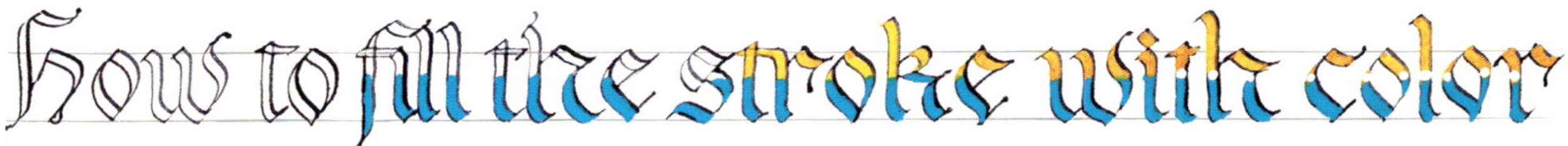

A brush or pen fills the lower half with a color . . . and a second color . . . and dots of white or a third color.

SPLIT PEN LETTERS   Extra versions of **a g k n p r s** are given on page 95.

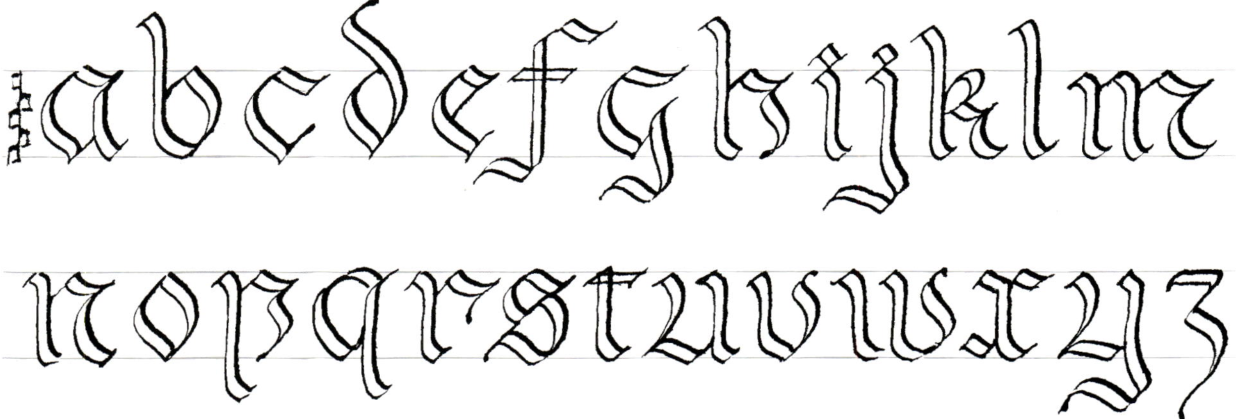

The same split pen can also render any pen capitals up to about 1″ tall (2.5 cm), like those on page 96.

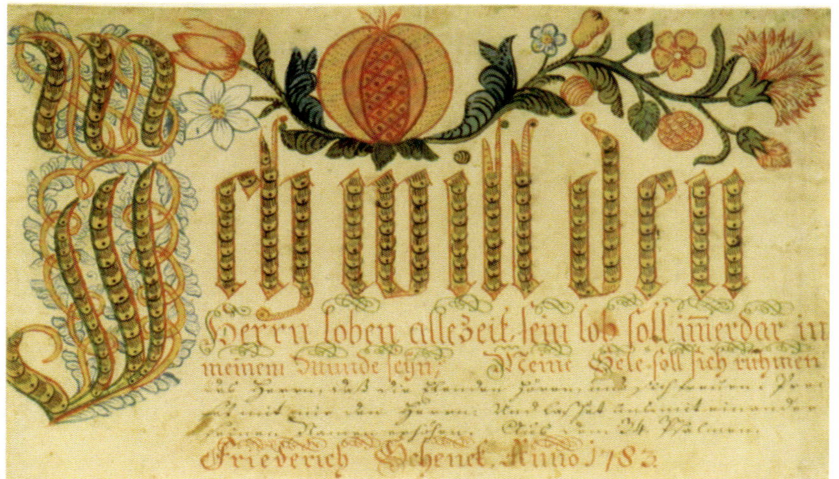

LETTERS THAT WERE LARGER than 1" tall (2.5 cm) required strokes that were wider than the quill nib, ³⁄₁₆" (.4 cm). Thus when Fraktur scribes needed large letters they had to outline each stroke by hand. Their deep familiarity with broad-pen letters helped them keep the thicks and thins in the right places.

Even the humblest text letterforms could blossom with color and decoration when they were enlarged. Filled strokes, already full of detail, might also then be repeated, like the dotted letter **I** *in "ich will den" above. From National Museum of American History, Smithsonian.*

Living among highly literate people, Fraktur calligraphers were careful to use proper grammar even in their display letters; when they enlarged a whole word or line, they did not presume to alter its distinction between capital and text letters. (Fraktur artists never spelled out whole words in all capitals, unlike scribes of the late nineteenth-century Gothic Revival.)

*Letter i, detail from above. The artist who enlarged the →
letter did not change its form; the word* ich, *which means the
pronoun "I" in English, is not capitalized in German.*

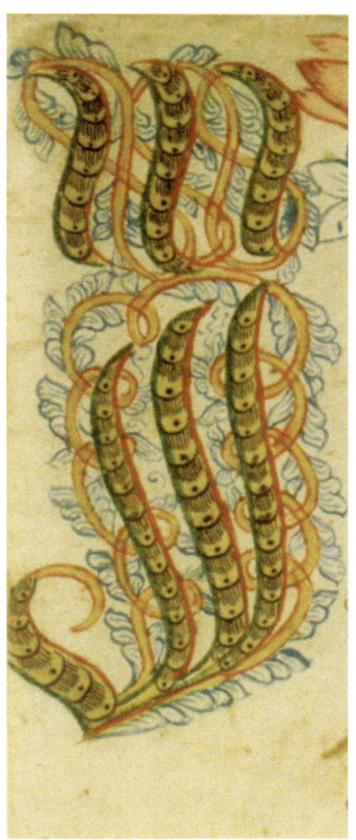

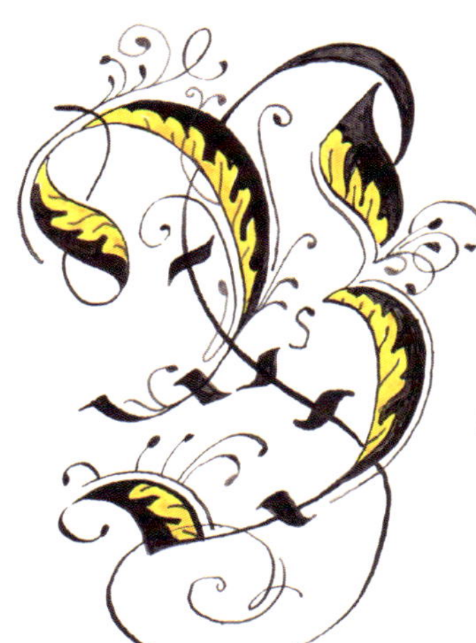

↖ Large leafy **B**, *based on a
Fraktur Vorschrift from 1821*

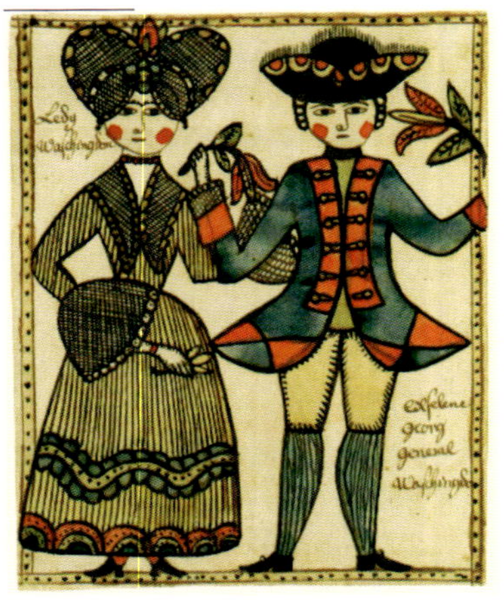

"Exselenc Georg General Waschingdon and Ledy Waschingdon," c 1780. Courtesy of Colonial Williamsburg.

THE TYPICAL FRAKTUR PAGE COMBINED a text, a symmetrical layout, and a wide range of vivid decorations, or what Fraktur artist Judy Brinck describes as, "birds, buds, and balance." Fraktur artists painted mostly what they saw around them, replacing their inherited German images with American ones: stylized roses and tulips; houses; native creatures, especially birds; and specific men, women, children, and babies mentioned in the text. Later designs added popular motifs of mourning such as urns, angels, and weeping willows. A few Frakturs depicted flags, revolutionary soldiers, or George Washington. Familiar motifs of village life were more common than sacred scenes from the Bible.

Any empty space remaining on the page was often filled with abstract ornaments such as repeated pen strokes, ruled lines, textured fill, geometric pattern, single swashes, and the intricately interwoven woven flourishes known as *paraphs*—swashes that zigzagged back and forth over themselves to form complex woven lattices.

Some virtuoso page layouts made images out of the lines of lettering. This was a favorite theme for love letters and valentines.

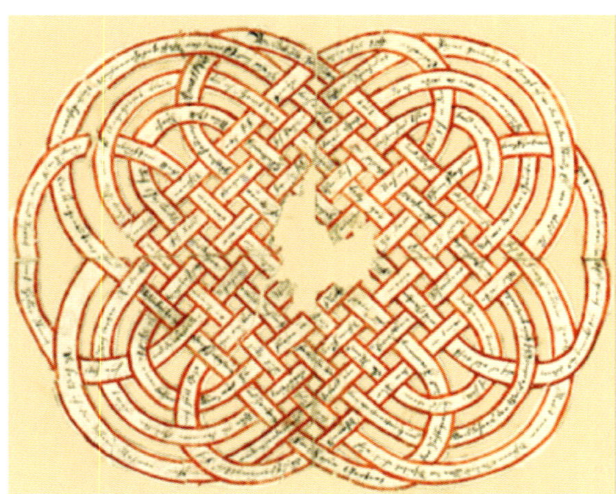

This intricately interlaced text delivers a love message. 1782. From the collection of the Mercer Museum of the Bucks County Historical Society. Used with permission.

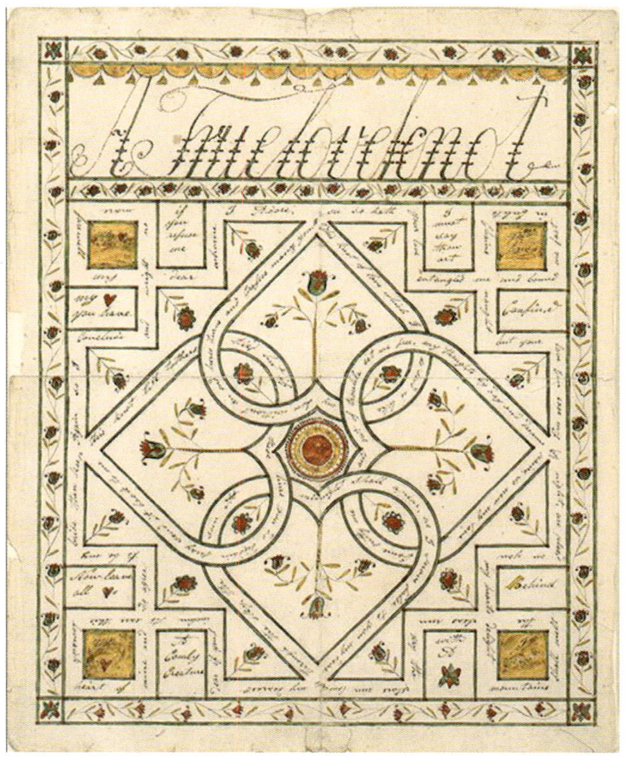

This overlapped knot is headlined with complicated script letters that read "A Trueloveknot." Courtesy of the Free Library of Philadelphia, Rare Book Department.

FRAKTUR ARTISTS HAD DAY JOBS as local schoolmaster, lay preacher, civil servant, pastor, or housewife. As part-time artists living far from cities, they worked with the kind of materials that could be made in a small town or bought from a market nearby or ordered from a city, not specialized items or expensive rarities.

PENS: Before about 1820, Americans used pens shaped from goose feather quills to write both formal calligraphy and everyday handwriting; after that, they began to buy metal nibs from importers; and eventually, from American manufacturers.

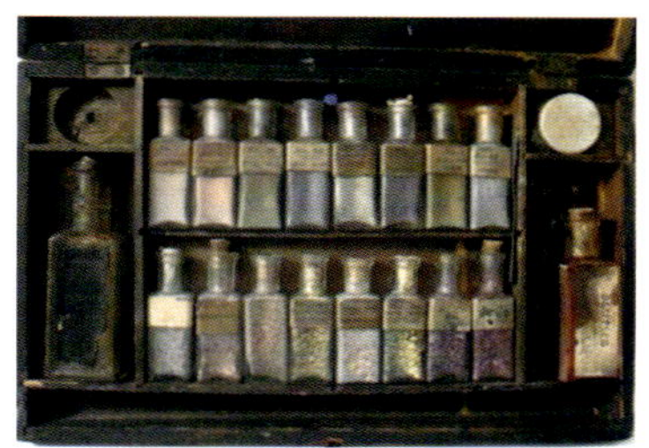

Fraktur paintbox with pigment powder in bottles, c 1825

INK: Ink was made using a recipe from late medieval Europe that blended oak gall, iron sulfate, soot, and gum arabic. Suppliers sold ink as powders or pellets to rehydrate.

PIGMENT: The Fraktur palette was limited to pigments that were readily available, resistant to fading or decay, and unlikely to damage the paper. They were bought from local shops, nearby towns, or traveling peddlers, or ordered from abroad; they came in corked bottles of powder, or after 1850, premixed in soft lead tubes. Fraktur artists gradually expanded their limited palette of blue, orange, red, and white into a wider range of colors: vermilion, red lead, chrome yellow, and verdigris, which made their designs more versatile but less distinctive. Artists today begin with Prussian blue and cadmium red, and add cadmium yellow, Hooker's green, and raw umber.

Gold leaf was not characteristic of Frakturs. Gold paint was sometimes added in small dots and burnished.

PAPER: American and Canadian Frakturs were virtually never written on parchment. Paper of that era, made of linen and cotton rags, was nearly as durable and much cheaper, and it would not buckle in the fluctuating temperature and humidity of northeast America. The country's first paper mill was established in 1689 in Germantown, New York. American paper was made in the laid style, shown on page 25, until wove paper was introduced around 1820.

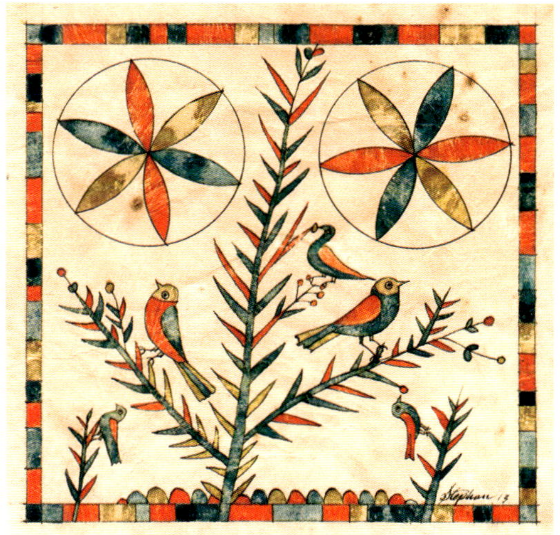

Fraktur "compass stars" in typical colors, created by modern Fraktur artist Dennis Stephan.

OUTSIDE INFLUENCES inevitably weakened the roots of Fraktur. As travel got easier, itinerant Fraktur artists began to circulate through clusters of towns, often carrying a stock of preprinted and decorated forms—some of them even set in type!—to fill in on demand. Originality dwindled as local styles became regional, undermining the personal connection.

Eventually, German Americans began to assimilate and move on from the customs of their immigrant ancestors. The brief popularity of Gothic letters in Nazi Germany during the 1930s stigmatized Germanic letter styles everywhere for a decade. Since mid-century, however, authentic Frakturs have been reevaluated as American cultural artifacts, historical records, and models of good design. Fortunately, the high quality of early American paper has left scholars and collectors with an estimated 8,000 to 10,000 documents in good condition. Much of the ornamentation offers insights into the details of daily life, making each Fraktur seem like a handcrafted window into the America of yesterday. Fraktur artists enriched life not just for their communities, but for the whole country. As Lisa Minardi, director at Historic Trappe Museum, writes, "Pennsylvania Germans actively participated in the formation of a national identity in which all could share, regardless of their ethnic background."

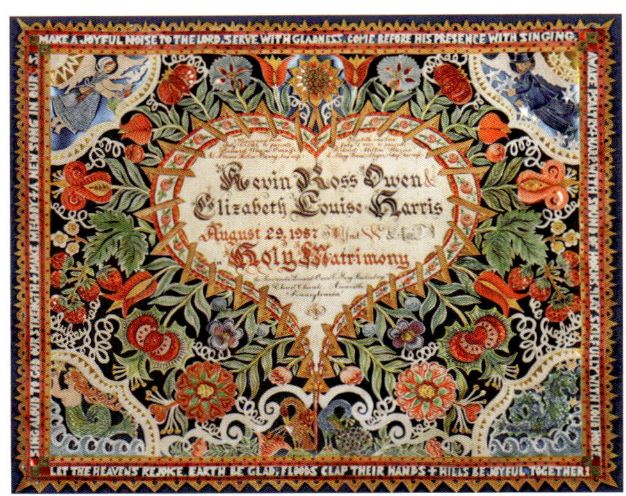

This modern Fraktur by Sukie Harris combines flowers, heart-shaped layout, angels, and cut-paper Bible verses around the border to celebrate the marriage of a musician and a calligrapher.

Fraktur's very assets—a distinctive color scheme, quaint imagery, and a naive view of a vanished world—have made it all too easy to copy. But a few American letter artists are trying to push it beyond its nostalgic comfort zone. Using its basic strokes, they invent art for their own era inspired by Fraktur from the past.

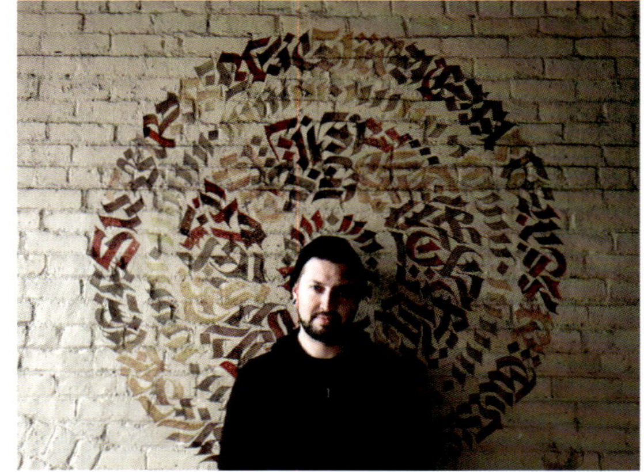

Using Fraktur strokes and Fraktur colors, letter artist Jake Rainis gives this abstract graffiti design Fraktur flavor.

- - - - - CAPITALS - - - - - - - - Height of capitals and ascenders

SMALL LETTERS _____ Height of letter bodies

Baseline _____________

*Broad-edge dip pen, marker,
or fountain pen.*

{ SMALL
  LETTERS

{ SMALL
  LETTERS

{ SMALL
  LETTERS

{ SMALL
  LETTERS

{ SMALL
  LETTERS

{ SMALL
  LETTERS

{ SMALL
  LETTERS

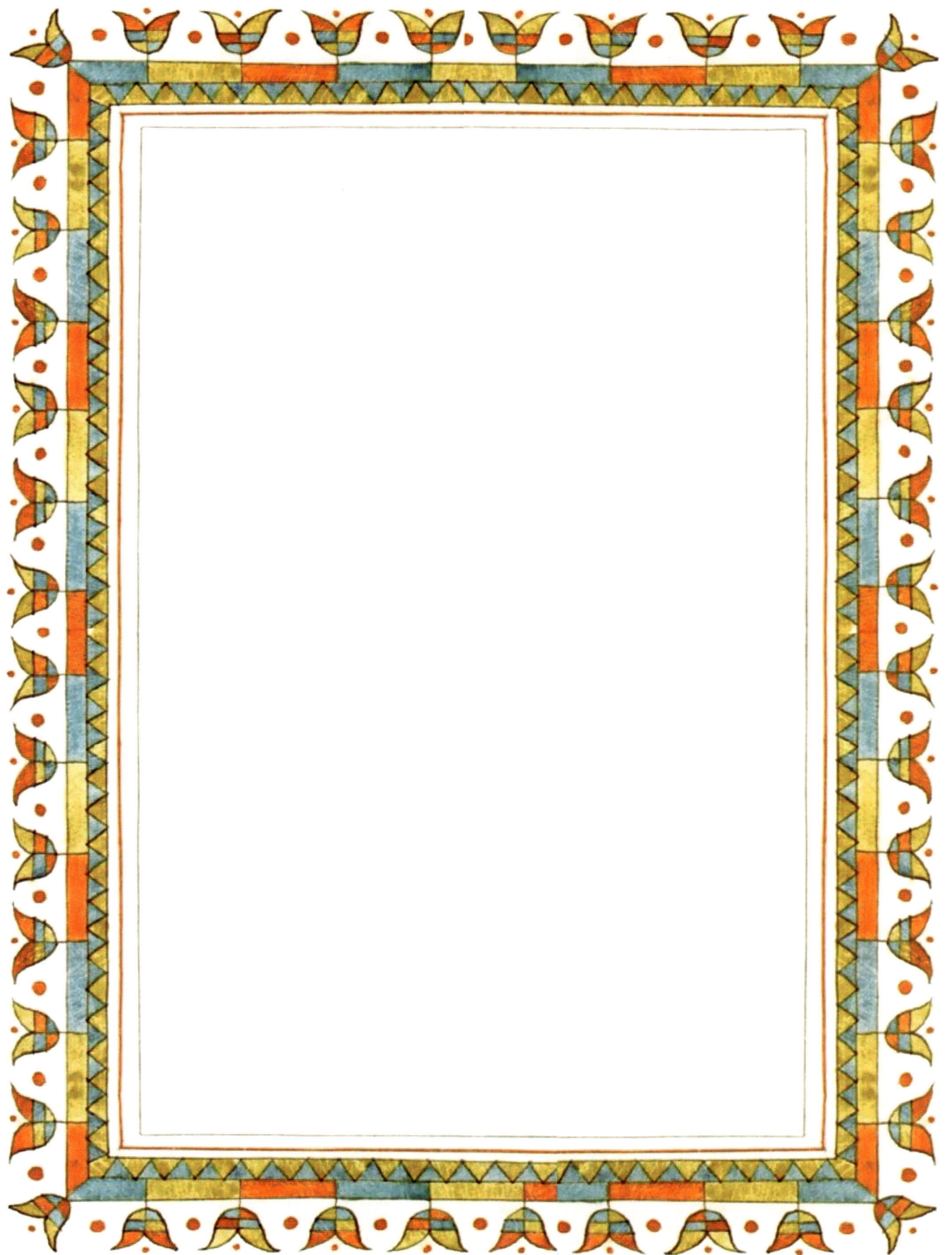

BLOCK

FROM 1860 TO 1970, HAND-PAINTED AMERICAN banners, signs, and showcards were everywhere, from corner grocery stores to national convention halls. Professional sign painters helped the new consumer economy to expand by creating the advertisements that prodded customers to spend money. In their heyday, they maintained busy workshops, organized labor unions, and gave whole neighborhoods a distinctive visual personality. Few urban photographs from this period lack their catchy sign, large or small. "Buy it now!" became a kind of slogan for the country.

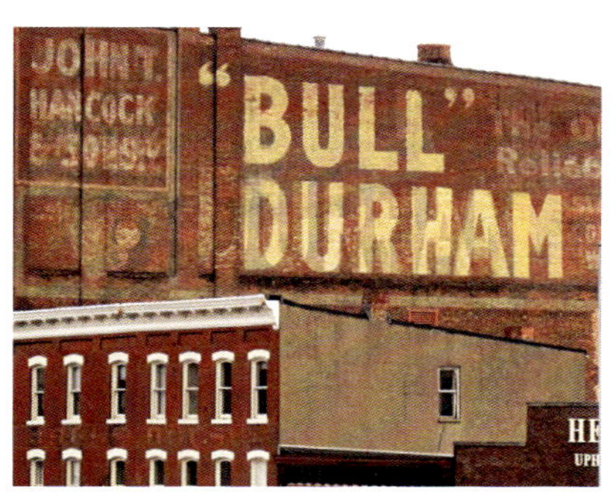

Wall-size letters on brick, decades after they were painted.

At one extreme, many whole walls were covered in long-lasting outdoor enamel paint with huge advertisements for patent medicines, chewing tobacco, beer, and clothing. Elaborately executed, incorporating all the latest graphic fads, and impossible to ignore in their era, these designs outlasted their original use. A few remain today, quaint and slowly fading, on city walls and country barns.

Big, splashy murals, however, were not where the most interesting letter innovations actually got started. Most sign painters depended on a daily stream of small-scale jobs to bring in a reliable income. For those, they evolved their own block alphabet—a workhorse rather than a show horse—that was easy to use for cheap, temporary signs and banners. Block letters were simple but could be dressed up for extra impact with just a few strokes. Utterly practical, they offered sign painters great flexibility with countless variations, such as the slab and Wild West alphabets shown in this chapter. Block also became the basis for the ubiquitous letterforms of typewriter and funnies. And although all these hand-lettered styles were eventually rendered into metal type, wood type, photo type, and digital type, they are still accessible to the pen or brush of an adventurous calligrapher today.

"After all, the chief business of the American people is business. They are profoundly concerned with producing, buying, selling, investing, and prospering in the world."

~ Calvin Coolidge

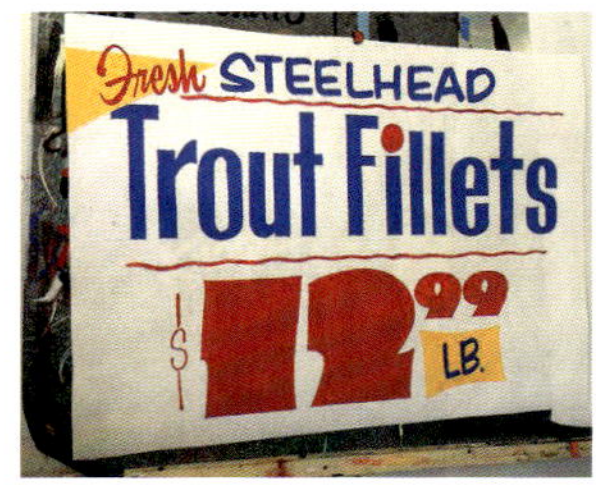

A typical grocery store sign is meant for a few days' use.

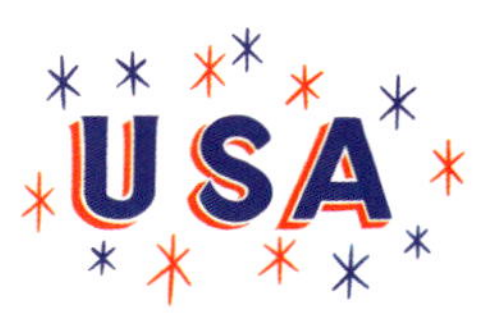

"You don't outline
a sign painter's
letter and then fill
it in with a Q-Tip—
that isn't really sign
painting. You use
the appropriate
size brush and do it
in three strokes."

~ *John Downer*

AMERICAN CALLIGRAPHY WAS A SEPARATE ART from sign-painting, because the tools, materials, sizes, and purposes were so unlike. Calligraphy limited itself to historical pen alphabets from Rome, the Middle Ages, and the Renaissance, written with a broad-edged pen in ink on a page of paper or parchment; and it added dignity to important occasions with permanent awards and diplomas that were carefully written and often elaborately ornamented. In contrast, everyday lettering on signs, showcards, and banners was written large, on cheap paper, with a flat brush and poster paint; it was meant for temporary display, designed to grab the viewer's attention, and aimed to sell things. The two worlds might overlap now and then, if a client requested large calligraphy or a small showcard. Both writers might use poster pens with nibs that made letters just small enough for calligraphers and just big enough for sign painters. Still, the purists did not think they had much in common with the promoters.

Calligraphers, however, can learn a lot from sign painters. Those who think that they mastered the ABCs in first grade or who have tried Roman capitals in calligraphy classes may be tempted to skip this style, not realizing how much the special rules of manuscript calligraphy have narrowed their view of how to make letters. Basic block offers the chance to start over, without traditional Roman's different letter widths, subtle visual adjustments, and set pen angles.

Block letters, written big with a wide brush, will refresh the eye of any writer who usually works small. The body's experience will be different, too: standing up and moving around; manipulating a wide flat brush; writing large letters with a free arm; and putting the thick and thin strokes exactly where they want them.

Anyone who learns the simple technique of changing the pen angle, both between strokes and during strokes, can use it to explore many more styles.

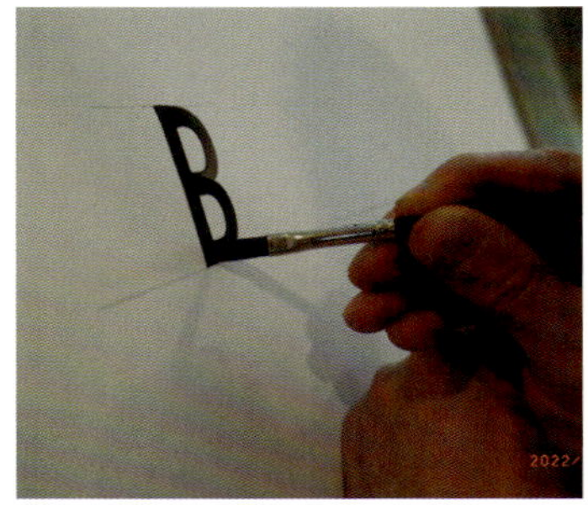

Single strokes take more skill than outlining and filling in.

BLOCK

Mid-strokes cross at the geometric middle (except **A**) not at the visually adjusted middle as in Roman.

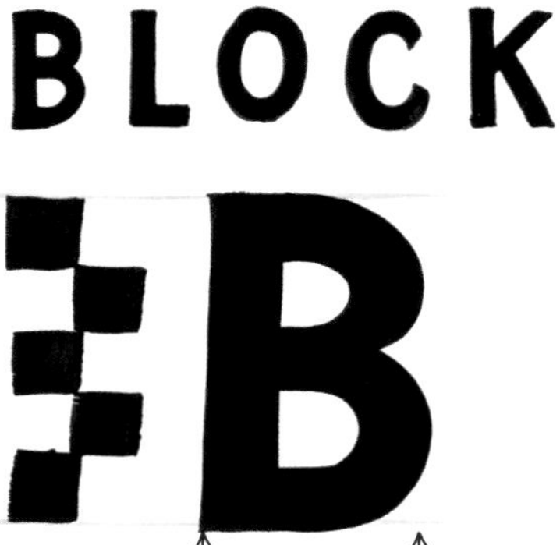

BASIC STRAIGHT STROKES

More than half the letters can be written using only straight strokes.

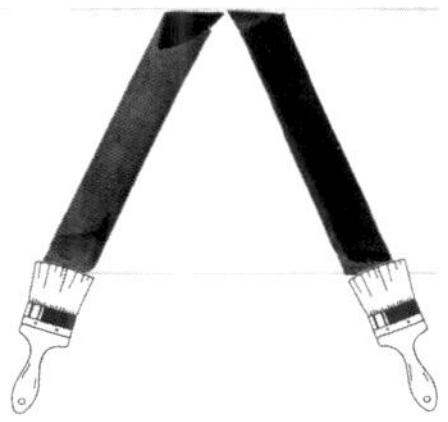

Changing the pen angle *between the strokes* will keep them the same width as the brush. There are no thin strokes in this alphabet. Choices of two angles for diagonals.

LETTERS   VERTICAL AND HORIZONTAL

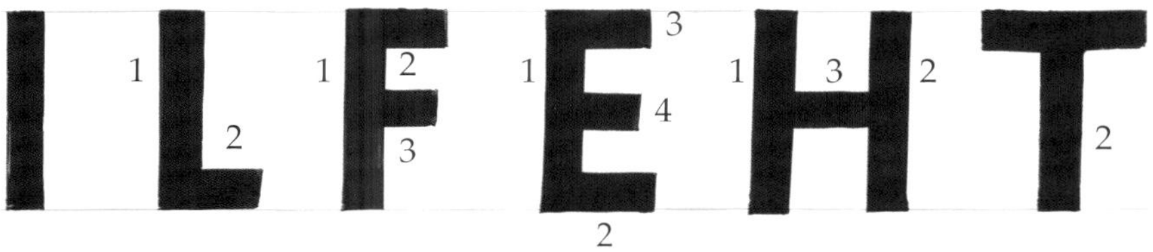

I L F E H T

DIAGONAL

V W X

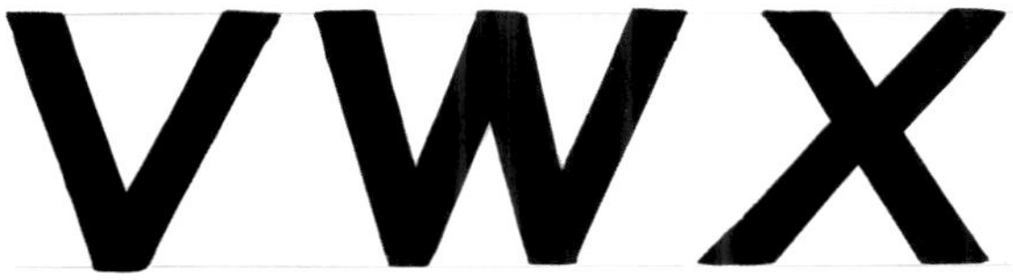

Strokes are written left to right and top to bottom. Strokes here are numbered in case the order might not be obvious.

VERTICAL, HORIZONTAL, AND DIAGONAL

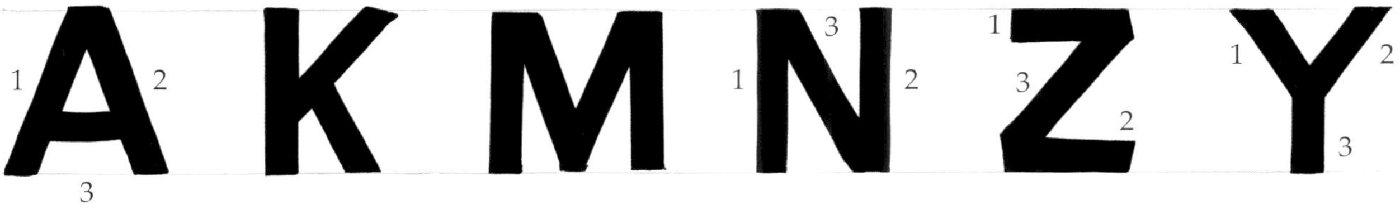

A K M N Z Y

BASIC CURVED STROKES

The pen angle turns steadily from the top *throughout the stroke*. Practice with quarter circles; then half circles; finally the other half circles. Virtuosos like to show their skill by completiong a letter O in one stroke.

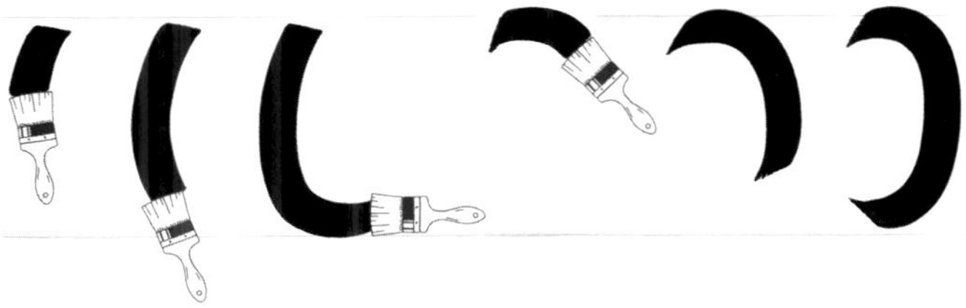

CURVED

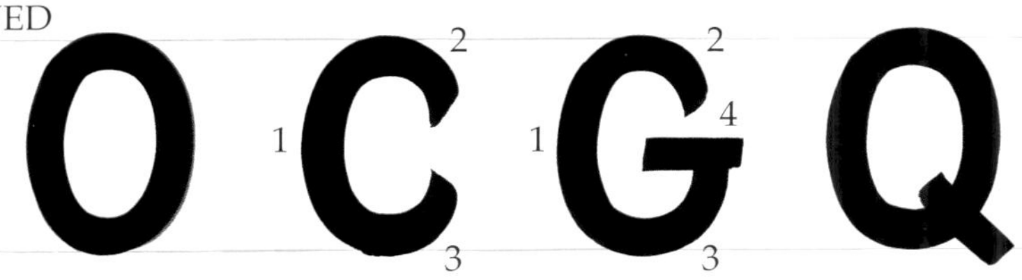

O C G Q

DOUBLE CURVE

S

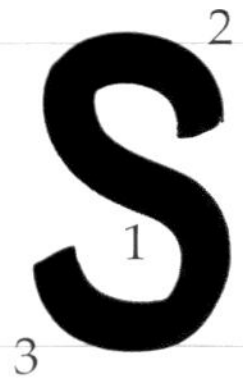

CURVED AND STRAIGHT

D B J P R U

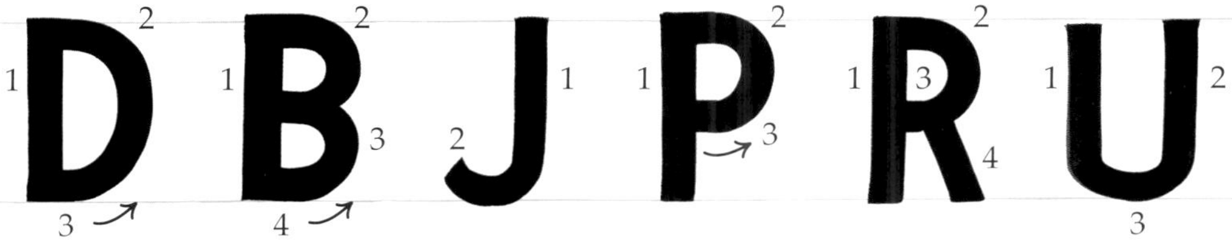

1234567890!?
¢ $ ¢ $ */? & @@?

Since so many signs are about price, here are basic block numerals, plus symbols for pennies and dollars.
1, 4, and 7 can be written using only straight strokes.

SOME VARIATIONS ON BASIC BLOCK CAPS

Sign artists have no trouble catching attention with huge letters painted on the side of a building, if their clients are willing to spend money on the buckets of paint and days of time that go into a big mural that will last for years. In contrast, it's the daily grind of short-lived signs like "**SPECIAL TODAY $1.98**" that have inspired many sign painters to develop a collection of simple, quick strokes that dress up the letters without spending much time. They can be fast, cheap, and appealing all at the same time.

A typical block lettered sign is limited to a few words—or just one—and a price. Lowercase letters, usually *much* smaller, may add a few details.

Dozens of quick extras can make block letters even harder to ignore.

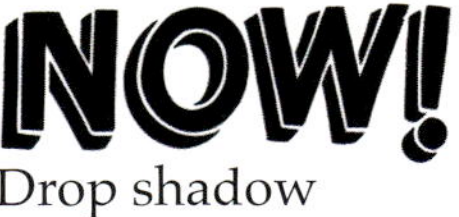
Drop shadow

Slant back

Slant forward

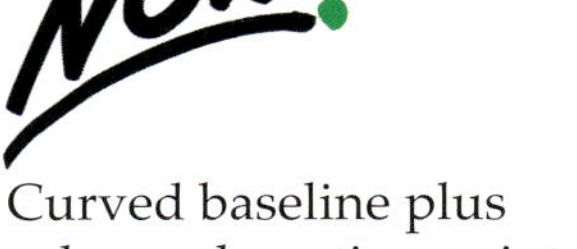
Squiggles inside stroke

Uneven baseline

Color outline

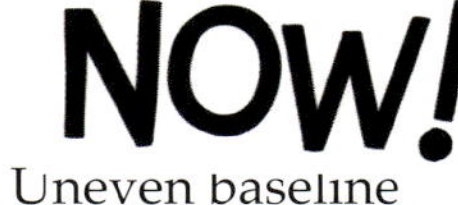
Curved baseline plus
color exclamation point

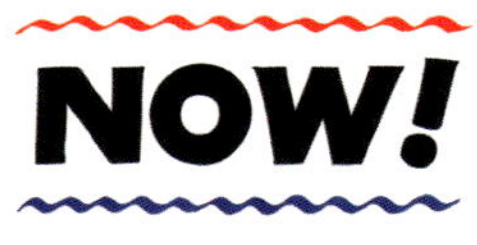
Wavy color
above and below

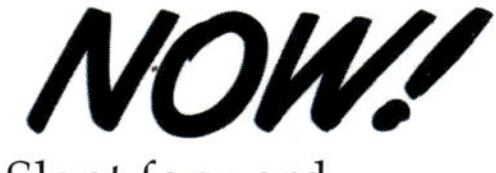
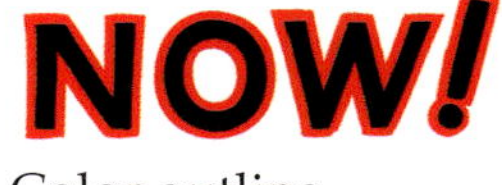
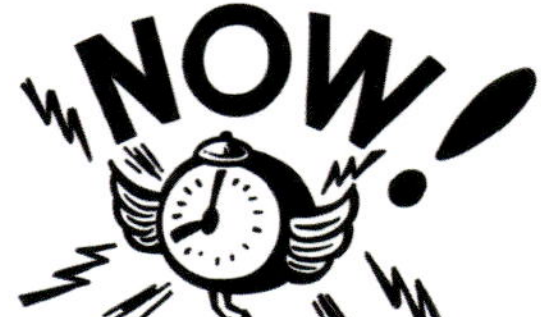
Spot art

AMERICAN SIGN PAINTING GREW . . .

SIGN PAINTERS used to cover everything from routine tasks to original art. Most of them learned by apprenticing themselves to a master sign painter for three to five years; by the early twentieth century they could also study at an art or trade school. They mastered their boss's alphabet styles, took care of clients, kept an eye on the successful designs of colleagues, and collected extra alphabets and problem-solving tips from dozens of manuals. Sign painting was a thriving profession in America until well after the 1960s.

. . . AND SLUMPED . . .

As the twentieth century wore on, however, hand-painted signs were gradually crowded out by cheap alternatives such as sticky notes, rub-on letters, printouts, and prefab plastic signs. Even hand-painted lettering on vehicles shrank to a magnetic sign or a glued-on vinyl cutout. Every store, every neighborhood, and every city started to look the same.

. . . AND GREW AGAIN

As with most changes in letter style, the pendulum has begun to swing back, so that today hand-painted signs are once more part of American life. For example, many local Trader Joe's grocery stores employ part-time artists who make friendly, informal signs by hand in marker, paint, and chalk. Restaurants have rediscovered the art of writing their menus on blackboards. Now many cities have a thriving visual culture of hand-painted signage. Individual sign artists have been inspired to set up their own shops, and they mentor rather than compete with new people entering the field. Women who used to be excluded from mid-century sign-painters' unions are finding new opportunities to earn a living with letters.

Most crucially, businesses are rediscovering the two biggest advantages of a hand-painted sign: it doesn't have to cost more, and it reaches customers with more oomph.

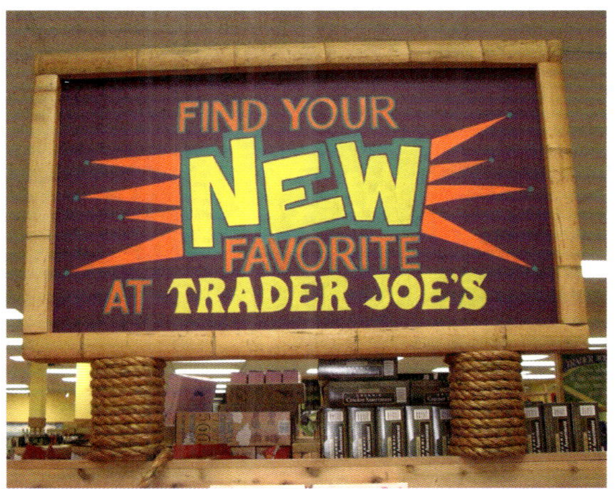

Grocery-store graphics in chalk, by Brigid Cowdrey.

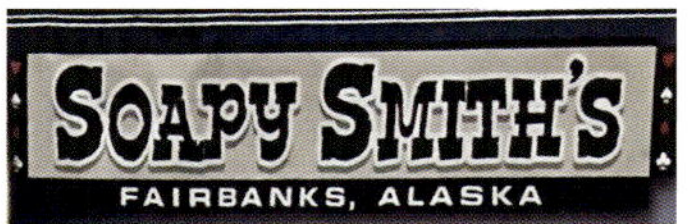

"Your feet's too big."
~ Song by Fats Waller

Slab lettering demands attention.

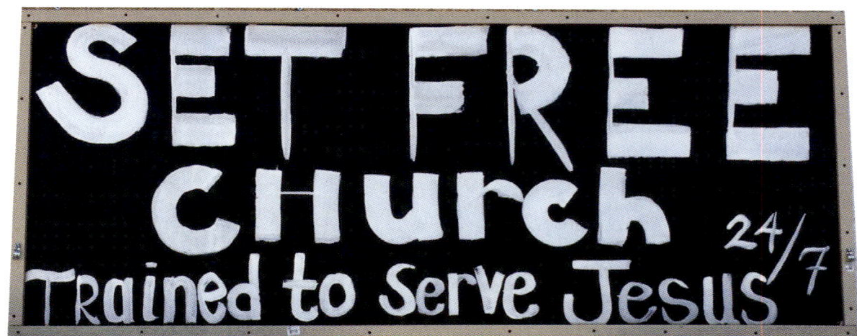

Slab serifs give this hand-painted beer sign a flavor of the Klondike gold rush from the 1890s. Photo courtesy of Sarah Friend.

THE BROAD PEN OF TRADITIONAL CALLIGRAPHY, held at a set angle, has always dictated which strokes would be thick or thin. Large block letters written with a flat brush, however, let the thick and thin strokes go where the writer wanted them. Because sign painters were not limited to one pen angle, they could explore nontraditional letter styles that added novelty without slowing them down. The structure of basic block, and the free movement of the brush, made it easy to experiment with other pen angles. At 90°, for instance, the uprights got spindly and the horizontals turned into slabs. This alphabet grabbed attention immediately because it upended its readers' expectations about the Roman alphabet.

This letter style was passed back and forth between type designers and sign painters for a century without calligraphers paying much attention, since heavy-footed capitals did not harmonize with their elegant traditional styles. But today they are discovering how a dramatic change of pen angle can transform letterforms. Slab will reset any calligrapher's habits. And it is a useful alphabet for anyone who wants to grab the reader's attention.

In the search for impact, however, it's wise not to overdo. This loud letter style makes all-capitals sound even louder; it is best to limit them to just a few words so they can speak, rather than shriek, "LOOK AT ME" to the reader. According to type designer Matthew Butterick, writing too many words in all capitals "make[s] text appear hectoring and obnoxious." Online, this is criticized as "flaming." These pushy letters work best for short, important messages.

Slab letters keep some of their impact even without slab serifs. Heavy horizontals and thin verticals are enough to carry the style. This talented amateur sign painter understood how to control the stroke thickness. In "SET FREE" E T F are written at 90°. For the other letters, the brush rotates smoothly in S R C U H using basic block technique. Tucson, Arizona, 2016.

Letter height = 7 pen widths.

These letters can be 2"
(5 cm) tall, written with
a ⅜" (1 cm) flat brush.

All letters are ⅝ the
width of their height,
except **I**.

Basic Strokes

Verticals
Not *too* thin.

Horizontals

Curves

Stroke   Serif   Half-serif

Diagonals

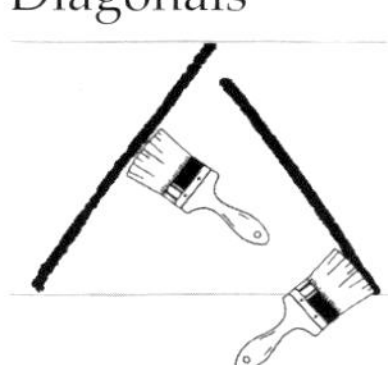

Thin diagonals
require turning
the brush at 90°
to the angle of
the stroke.

One corner of the brush
can make short S-curves.
And thin horizontals for **A**
B H and optional **E F G**

Letters

One-stage straight

I L T E F H

Two-stage straight

One-stage straight + curved

O D G J O Q U

Two-stage straight + curved

B P K R

The legs of **K R** and the tail of **Q**
can be shaped into tight curves
using the corner of the brush.

S

One-Stage diagonal

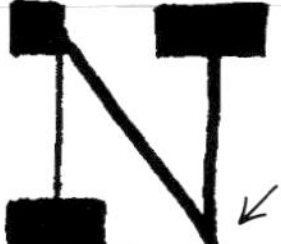

This corner
of **N** can have
a half-serif.

This corner
of **N** has
no serif.

No serif
on the lower
corner of **V**.

N V Z

The middle
strokes of **M**
and **W** save
space by
connecting
halfway up.

Two-Stage diagonal

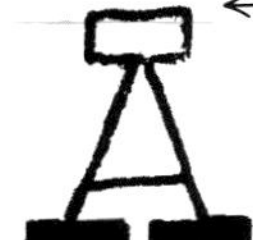

← Optional serif on
upper corner
of **A**.

A

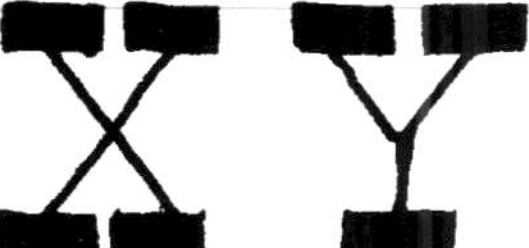

X Y

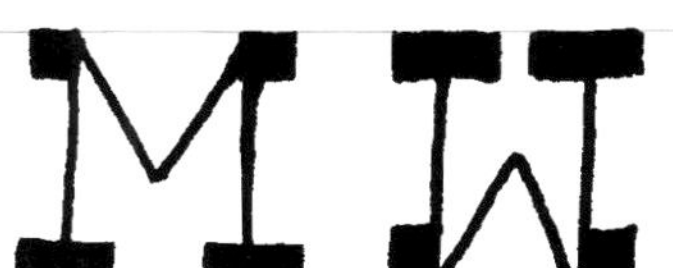

M W

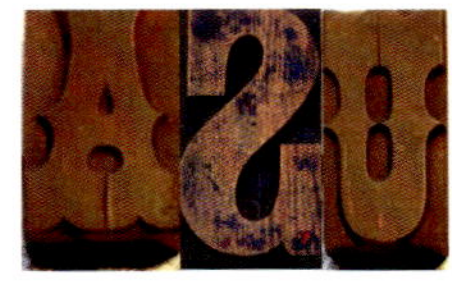

THIS CLASSIC AMERICAN ALPHABET evokes the Western frontier of both history and legend. Though it was best known as a wood type for printed posters, its bold, extroverted letters can be easily turned back into calligraphy with a few strokes of a broad-edged pen. It has thin verticals with thick horizontal serifs made of two short strokes. It may be flamboyant and time consuming, but it still belongs in the block family because of its uniform letter body.

These letters looked unmistakably American because the conditions that created them didn't come together in quite the same way anywhere else. The era of wood type lasted from 1830 to 1910, during a period of national expansion, railroad building, and technological progress. Wood offered a number of advantages over metal: it was cheaper; it was available in most regions and easier to transport; and it did not dent or break if dropped (or break something else). Unlike metal letters, which risked warping while they cooled if they were larger than 1" (2.5 cm) tall, there was no upper limit on how big wood type could be. America's old-growth forests provided plentiful hardwoods to carve into type, with a stream of new techniques that kept the price low. New industrial chemistry for producing pulp from softer woods made large paper cheaper, too.

Wood type was less durable than metal for long print runs, but it was the best choice for short runs on large paper. As the nation expanded, each new local printery needed its own supply of large type for posters and announcements.

Extremely popular at home, many styles of wood type carried a whiff of American brashness abroad, where wood type was scarcer. Purists gave its melodrama mixed reviews. "The period 1815–44 was perhaps the worst of all from the point of view of type-design, though at the same time it was one of the most prolific of novelties," wrote British scholar Ronald B. McKerrow in 1927. But the American public loved it.

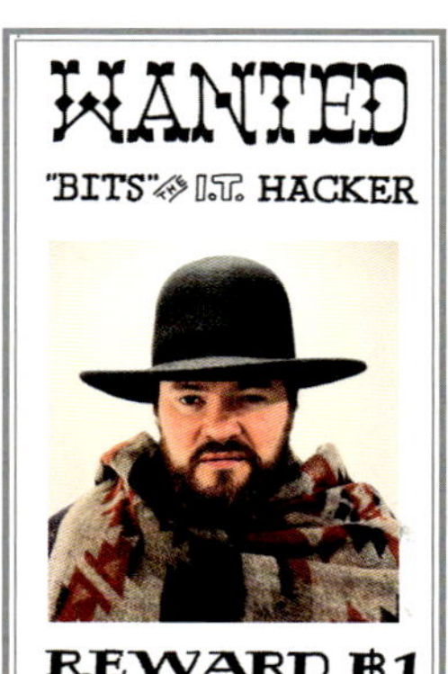

←*The humorous "WANTED" poster is an American cliche that never seems to grow old. Many websites offer free downloadable templates, usually set in Wild West letters to make the joke obvious.*

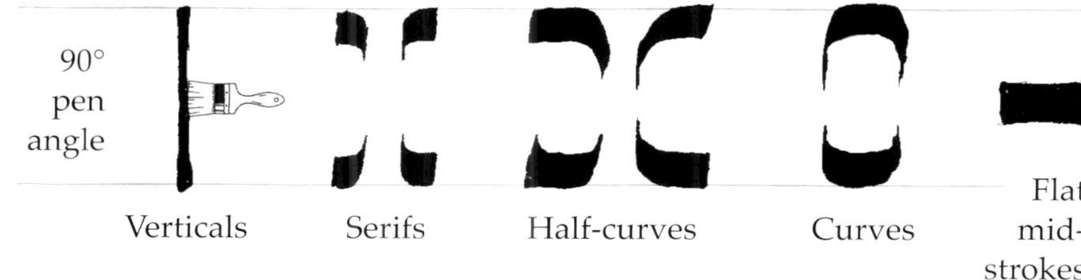

Letter = 7 pen widths tall.

↑ Letter's width = ½ its height. ↑

A pen, brush, or marker wider than ¼" (6 mm) will make it clear how the strokes fit together.

Rotating the paper can make the 90° pen position feel less awkward.

LETTERS

Type designers have nicknamed this stroke the "spur" in honor of its frontier origins.

BASIC PRACTICE STROKES

90° pen angle

Verticals — Serifs — Half-curves — Curves — Flat mid-strokes

45° PEN ANGLE

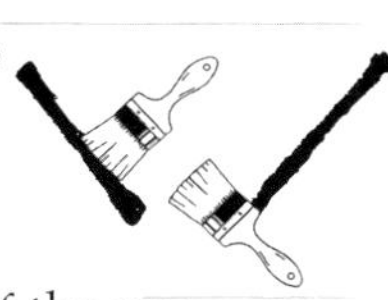

The angle for most squares is 45°, except in the optional **N X Z**.

VARIOUS PEN ANGLES

Thin diagonals require turning the brush to follow the stroke's angle.

Dragging one corner of the pen can also make short thin strokes.

LETTER CONSTRUCTION

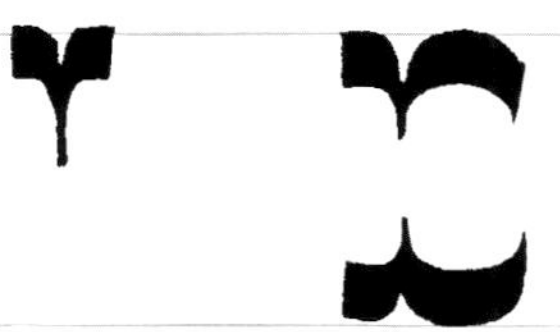

Two-stroke serif.

One-stroke serif plus a curve.

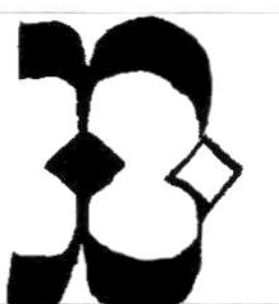

Most verticals have a square in the middle that neatly covers where they join. ◆

Squares shown here in outline are optional. ◇

ONE-STAGE STRAIGHT

TWO-STAGE STRAIGHT

→

ONE-STAGE CURVED

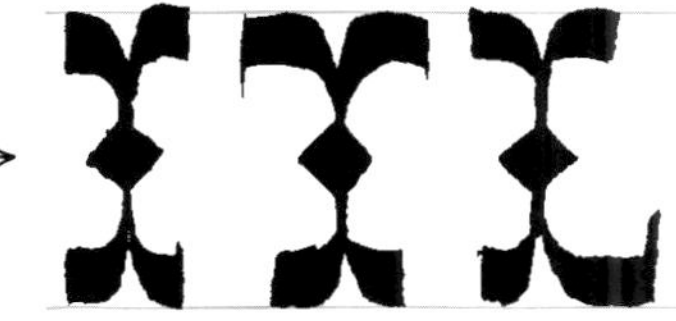

TWO-STAGE CURVED

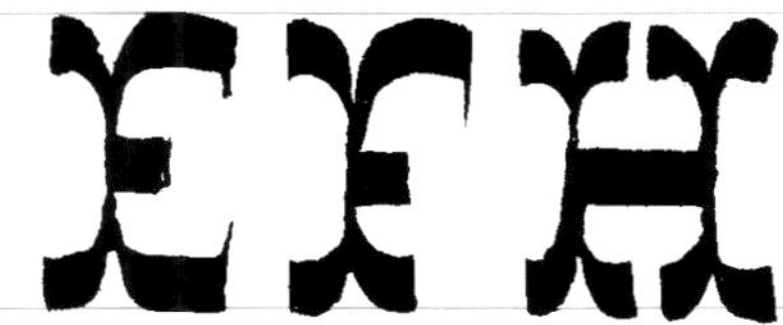

ONE-STAGE DIAGONAL

TWO-STAGE DIAGONAL

EXTRA-WIDE

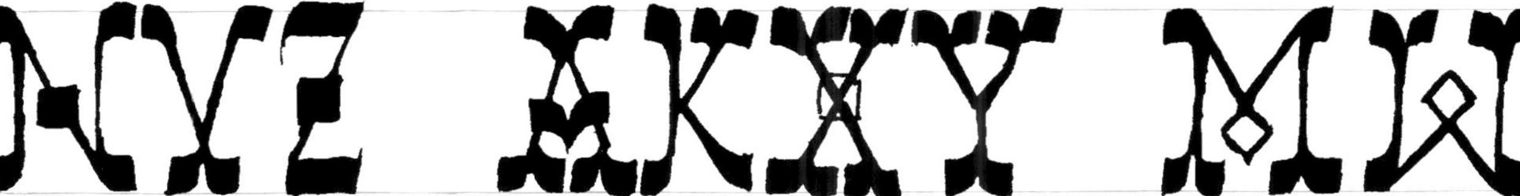

The serifs are placed first, then connected with diagonals.

M W Can be wider.

CALLIGRAPHERS AND TYPE DESIGNERS could easily simplify or embellish Wild West letters by manipulating their stroke weight and adding or subtracting square dots. In all these versions the heavy split serif is the essential ingredient that gives it flavor.

Five variations are shown here, for calligraphers to mix and match. Some are easy; some are challenging. A flat flexible brush makes these experiments easier.

The mid-strokes of **A B E F H P R** can be thinned.	The thin strokes can be thickened for less contrast.	The square in the middle can be omitted.	A white dot can be added inside the square.	Extra squares can embellish the split serifs.

PAGE DESIGN

Posters of the era typically grabbed attention by combining block, slab, and Wild West letters of different sizes and proportions on the same page. The classic layout shown here, though made with modern type, can still inspire experiments with the pen.

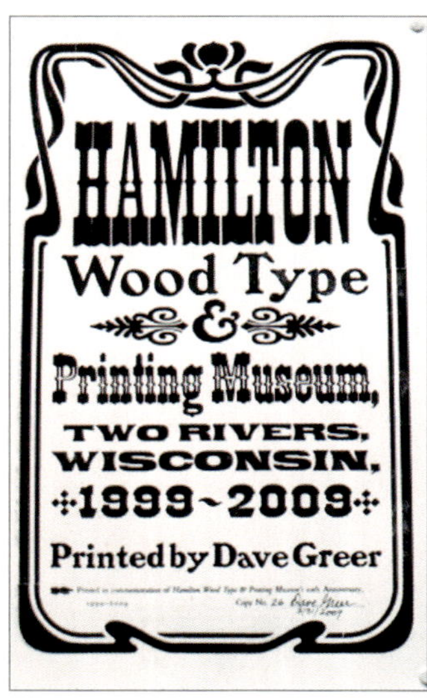

← *Poster courtesy David Greer, designer.*

→ *Even charcoal gets cowboy flavor from Wild West calligraphy. The letters in "cowboy" have two decorative spurs; the letters in "lump" have one.*

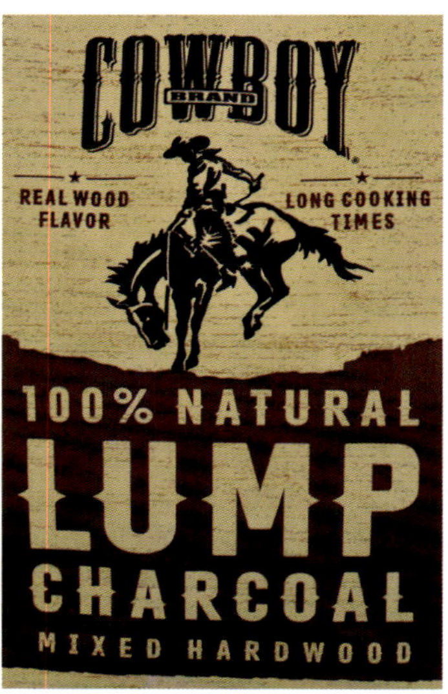

WILD WEST LETTERS IN AMERICAN CULTURE

AFTER 1900, printing with wood type was crowded out by lithography and photo-offset, which offered lower costs, easier setup, quicker turnaround time, longer print runs, and a wider choice of letter styles. With the passing of wood type, many of its most characteristic styles dropped out of fashion too, replaced by the sleeker, suaver letters of the 1920s and 1930s. Even though printers emptied whole cabinets of wood type onto the trash heap or into the

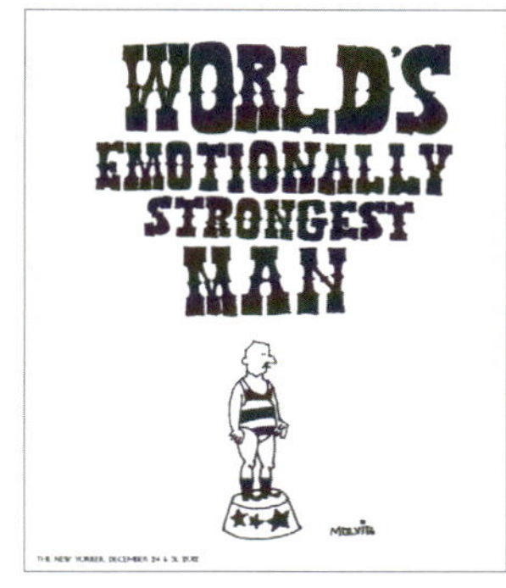

fire, so much remained that most flea markets and antique shops offered vintage wooden letters for sale, which decades of hobbyists turned into crafts projects.

The imagery of Wild West letters was so appealing, however, that they found other roles in America's visual life. They can be seen in logo designs, cartoons, sports team uniforms, and movie sets, always carrying the nostalgic echo of a bygone American era.

Boston Red Sox baseball team logo.

THE FUTURE

A small, dedicated group of scholars and enthusiasts are conserving wood type and finding new artistic uses for it, hoping to engage a new generation of letter artists.

This New Yorker *cartoon spoofs the tough-guy image* →
evoked by Wild West letters. Artist Ariel Molvig.

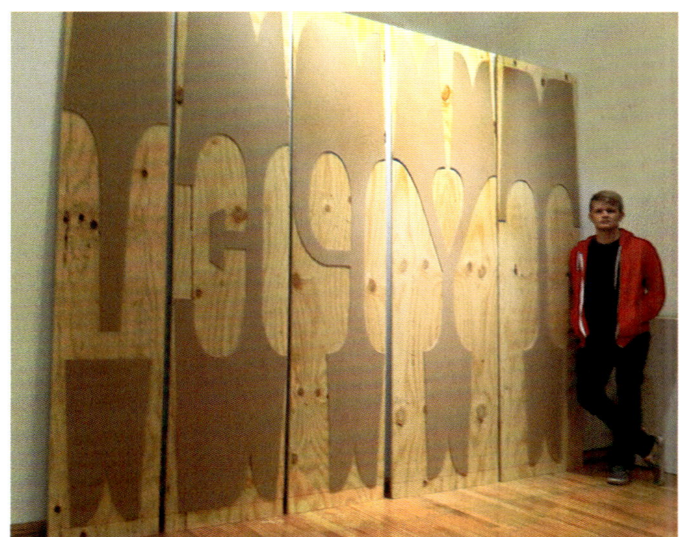

← *These huge letters make a dramatic statement about this alphabet's scalability. Created, inked, and printed to publicize a 2011 exhibition at Columbia College, New York, they are still the largest printable type in the world. Now housed at the Hamilton Museum. Photo courtesy of Nick Sherman.*

usa

"Procrastination is the art of keeping up with yesterday."

~ Don Marquis

TYPEWRITER

A CENTURY OF PROGRESS in communication brought the typewriter into virtually every American home, office, and dormitory. Many early typing machines were made and patented in the United States, some as early as 1830. Available commercially by the 1870s and standardized by 1910, the typewriter helped modernize American businesses, which readily abandoned pen and ink for the keyboard. Private citizens and students followed suit as the typewriter got ever cheaper and easier to use, launching major changes in American life. It sped up women's entry into office jobs. It accelerated the decline of handwriting. With the aid of simple duplication techniques, it let anyone make copies without needing typesetters and a press.

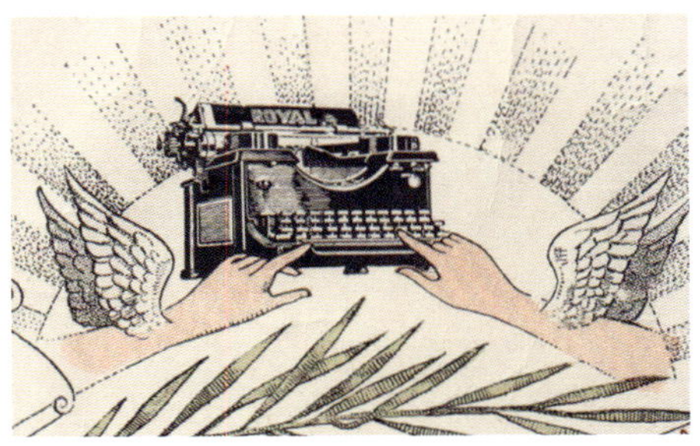

↗ In a detail from the 1944 Canadian diploma shown below, angelic hands press the keys of a deified typewriter. Sharp-eyed readers can count some fourteen different letter styles (including shorthand and a date stamp)—but no typewriter type.

Typewriter letters started out visually blunt and stayed that way. While type designers continued to refine the Roman type that was widely used in books and newspapers, the internal mechanics of the manual typewriter kept its letters from progressing much until 1961.

IiIiIi

MmMmMm

Paul Shaw describes typewriter spacing: "Take the letters i and m, for example. It's like putting an elephant and a mouse in the same space. You can't do it without making the mouse too big or the elephant too small."

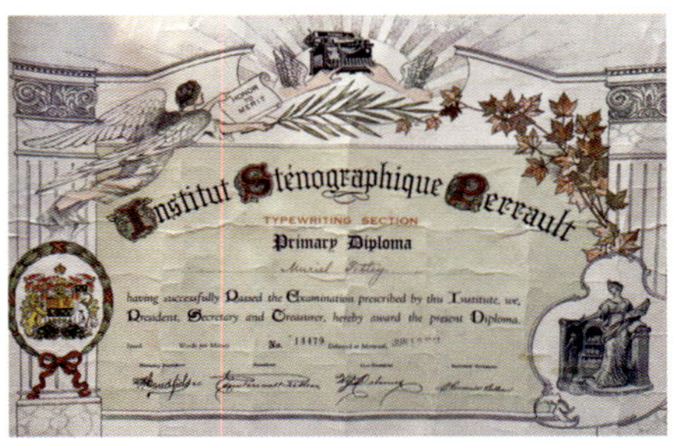

← *Monospacing forces all letters to be the same width.*

While most typewriters survive today only in the collections of a few die-hard fans, the letters are surprisingly fun to write by hand. Their lack of refinement makes them easy for beginners who may feel intimidated by more elegant alphabets. The letters actually look more authentic if they are *not* evenly aligned. They are equally accessible to right- or left-handers. And they are useful for many practical projects.

Even though typewriters have evolved into laptop computers that offer digital fonts of every alphabet style, type designers today are still fond of reviving the letters that were formed by those antiquated machines. Calligraphers too can recapture the charm of that vintage alphabet.

Typewriter

Capitals, ascenders, and numerals = 8 pen widths tall.

Speedball B3 nib or blunt marker. held at any angle.

PRACTICE STROKES

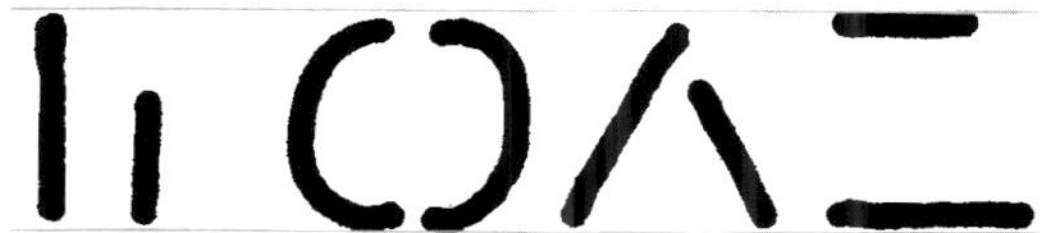

Ball serifs are added to stroke ends of **J c f g j r y 2 3 5 6 9**

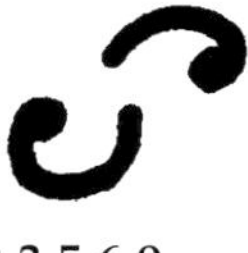

CAPITALS

CURVED

C G O Q S

STRAIGHT

E F H I L T

B D J P R U

CURVED + STRAIGHT

A K M N V W X Y Z

Small letter bodies = 5 pen widths tall.

SMALL LETTERS

a c e g o s   i l

CURVED   STRAIGHT

k v w x y z

DIAGONAL

b d f h j m n p q r t u

CURVED + STRAIGHT

Early keyboards offered fewer characters. Typists had to use lowercase l for numeral 1, and capital O for zero. Backspacing let them make ! from a period under an apostrophe, and ¢ by adding a slash to c.

NUMERALS

1 2 3 4 5 6 7 8 9 0 !

HIGHWAY

THE BLOCK ALPHABET that Americans knew best was perpetually reshaped by where they were, and increasingly where they were was in a car. People no longer had time to stop and read the eye-catching posters of the late nineteenth century (see page 42), which were replaced by terse messages that drivers might have only a few seconds to catch.

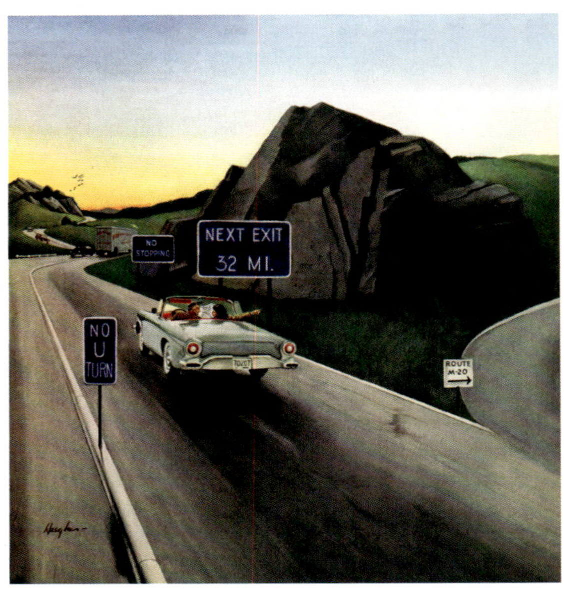

Missed Exit, *by George Hughes, 1957. From the* Saturday Evening Post *cover, used with permission.*

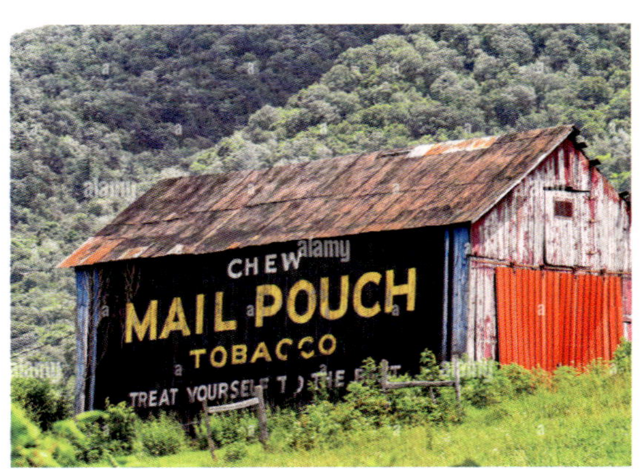

← *Barn-size advertisements for Mail Pouch Chewing Tobacco were part of the southern and midwestern American landscape for virtually the whole century. At one time they numbered 20,000.*

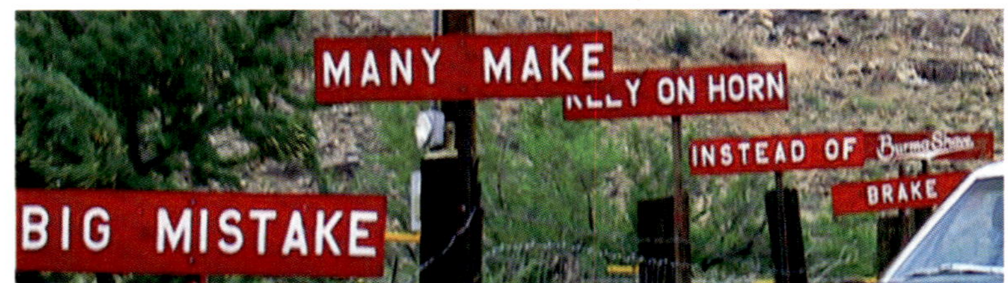

↑ *From the 1920s to the 1960s, Burma-Shave's iconic signs provided serial roadside humor for long car trips. Block letters on signs one hundred feet apart were easy to read at mid-century car speeds.*

By the 1960s the sprinkling of signs by America's roadsides had become a crowd, distracting drivers with a jumble of signs and huge billboards. As speed limits rose, the legibility of official signs became even more important. The Highway Beautification Act of 1965 cracked down on this visual clutter, banning commercial signs on federally funded highways. Today, typefaces on the signs that are allowed on highways have been honed by intensive research, including where to capitalize them, how to space them, and what colors are most readable.

Fine points of legibility

Highway letters today have been carefully analyzed and minutely specified. As type, of course, they are far too refined for calligraphers to write by hand, but knowing why they look the way they do makes them more interesting to look at:

- Capitals and lowercase letters are easier to read than all-capitals. "If a word is set in all caps, all you will see are little white rectangles," advises type designer James Montalbano.

- The traditional forms of **a** and **t** are actually more legible than their newer forms ɑ and t.

- Letters and numerals should be 1" (2.5 cm) high for every 40 feet (12 meters) of reading distance.

- Though they knew they did not want to simply use highway type from Europe, American designers took decades to settle on a uniform letter style with the virtues of block. First issued in 1948 as Highway Gothic, it was a blend of several twentieth-century sans serif types. During the 1990s type designer Don Meeker created an improved highway alphabet, Clearview, with better spacing and x-height. Initial testing seemed to support its superiority, but type critics promptly divided into two camps that battled each other and the bureaucracy. There is still no country-wide ruling about which to use, leaving states to make their own choice—a classic American solution.

- Color choice of pale yellow letters on dark green background made reading easier in low light or fog. Simply coating the letters with tiny reflective beads turned out to make them reflect *too much* light, giving the letters a blurry halo. New pigments and materials continued to complicate the search for the ultimate alphabet.

One of calligraphy's core lessons is that *small differences matter.* Highway signs ought to be stripped down to the essentials, but even the experts disagree about what those essentials are. While they work it out, ordinary drivers can enjoy noticing telltale clues to which alphabet they are reading, such as the small stroke at the bottom of small **l** and the slightly larger space inside **e**.

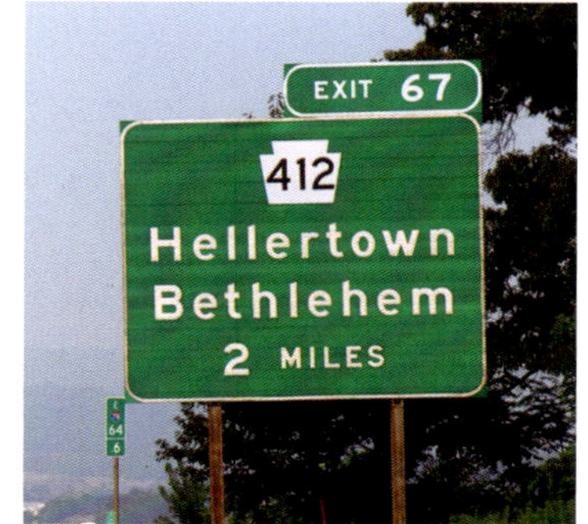

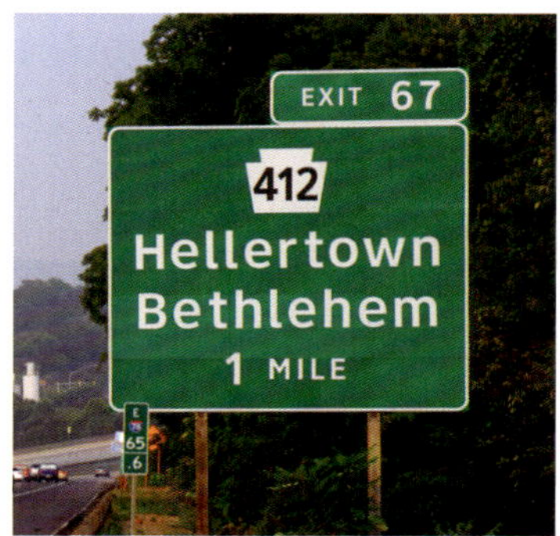

Comparison of Highway Gothic and Clearview type. Photos courtesy of Don Meeker.

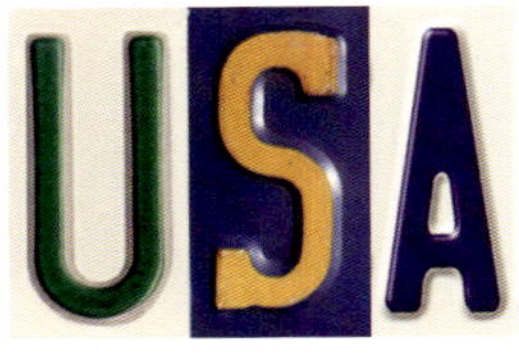

"GAS LOL"

~ *Custom license*

plate on an

electric car

LICENSE

AT THE SAME TIME that letters by the side of the road were being carefully engineered to be legible at cruising speed, letters on license plates were being modified to protect against problems of wear and tear at ground level. Fabrication demanded robust characters that could be machine-stamped into thick sheet metal, screen-printed, and kiln-fired to help them resist abrasion, impact, chemicals, and extremes of weather. This required rounding the corners, and made an asset of the heavy weight, equal width, and uniform spacing of block letters.

Even while they allowed for these physical limits and complied with each state's protocols, designers still managed to transform license plates into tiny graphic gems of regional American identity, a kind of haiku of the highways. Like many calligraphic designs, they combined color, spacing, background, and borders. Because design rules were different in every state, licenses carried a lot of regional identity. Bureaucrats labored to choose short, unique, upbeat slogans, often in the face of competing interest groups and constant critics. Watching for a plate from each state was a classic American game for children in the back seat during a long trip.

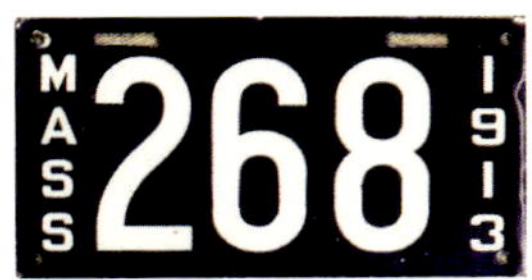
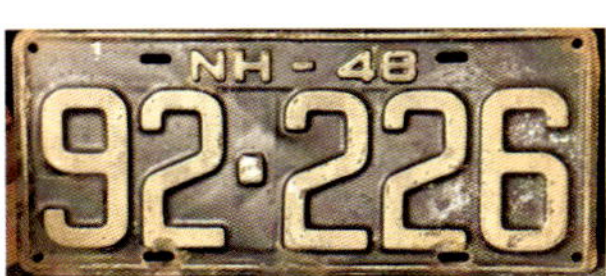
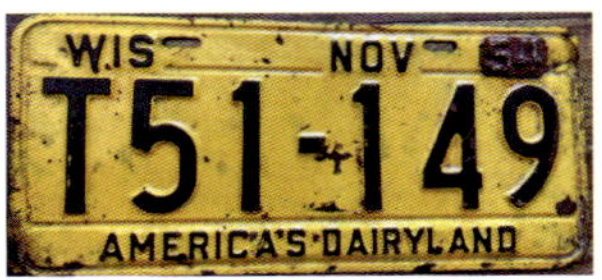
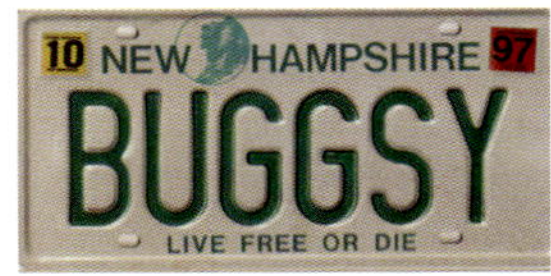

Typical license plates, from 1913 porcelain collector's item to a 1997 vanity plate.

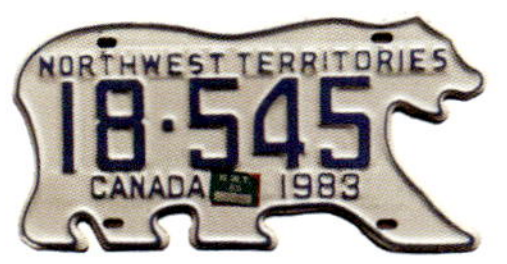

← *This modern Canadian license plate is elaborately silhouetted but still within the North American template of 6" x 12" (9 cm x 18 cm) with 3" (7.5 cm) letters.*

*Most plates today contain 5–8 random letters or numerals, or a mix of both, unless owners pay extra for vanity plates that let them choose their own word. In this absence of context, alphabet design has to keep letters from being mistaken for numbers, such as **B** for 8, **1** for **I**, **S** for 5. A few states and territories prevent this by separating groups of numerals from letters or using one or the other exclusively, and some don't use zero at all because it looks so much like **O**.*

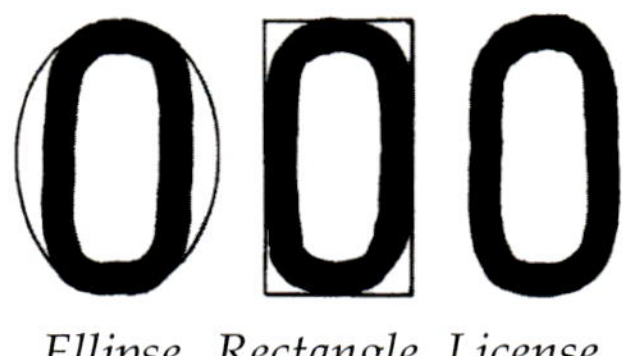

This alphabet's basic shape is harder to handwrite than it looks. The oblong letter body is midway between round and square; the vertical strokes are parallel, not like the constant curvature of an ellipse. (In practice, this letter shape varies from state to state and era to era.)

Ellipse Rectangle License

LICENSE

Height = 8–10 pen widths.

Letter width = ½ of height.

Blunt marker or Speedball B

→ Seen in cross section, the raised stroke is ½″ (12 mm) wide and the painted stroke is ¼″ (6 mm) wide.
→ A thin gray line around the letter can mimic this 3D effect on paper.

BASIC STROKES

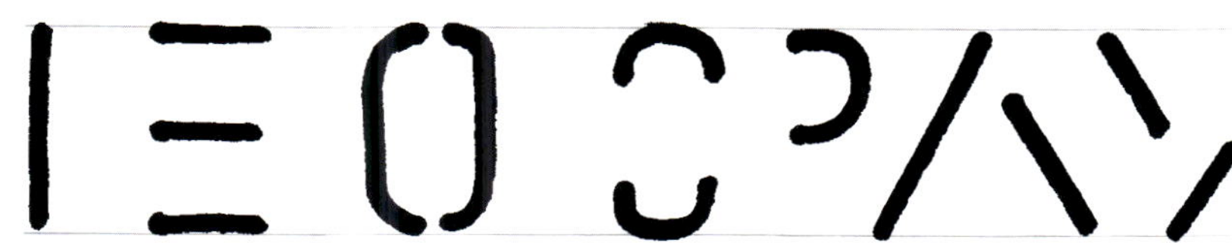

Flat sides

Round tops and bottoms

STRAIGHT

Alternative choices are shown by outlined strokes.

E F H I L T

STRAIGHT PLUS CURVED

C G O Q S S

The middle stroke of **S** can curve or slant.

B D J P R U

MAINLY DIAGONAL STROKES

EXTRA-WIDE

A K N V X Y Z M W

NUMERALS

Diagonals can straighten this curve.

Small adjustments make numerals more legible and help distinguish them from letters.

Extra stroke

1 2 3 4 5 6 7 8 9 0

Serif

↑ The middle stroke can be lower and longer.

↑ These ↑ diagonals can curve. ↑

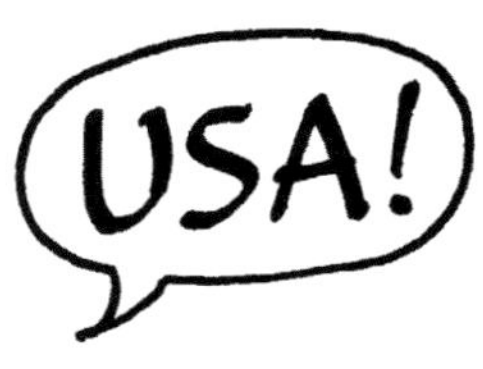

THE FUNNIES

FOR SHEER VISUAL VARIETY, it would be hard to beat the comic strip pages of an American daily newspaper from the 1950s. They dished up a generous buffet of superheroes, soap operas, and gags, with something for every reader. Individual cartoonists did their own lettering, in their own individual style, and used every technique of calligraphy to give their strip a distinctive look. A special format on Sundays featured longer strips, color, and inventive touches of calligraphic drama. In previous decades, comic strip art had already spread into comic books and magazines, and by 1970 it had fostered underground comix and graphic novels. Each genre evolved its special letter styles to play an important role. This abundance of images and letters was an integral part of American life, absorbed and taken for granted, but not common anywhere else.

To make their comic strip characters talk, cartoonists modified block letters and wrote them with a variety of pens.

Samples of lettering from the funnies 1970–2000.

Cartoonists drew their black and white art larger than final size, which let them control the details. They mapped out each panel of a strip first in pencil, to control exactly where the words should go when final inking was done. They usually wrote in all capitals, which are still preferred today, because this made it easier to space the letters and lines. Each cartoonist seems to have kept a favorite pen just for lettering. Until digital lettering, no two cartoon strips had quite the same letters.

Cartoonists complained about the drudgery of writing small. But in those tiny spaces, they crafted letters that expressed every nuance of their imaginary characters' voices, from *Krazy Kat* to *Fritz the Cat*.

FUNNIES

Slanted horizontals and a steep pen angle add subtle energy to this all-purpose alphabet.

Letter width = ¾ height.

Letter height = 6–7 pen widths.

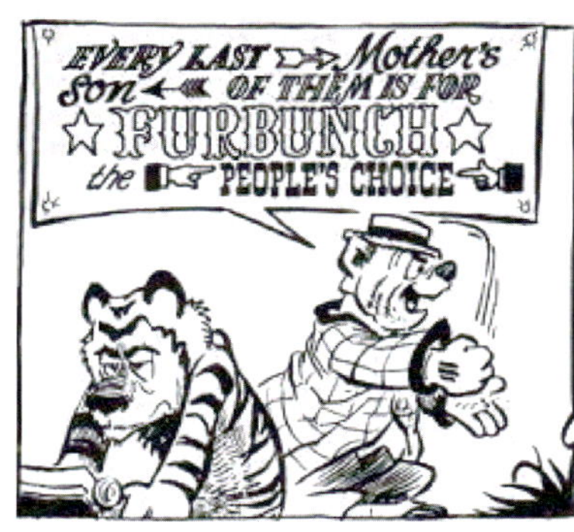

Pen angle 50° - 60°.

Choice of pen shaped a cartoonist's style. Many preferred the Speedball D for its moderate line contrast.

PRACTICE STROKES

Horizontals and half-curves tilt about 5° and can overlap the guidelines just a bit.

LETTERS

L E F T H I Z

ROUND VERTICAL AND ROUND

O Q C G

↑ To prevent confusion, serifs were usually added to **I** and sometimes **J**, even though the other letters might have none.
↓

VERTICAL AND ROUND

D B P R S U J

DIAGONAL

A K M N V W X Y

PEN VARIATIONS: Light   Wide   Narrow   Back   Ahead

YES YES YES YES YES

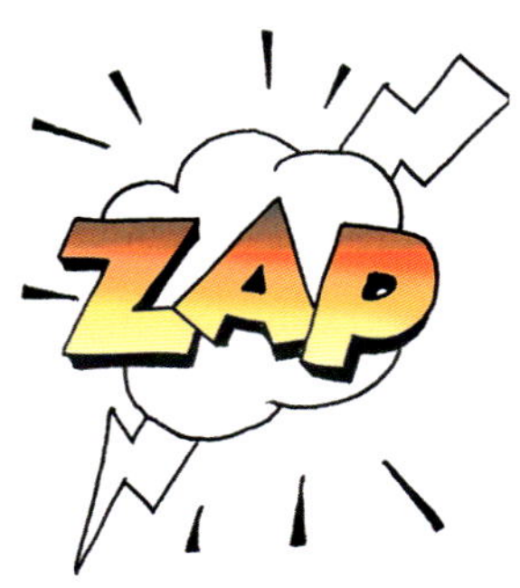

OUTLINED LETTERS

In addition to pen-lettering, some cartoonists also drew larger words in outline—but only a few, because that needed more time and different pens.

← *P. T. Bridgeport spoke like a circus poster, in outlined Wild West letters, slab capitals, and wingdings. From* Pogo, *by Walt Kelly.*

Superhero comics turned their outlined letters into a major design element. ↑

COMIC STRIP DESIGN

ABOUT HALF OF THE DAILY STRIPS on the funny pages simply presented serial episodes from an ongoing story, full of familiar characters but without any final outcome. These domestic sagas seldom needed to vary their lettering. Superhero tales, however, quickly magnified the action in their stories by exaggerating the lettering.

In other strips, the classic three-panel joke typically consisted of set-up, situation, and punchline. Almost all of the drama—emphasized by the lettering—happened in the third panel. Some added a fourth panel for aftermath, which might be a kind of punch line in itself.

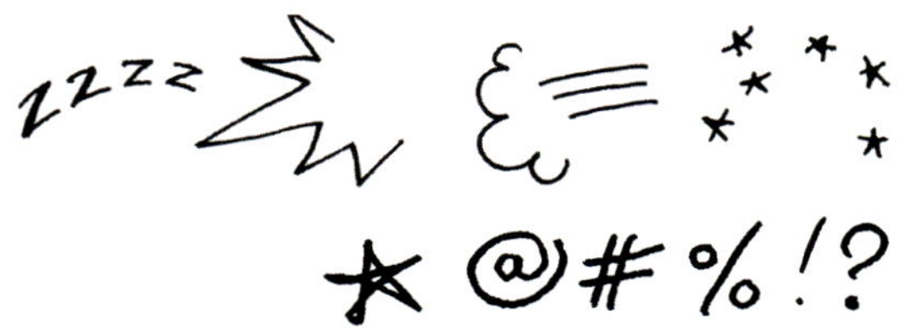

↗ *Mort Walker, creator of Beetle Bailey, coined the term "grawlix" for the string of wingdings that means swearing.*

→ *Walt Kelly's Deacon Mushrat always spoke in the dismal tones of Gothic letters.*

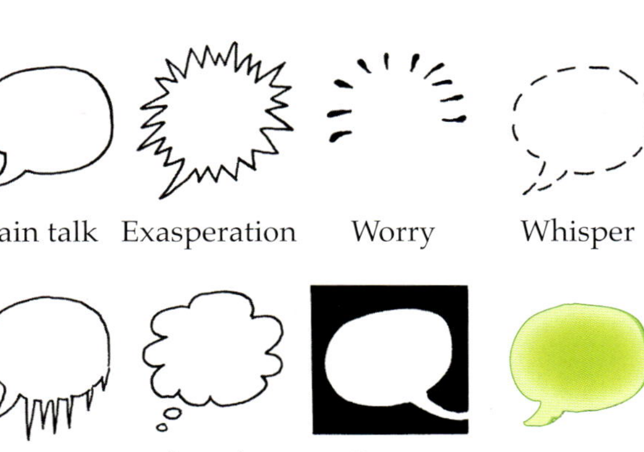

Changing the weight, width, size, and slant of the letters changed the tone of voice. In addition, cartoonists also invented their own graphic language, with special symbols for sleep, exertion, escape, and concussion.

A few virtuosos added letters in other calligraphy styles to imply other tones of voice, hidden agendas, or national accents.

BALLOONS

Speech balloons (also called speech bubbles) evolved to be almost as important as the words inside them. The idea itself is not new; banners with spoken words in them had appeared in medieval manuscripts before 1300 CE, and the very earliest speech balloons can be seen in Mayan paintings from before 600 CE. Twentieth-century cartoonists first filled them with a lot of dialogue, then grad-ually cut down the word count and let the speech bubbles convey more of the meaning.

Plain talk Exasperation Worry Whisper

Snarky chill Thought Offstage Envy

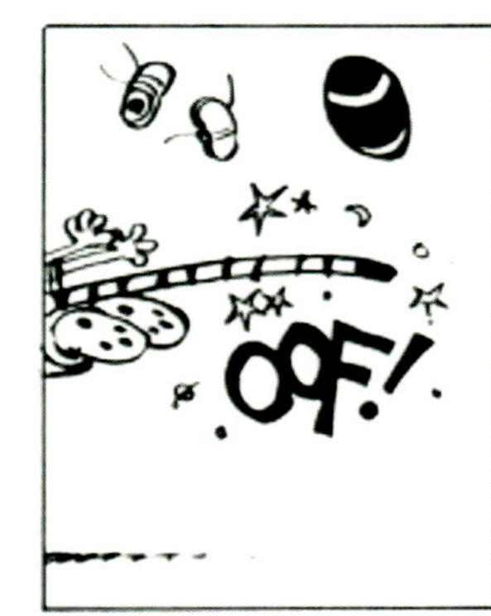

Sometimes a punch line needed no speech balloon. From Calvin and Hobbes *by Bill Watterston.*

Beyond the funny pages

From its roots in family-friendly comic strips, cartooning branched out and specialized: comic books for adolescents and preteens; "comix" for counterculture twentysomethings; graphic novels for serious adults; plus greeting cards and graffiti everywhere. Meanwhile, for half a century 1952–2018, the subversive graphic creativity of *Mad Magazine* energized cartoonists in every category, and in the culture at large.

New formats and audiences sparked new lettering. Counterculture comix in the 1960s and 1970s had raised the bar, not just by probing topics of greater depth—social injustice, complex characters, ironic humor, quotable dialogue—but also by their over-the-top calligraphy. Independent artists like Robert Crumb did not have to follow newspaper rules, or avoid controversial topics to keep their syndicators happy. Spreading from the underground, these books matured early into such black-and-white masterpieces as Art Spiegelman's groundbreaking *Maus*, serialized 1980–1991. And letters in action comics just kept getting more colorful and creative, more exaggerated and heroic.

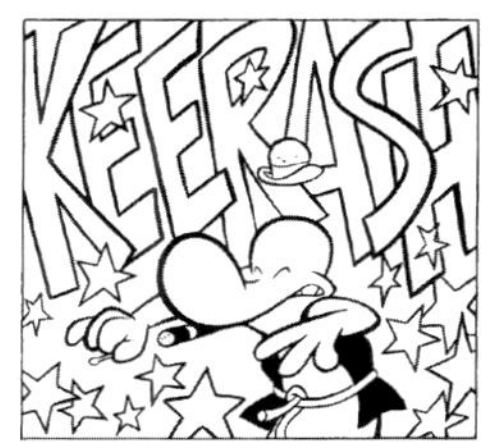

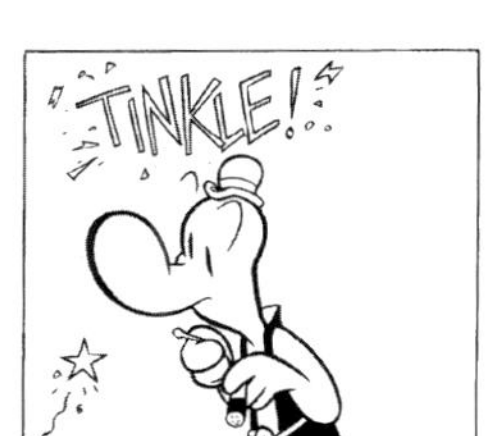

← *Cartoonist Jeff Smith uses letter size (and the reaction of his character, Bone) to show loudness.*

Decline of the funnies

While letter innovation thrived in other parts of the comics world, comic strips themselves were fading from daily life. Fewer people read newspapers at all, preferring to get their news—and humor—from radio, television, or the internet, and newspapers economized by shrinking to barely two-thirds of their former page size. A few strips were collected and printed in books.

Daily comics also weren't such individual works of art anymore. Syndicated strips limited their cartoonists to inoffensive topics. At first, comic strip artists had done their own lettering on their own drawings; soon, tired of the toil, some delegated it to specialized lettering artists; and eventually most changed to digital fonts, which certainly made it easier to control spacing and make corrections.

Today, some cartoonists compromise by using type digitized from their own handwriting. It doesn't quite replace the human hand, however. Calligraphers can still learn a lot by trying out this this readable, useful, fun, and friendly alphabet.

BLOCK LEGACY

BLOCK LETTERS WERE FIRMLY ROOTED in the practical side of American life. Their creators shaped them to do a job, without elegance or subtlety; they became beautiful because they were *useful*. Sign painters had a clear goal; to help their clients to sell things in the marketplace. In doing this, block letters got boiled down to their calligraphic essence—easy to read, fast to write, and impossible to ignore. This modern American aesthetic was concisely summed up by grammarian William Strunk Jr.,

"A sentence should contain no unnecessary words, a paragraph no unnecessary sentences, for the same reason that a drawing should have no unnecessary lines and a machine no unnecessary parts." Block letters elevated modest pragmatism into real beauty.

Over the decades, the simple block letters devised by sign painters proliferated into an extended family of specialized styles that spread to the world of calligraphy and type. In its era, each alphabet filled an important niche in American life, and though their moment may have passed, the underlying block structure can inspire a new generation of calligraphic innovators.

↗ For over 150 years, ranchers in the Southwest have made block-letter branding irons like this "Rocking R," to burn marks of ownership into their livestock's hide.

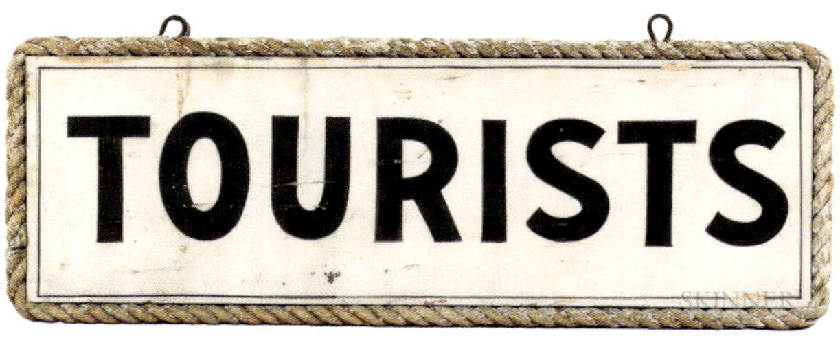

This early twentieth-century sign is carefully spaced and confidently written—a small calligraphic masterpiece. Courtesy of Richard Herold.

BASIC BLOCK | SLAB | WILD WEST | TYPEWRITER | LICENSE | FUNNIES

Broad-edge pen or marker, flat brush, or Parallel pen

Blunt marker or Speedball B.

AMATEUR

AMERICAN CALLIGRAPHY GETS VITAL ENERGY from its amateurs, who bring a fresh perspective to the art of making words visible. This began with the ingenuity of the earliest colonists, who arrived in an unfamiliar land with only a few tools, skills, and materials, and immediately had to improvise necessities for themselves instead of importing them. This "can-do" spirit continues today. Beyond simply helping to improve daily life, these letters inspired other artists to innovate, and over the years distinctive American letter styles have emerged.

In addition, Americans respected manual work. Settlements that were made up only of gentlemen were doomed to fail. People who could make things with their hands survived and thrived, improvising with the tools they had and the techniques they knew. In the colonies, even patricians like Thomas Jefferson prided themselves on cultivating manual skills.

This problem-solving frame of mind is so basic to the national spirit that it is easy to forget that being an amateur is not always so admired in other cultures. They prefer training and certification. But in the country that invented the term "do it yourself," hiring a professional is often impractical and is sometimes seen as admitting defeat.

Amateurs, however, are not the same as beginners. Even though some may feel energized to study more calligraphy after their first experience, amateur lettering does not have to lead anywhere else. It deserves to be seen and understood on its own terms.

The human need to be heard and remembered was turned into art by untrained people who did the best they could with what they had on hand. Calligraphy by amateurs, from seventeenth-century gravestones to twenty-first-century protest signs, illustrates the range of American resourcefulness.

A rubbing from a 1717 Rhode Island gravestone.

The Passion of Sacco and Vanzetti, →
Screen print by Ben Shahn, 1958

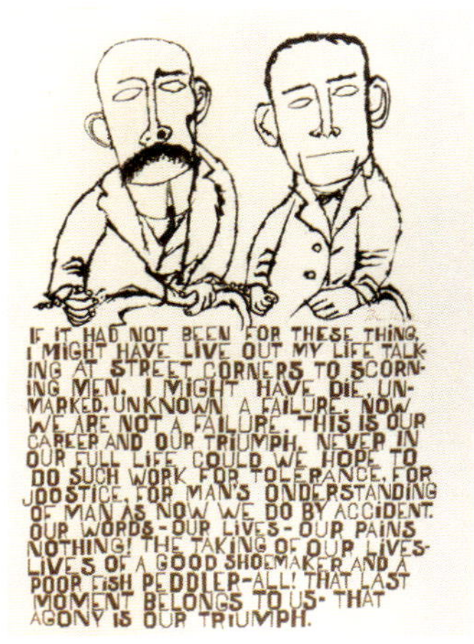

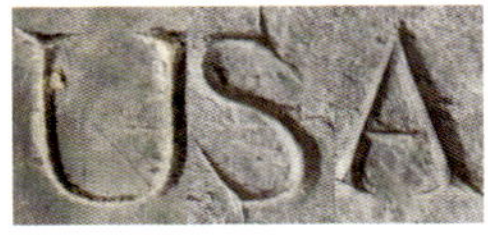

"By looking at cemeteries
with a mason's eye,
an artist's heart, and a
historian's curiosity, I have
gained admiration for
the artistry of our colonial
ancestors."
Jonathan Appell,
gravestone conservator

Vernacular letters carved in slate have been called "America's first sculpture." They open a special window into life—and death—some four hundred years ago, when harsh conditions in North America meant that gravestone inscriptions were among the first lettering a new community needed. Gravestone carving, by its nature, was a local art for local use on local stone for local people in styles tailored to local tastes. Early carvers made do with masonry tools to shape whatever material was available: slate in Boston, sandstone in Connecticut. (Granite was too hard for carving letters with hand tools.) The letters that they created mainly from memory have an endearing openness, vulnerability, and charm that is not found anywhere else. Later letter styles became more standardized.

Hundreds of thousands of slate gravestones that remain today bear witness to life in early New England, with a few dozen surviving from the first seventy-five years. While serving the age-old human need to commemorate the dead, they are also a rich source of information for historians. Unlike many early colonial artifacts, they are almost always found in their original locations. They document each person's name, family, lifespan, birthplace, occupation, and rank; some even bear the signature of the carver (town records occasionally hold a copy of the carver's invoice). Gravestones provide details about a whole community's geology, folklore, economic life, demographics, kinship patterns, public health, and aesthetics. And of course, they preserve its calligraphy.

The freshest, most original calligraphy came from those first American carvers. Within two generations, for better or worse, gravestone carving was in the hands of the professionals.

*How carvers made letters fit into layouts: Letter pairs **HE TH MB** make long lines a bit shorter. The elevated small e in **YE i**s a common space-saver. **AND** is often represented by &. The reduced N in **ALLYN** appears to compensate for a layout miscalculation. The elevated **TR** of **DAUGHTER** stands for the omitted letters **G H E**. Detail from gravestone of Elizabeth Allyn, Cape Cod, 1698.*

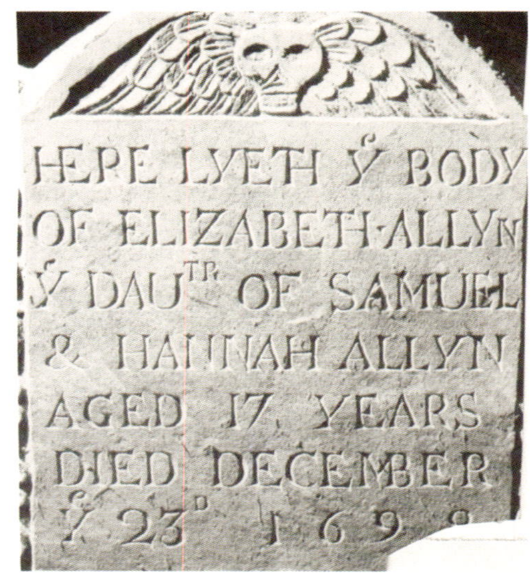

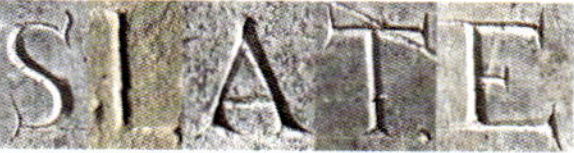

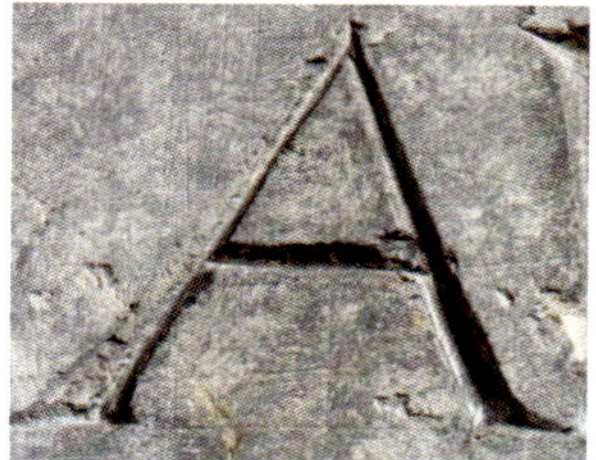

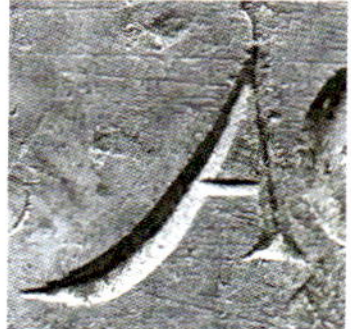 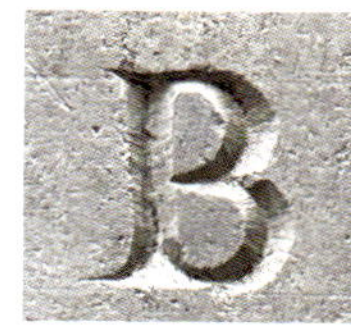 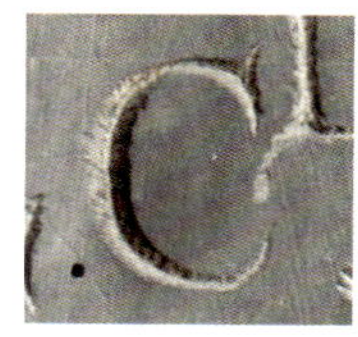 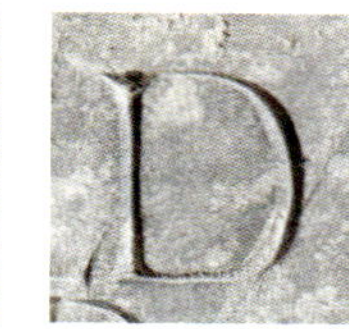 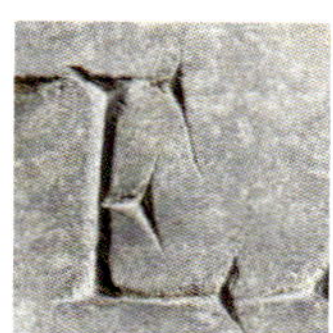

A might spread, tilt, or extend.

E was top-heavy and wasp-waisted.

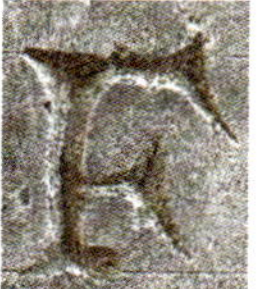 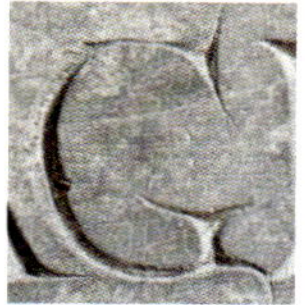 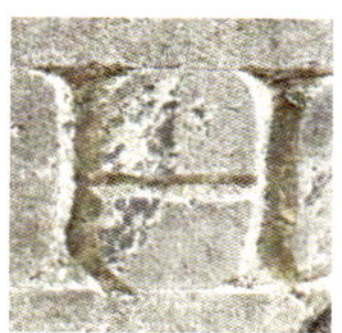 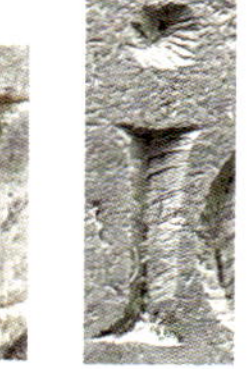 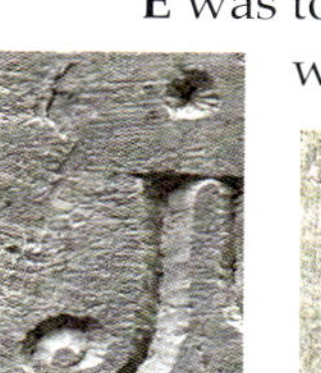

ROMAN LETTERS OF EARLY NEW ENGLAND were several steps removed from the classical capitals they were modeled on. While some carvers got some letters right, (**B L V**), many of their letters were not quite correct: either they had not studied the originals (extra-wide **M W O** or symmetrical **Y**); or their skills were unpolished (crooked crossbar of **H**); or they preferred to use forms they had thought up themselves (**E K**).

The cross stroke of **F** might be above center.

G's vertical was often shortened.

Some carvers dotted **I J** and used them interchangeably.

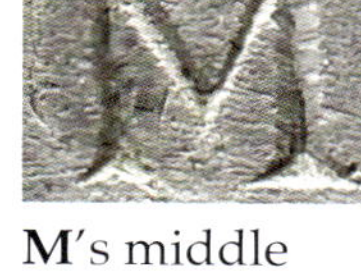 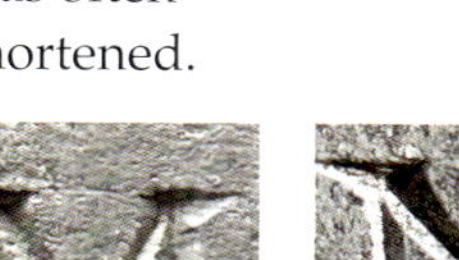 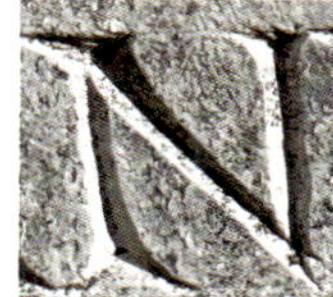 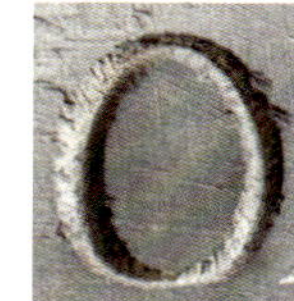 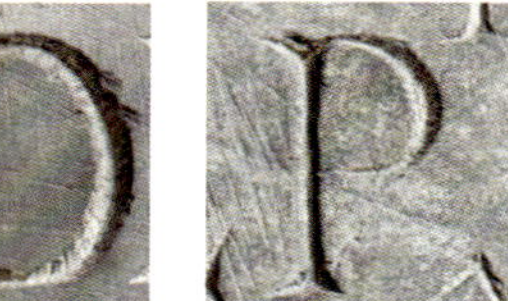

M's middle strokes joined halfway down.

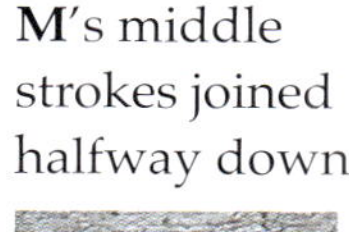 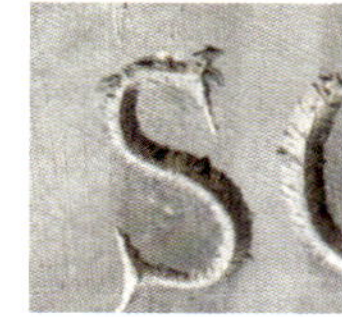 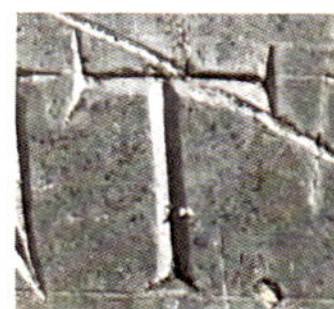 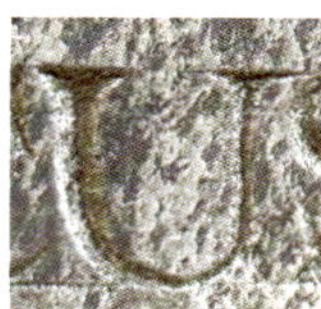

Q could have a decorative tail.

S often had an unbalanced slant.

Before 1750, **V** was often used for **U**.

Scholars can identify many carvers based on individual habits such as: stroke length (**A**), extra marks (**I J**), letter construction (**E**), visual errors (**S**), strokes that were done just for fun (**Q**), and telltale chisel marks like the dot enlarged here ↓ .

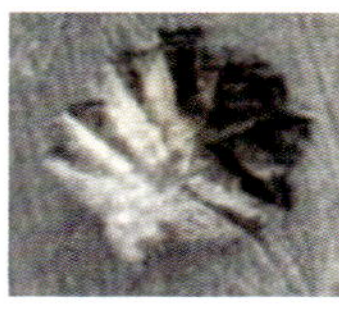

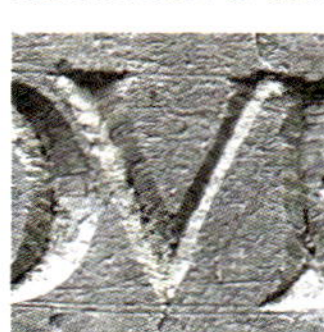 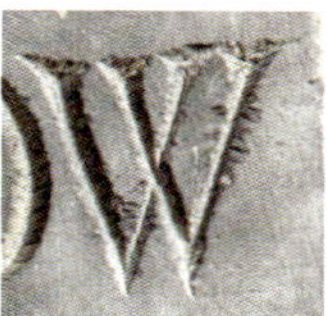 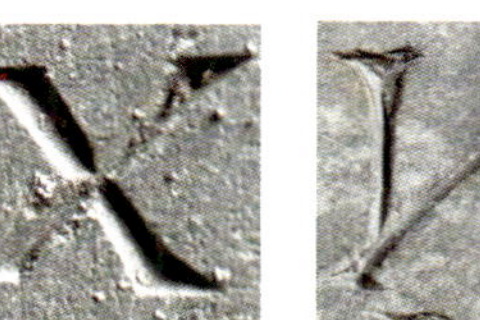 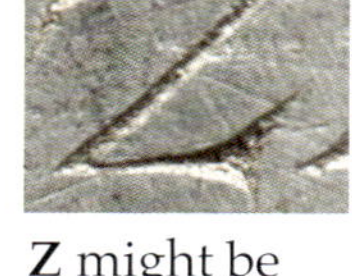

The height of the **X** or **Y** intersection might vary.

Z might be top-heavy.

NUMERALS

The Gregorian calendar was phased in during the 1700s in Great Britain and its colonies to replace the old Julian calendar, dropping eleven days and shifting the New Year from March 25 to January 1. For a few decades, carvers used double dates, as shown here, to clarify which year was meant.

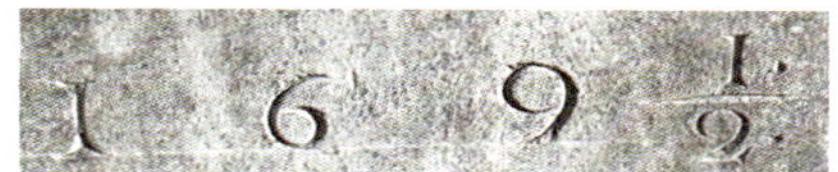

ARCHAIC LETTER; **y**^e = the.

Early printers and carvers substituted **Y** for **þ**, the medieval thorn, a rune for the "th" sound. It was still in occasional American use until 1800. →

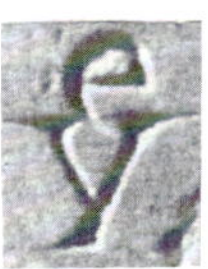

DIFFERENT REGIONS OF AMERICA offered different kinds of stone: schist, soapstone, sandstone, greenstone, fieldstone, marble. Slate was the friendliest material, soft enough to carve with hand tools but strong enough to survive winter weather. The white layer just beneath the surface made even the thinnest lines clear. It could be split readily into roof tiles, floor pavers, and gravestones. The slate found in the area around Massachusetts Bay, where colonists from England first settled in 1620, seemed particularly hard and durable. Carvers today still choose slate for its association with New England of that period.

Lettering on slate, by beginners or masters, has two main parts: laying out the design and carving the grooves. From what historians can tell, early carvers sketched layouts directly onto the stone without a full-size rough draft on paper, compressing words in various ingenious ways to fit them all in.

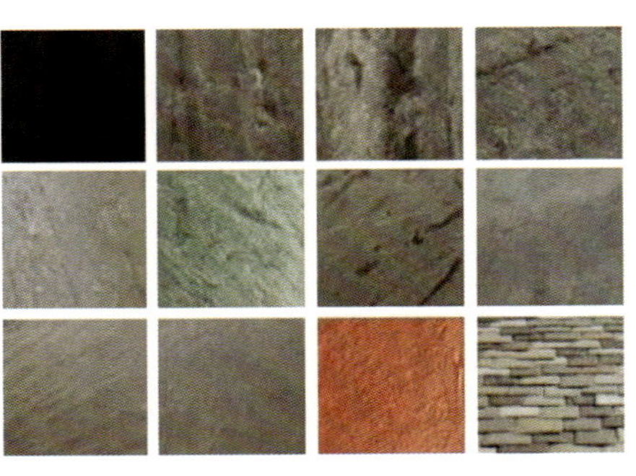

Samples show the range of slate colors.

DESIGN

Slate gravestones were shaped into silhouettes of different sizes and proportions. Letters were usually centered between the margins, along with a very few decorations—usually lines, dots, vines, or a skull. The back and edges were sometimes carved, too.

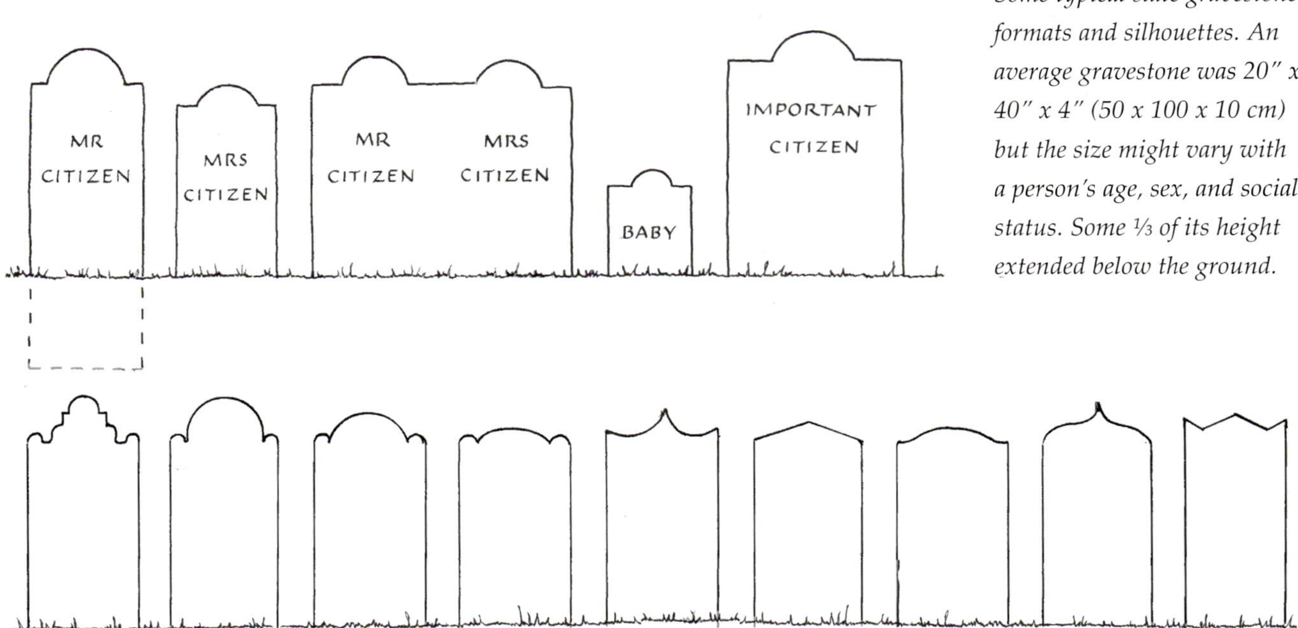

Some typical slate gravestone formats and silhouettes. An average gravestone was 20" x 40" x 4" (50 x 100 x 10 cm) but the size might vary with a person's age, sex, and social status. Some ⅓ of its height extended below the ground.

DECORATION

The religion of early New England focused on sin and punishment and the corruption of the body. Early gravestones reflected this with the skull and bones motif.

The skull was given wings in the "death's head" motif, used frequently in New England.

The skull evolved into a winged cherub. Some scholars think this meant that death was now regarded not as a time of reckoning for misdeeds but of reward for a life well lived.

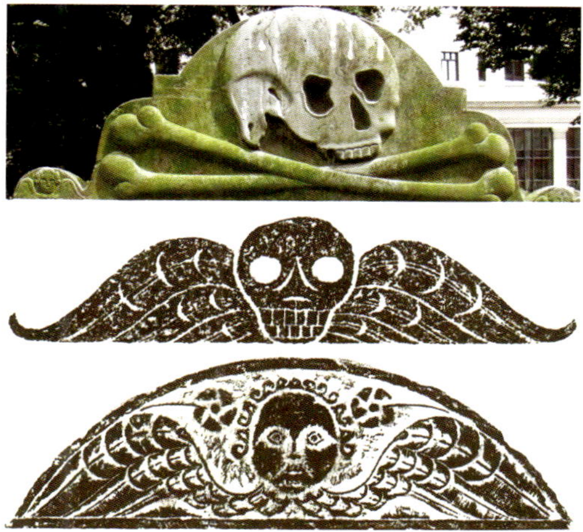

CARVING THEN AND NOW

For many decades, even expert American carvers worked only part-time at their trade, often needing to combine it with painting or farming. Somehow gravestone carvers never attained the social status accorded to other skilled local artisans. Eventually this lack prompted one prosperous Yarmouth carver, Jabez Fisher, to designate himself a "marble monument manufacturer" instead. A few carving studios survived through generations, epitomized by the John Stevens Shop of Newport, Rhode Island.

Traditional techniques for carving letters by hand into slate do not vary much around the world or over time. The carver holds a flat chisel (not, as logic might suggest, a V-shaped chisel) at about a forty-five-degree angle and taps it with a wooden mallet. The main cuts are perpendicular to the line of the stroke, finished off by a serif at a right angle. Slate carvers typically make a capital letter using just one chisel and many small cuts, while some carvers use a different chisel for shaping the serifs.

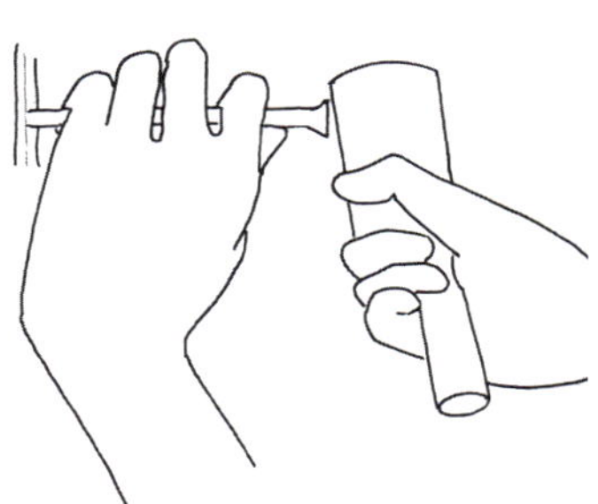

Carvers can carve outdoors on upright stones and walls, but prefer horizontal surfaces in the studio.

In addition to exposing the layer of whitish material below the surface of slate, carved letters in any material are legible because the grooves either cast shadows or catch extra light. Using a technique from the original Roman artisans, later carvers might add paint or gold leaf to the finished cut to heighten this contrast.

Slate gravestones do not last forever, and grow old in several ways. While slate gravestones were weather-resistant, they were not weather-proof. Freezing and thawing eventually split some of them. Some were overgrown with moss, mold, vines, and lichen. Vandalism, as well as neglect, damaged a few. And even acts of homage took their toll; recent admirers who made rubbings from old gravestones soon found that they were wearing the letters away.

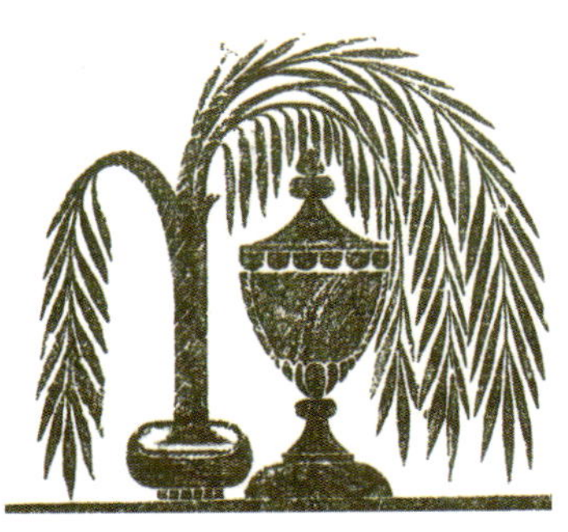

Classical symbols of mourning

*Different tools and materials
make different cross-sections.*

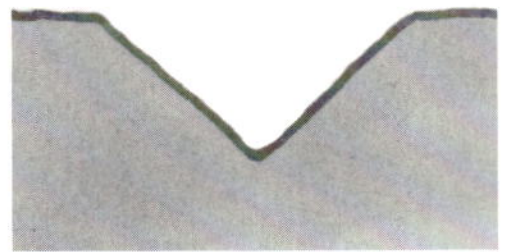

*Hand chisel
on slate*

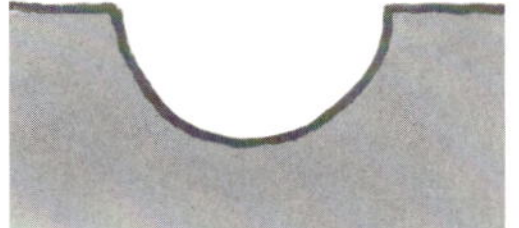

Sandblaster on granite

SLATE'S SLOW DECLINE

AS TRANSPORTATION IMPROVED and America's population grew, carving became the job of full-time experts in urban centers. Gravestones soon grew bigger and more ornate. Grim gray death's heads of the Puritan era gave way to soft-winged cherubs and then to the weeping willows and graceful urns of Greek Revival. As historian James Blachowitz put it, "Remember death" is replaced by "Remember me."

Words, and lots of them, appeared more often in upper and lowercase than in formal capitals, on massive pillars rather than flat slabs. By 1831 when Mount Auburn cemetery was founded in Cambridge, Massachusetts, Americans had begun to abandon the burying grounds of crowded urban churchyards for the parklike landscapes of secular suburban cemeteries; they felt more comfortable referring to gravestones as monuments, headstones, or markers.

Local material was gradually superseded by other stone. People came to prefer the hardness of Vermont granite and the dazzling whiteness of Italian marble over the austerity of native slate. Many slate graveyards fell into disrepair.

Slate was further outmoded by power tools for carving, that made it easier to sandblast inscriptions into granite, or to dig them out of its shiny, speckled surfaces using miniature versions of jackhammers. Even though the machines were soon found to be unhealthy for artisans' lungs and hands, the din heralded a new era. From 1904 to 1949, Americans everywhere could mail-order a gravestone, with custom carving, from Sears, Roebuck.

SLATE'S RECENT REVIVAL

Since 1950, however, interest in carving slate with traditional hand tools and classical techniques has been revived. Old ways have gotten a second look. New devotees are finding, cataloging, photographing, mending, and preserving America's early slate inscriptions, recognizing graveyards as "outdoor museums." Letter artists, energized by the revival of this calligraphy tradition, have updated their cultural legacy with new letterforms, colors, and designs.

Those charming, inventive amateur letters from America's first years, however, are probably not coming back.

USA SOMETIMES LESS TRAINING makes for better art. For years, the boundless creativity of amateur letter artists in the United States has made up for their lack of expertise. In the twentieth century, some of the most eye-catching signs were made not by professional sign-painters but by the people who needed them: local garage mechanics, motel managers, and diner owners.

America's handmade signs attracted the critical eye of classically trained calligrapher and master lithographer Ben Shahn, who wrote:

It was during the Thirties . . . that I first became aware of hand lettering by amateurs. Here was folk art of great quality. . . . The lettering was laborious and of an impressive variety. On a good day, one could count as many as twenty different versions of the figure 2 alone. . . . There is also flavor and a sense of place.

An immigrant from Lithuania at age eight, Ben Shahn used the folk letters of his adopted country to advocate for social justice in many of his posters, lithographs, and book covers. He admired original thinking more than unquestioning obedience, not just for the letter's shape but for page design and for society in general. Shahn said that "Probably as a reaction against the mechanical perfection of type, I began to free words and letters from the set line" and encouraged others to follow him.

Shahn's letters were influential for decades, and they still evoke a timeless blend of country roads and city streets. Calligraphers who follow his philosophy will continue to open people's eyes to the power of letters made by amateurs.

"Don't tell people how to do things, tell them what to do and let them surprise you with their results."
~ George Patton

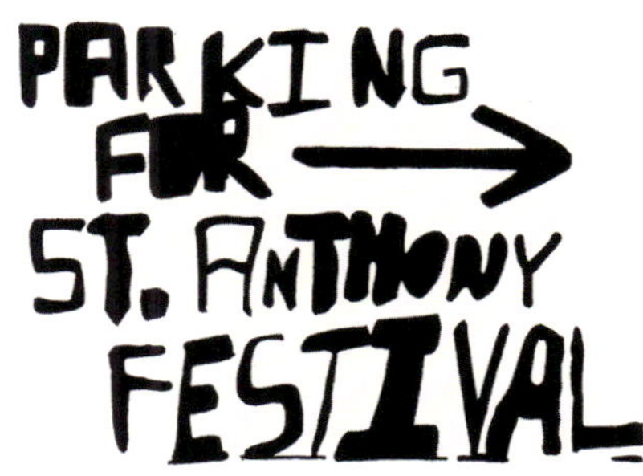

Hand-painted parking sign, Boston 1974.

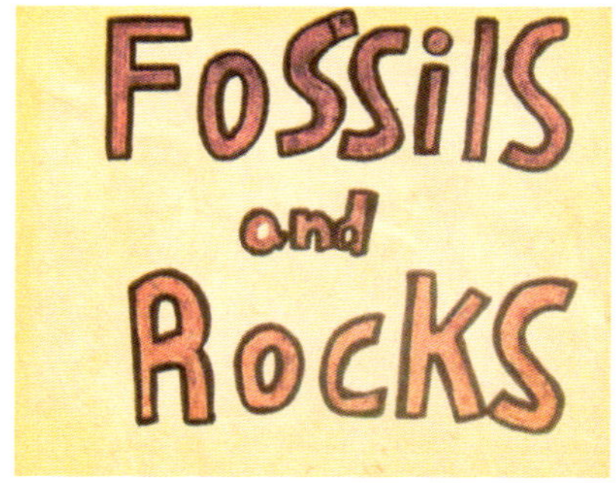

Fossils and rocks, Tucson, Arizona 2014

FROM THE VERY BEGINNING, WE V
THE RULES AND TEST TYPOGRAPHi
BUiLD A LiBRARY WiTH A COLLECT
A RANGE OF TYPEFACES THAT HAC
DiFFERENT PURPOSES, THAT WAS

Sample card showing type in Ben Shahn's letter style.

HANDWRITTEN SIGNS HAVE PLAYED different roles during different American eras. Early in the twentieth century, the new phenomenon of automobile travel spurred small-town amateurs to create signs to catch the eye of people passing through and persuade them to stop at local gas stations, coffee shops, and farm stands. Every village street and gravel road needed signs.

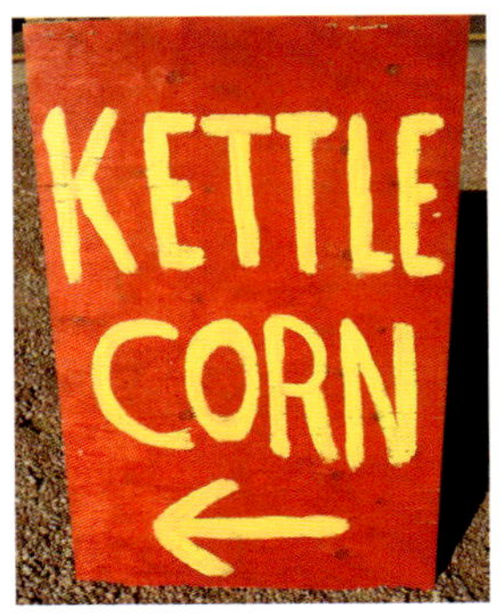

Robust letters in vibrant colors point to a snack stand. Tucson, Arizona, 2014.

In a regional style, cabin owners on 1950s Cape Cod made their own rustic backroads signs.

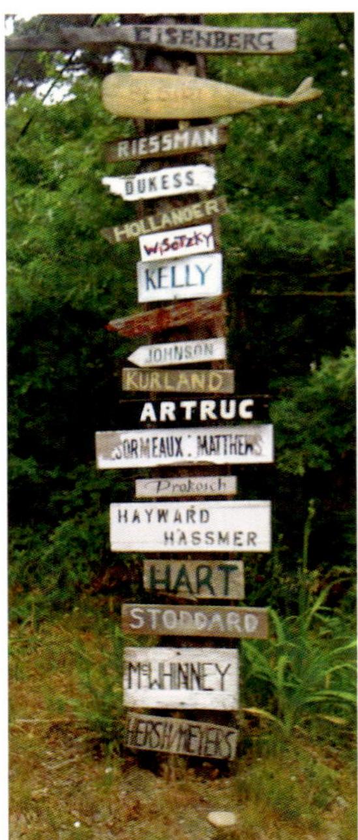

It was a short step from putting up signs that offered food or directions, to holding up signs that asked for help or demanded justice. Depression-era signs pleaded for decent jobs. Protesters in the 1960s and 1970s made hand-lettered placards to express anti-war slogans, and through five more decades, amateur signs proclaimed their opposition to poverty, racism, and sexism. Signs carried by the jobless or homeless, especially, have borne witness to personal trauma. For decades, the US constitution has guaranteed Americans the right to advocate for the issues they care about, in letters they make themselves.

Though cheap and convenient machine-made signs are now edging them out, signs by amateurs will always matter. They deliver a message; they often expand the craft; anyone can make them. Recently collectors have started featuring them in gallery shows. These physical reminders of the country's social challenges have Ben Shahn's crucial virtue of *sincerity*. People trust what the message says because they sense the individual effort it took to write.

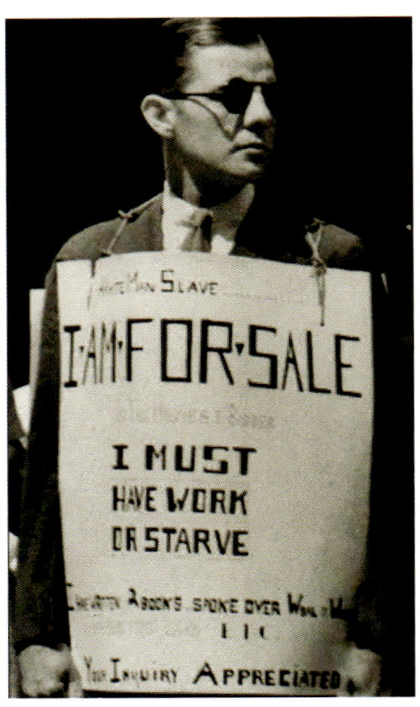

A Depression-era worker's sign seeks a job.

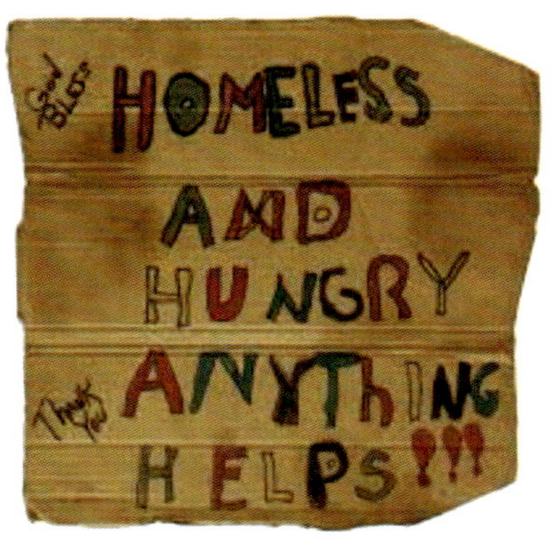

A homeless person's sign asks for help.

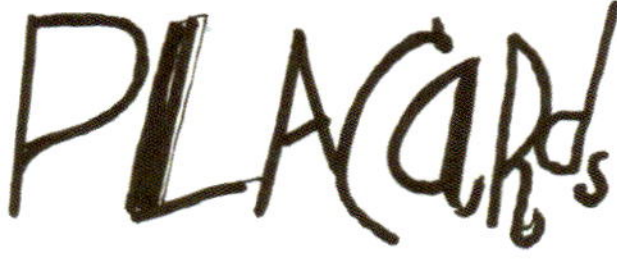

While there is no wrong shape for amateur letters, here are two of the easiest ways to construct them:

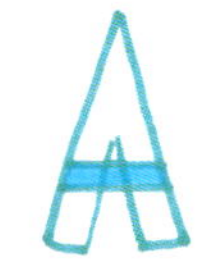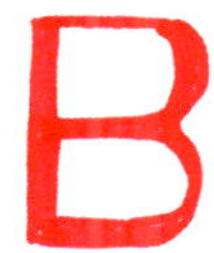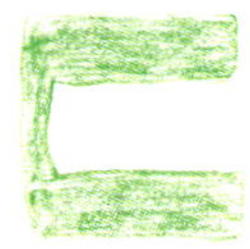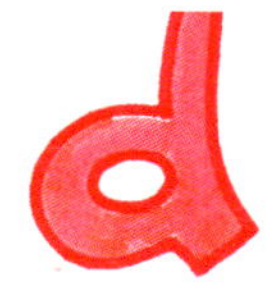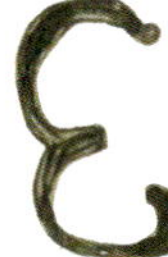

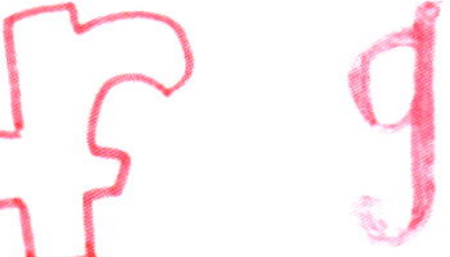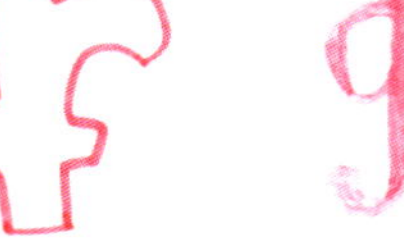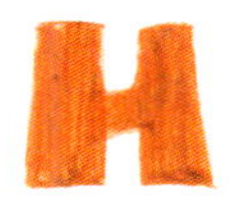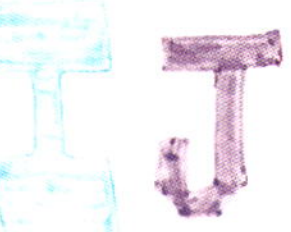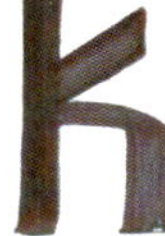

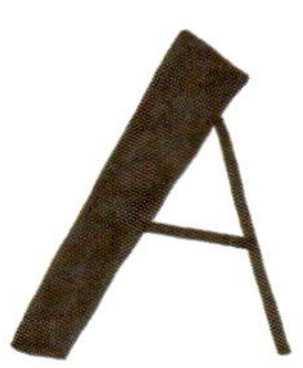
A blunt marker can write the thin strokes, then outline and build up the thick strokes.

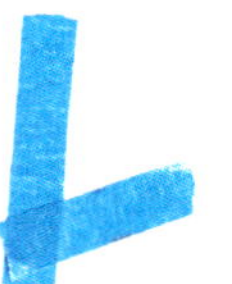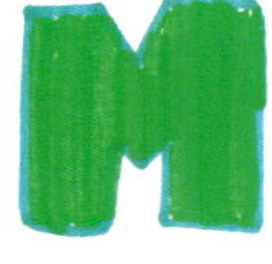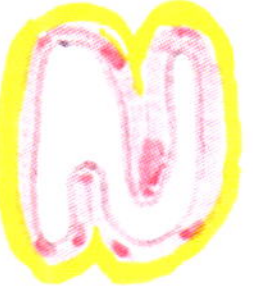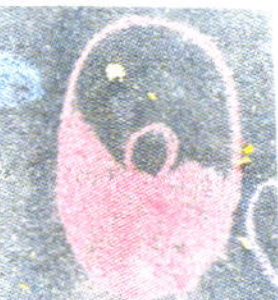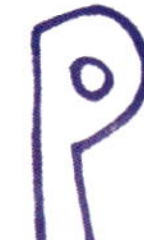

or

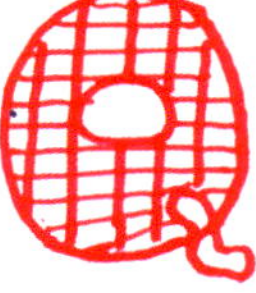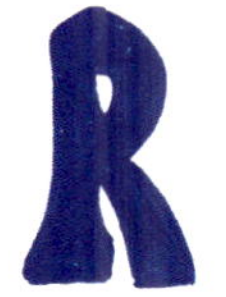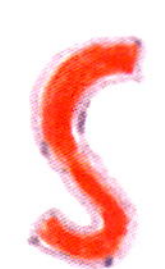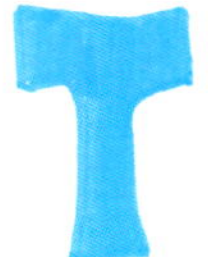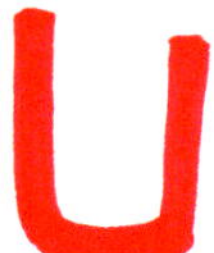

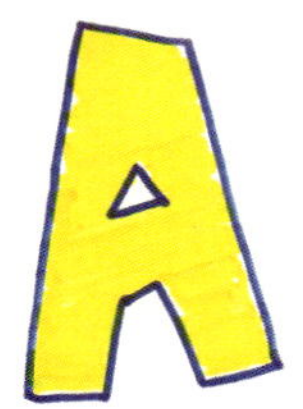
A set of children's markers can outline the whole letter then leave it empty or fill it with lines, dots or solid color.

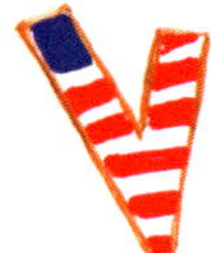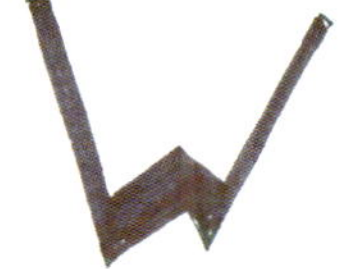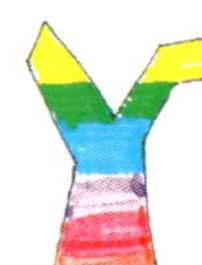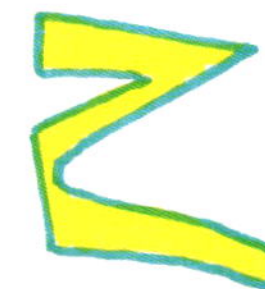

There is also no wrong material for placards; they can be made with poster paint, crayons, masking tape, house paint, or chalk, on cardboard, wood scraps, paper plates, posterboard, or cloth banners.

AMATEURS CAN EMBRACE INCONSISTENCY

Type designers began expanding Ben Shahn's alphabet as soon as phototype in the 1960s made it practical to offer choices for each character, providing a new way to control the texture of the page. Shown here, "Ben's Folk," reissued by Harold Lohner in 2000, with two versions of **E** *and* **T** *in its red headline.*

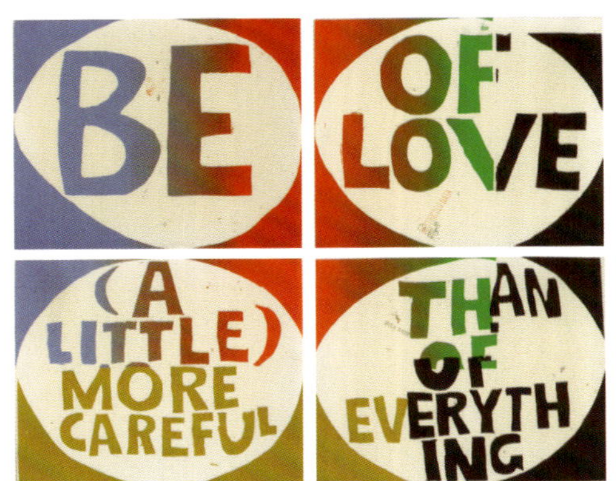

Corita Kent 's silk screen prints gave a voice to a generation of idealists. This 1967 poster captures the poetry of E. E. Cummings.

AMATEUR CALLIGRAPHY inspired artists in many other fields: printmaking, logo design, book cover design, artists books, and poster design. After decades of being written on corrugated cardboard, these letters went mainstream. Ever since the 1930s, the idea of vernacular letters has gradually gained acceptance, elevating them from American roadsides to museum collections.

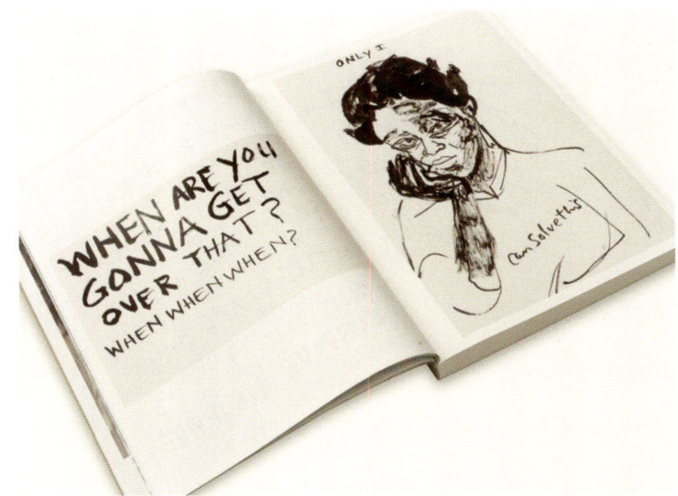

Skepticism in 2021 speaks with a blunt visual tone. From A Black Hole is Everything a Star Longs to Be, by Kara Walker.

COMMERCIAL USES

Inevitably, corporate America caught on to the branding power of these populist, popular letters, and revived them for a whole new generation of consumers.

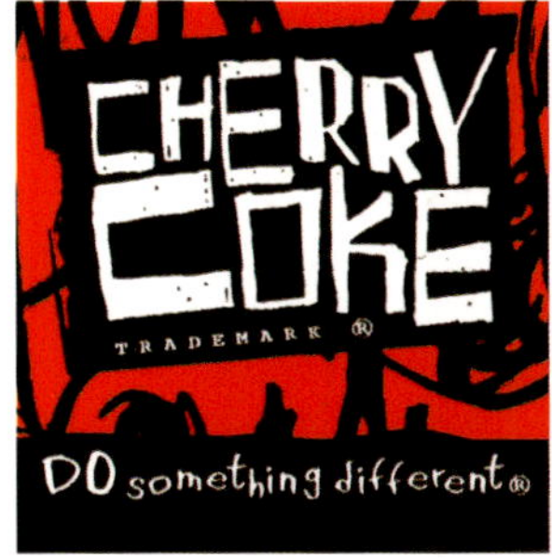

Cherry Coke logo, 1995, urges people to "DO something different."

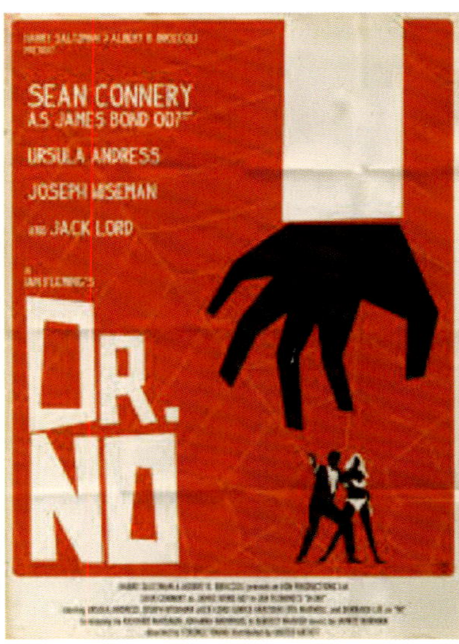

"Dr. No" movie poster from 1962. Designer, Saul Bass.

CHILDREN GO THROUGH A BRIEF PHASE when they want to construct big letters and have to figure out how. They find that their handwriting lessons, if any, don't give them much guidance, so they use what they know from art class instead, treating the letter as a shape to be drawn rather than a symbol to copy. Some children may have already noticed that the letters they read include extra touches—serifs, thicks and thins, bold weight, and color—but haven't recognized any system behind it, freeing them to experiment. And they don't have to worry about trends in graphic design.

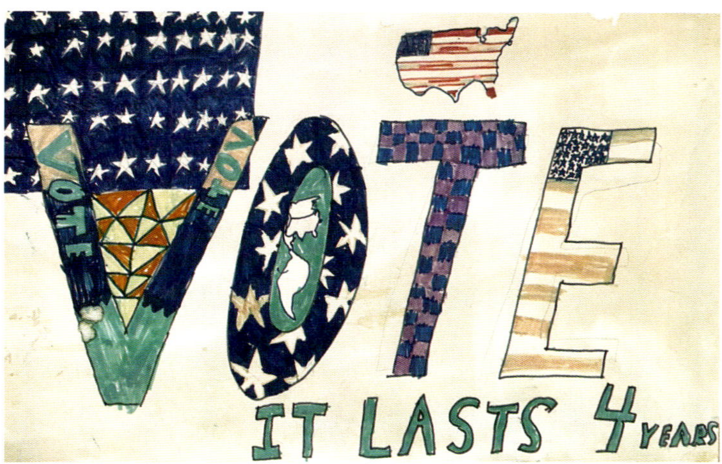

*This eleven-year-old included every symbol she could think of to catch the reader's eye and make her point. "Vote" is repeated, in mirror image, inside the strokes of the **V**.*

Dimensions 12" x 18" (30 cm x 45 cm)

"Vote" poster and "Ice Cold" sign courtesy of Zoë Friend.

Signs from this magic age carry built-in appeal that is not just limited to friends, neighbors, and doting parents. Signs really *do* sell lemonade. In addition, the children who undertake and carry out these projects learn a lot about materials, planning, and scale. They learn what makes a sign appeal to people. They gain confidence from making something themselves. They use their eyes *and* their hands. Now that type and printout have gradually replaced handwriting, constructing letters gives them a chance for hands-on learning.

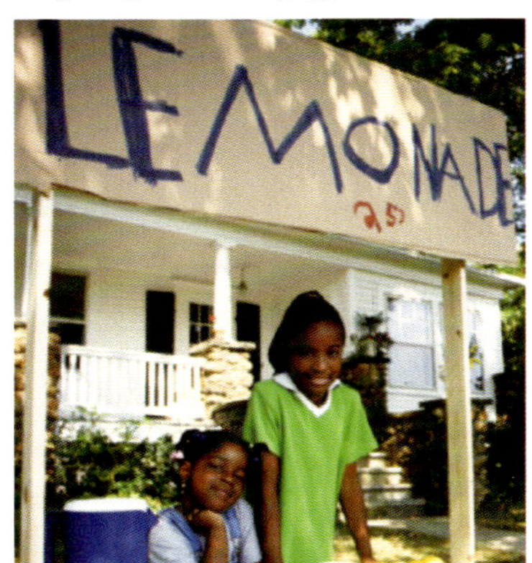

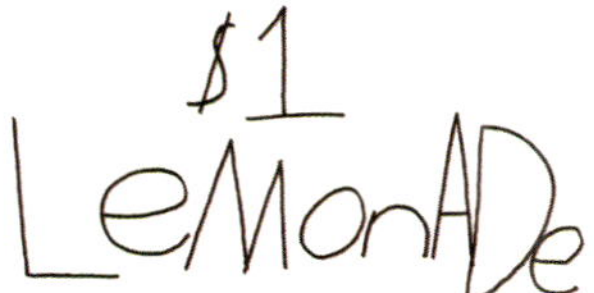

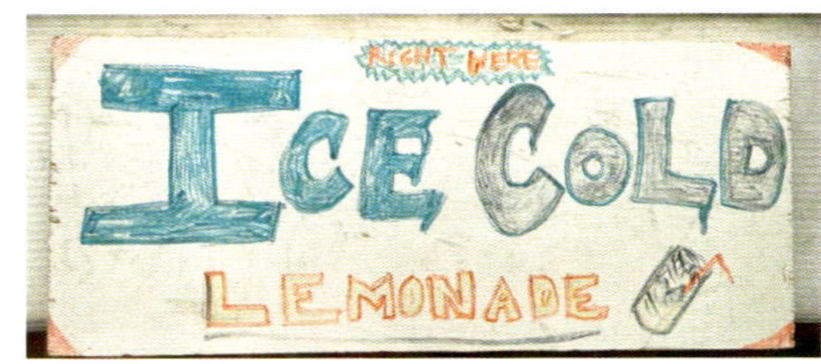

In an American rite of passage, kids make signs for their lemonade stands. Spacing is often a challenge. Outlined "Ice Cold" letters above have stylized icicles hanging off them.

AMATEURS WRITE WHAT THEY THINK

UNTIL RECENTLY, SCHOLARS AND CURATORS did not apply the standards of fine art to calligraphy, let alone to the work of amateurs, hobbyists, crafts people, folk artists, and outsiders. Readable art was usually relegated to a second tier, undervalued because it was useful. Definitions and minds have been broadening since mid-century, however, so that designs based on grassroots letters have begun to receive the critical books, studies, and exhibitions they deserve. Today, the Smithsonian Museum, among others, takes special care to archive the placards left over from protest marches.

Amateur letters of many eras share common traits, whether the medium is durable slate or corrugated cardboard. Beyond how they look, amateur letters also highlight some uniquely American qualities.

- Amateurism: Art is seen as accessible to all, not only the professionally trained. In the pursuit of happiness, people are encouraged to do what they love—the literal definition of "amateur."

- Faith in Innovation: Americans have always tended to think that the best answer to a difficulty lies in the future rather than the past. A typical attitude to problems still is, "There's got to be a better way."

- Oppositionality: From the beginning, Americans tended toward rebellion and defiance rather than orderliness and obedience. The struggle for political independence from England set the tone for the next 250 years more of rejecting old-world dominance in art, fashion, music, philosophy, poetry, and cuisine. Even spelling was Americanized after the 1840s.

- Goal orientation: Amateur letterers get the job done, *now*. All a sign has to do is be readable; everything else—polish, stylishness, or beauty—is secondary.

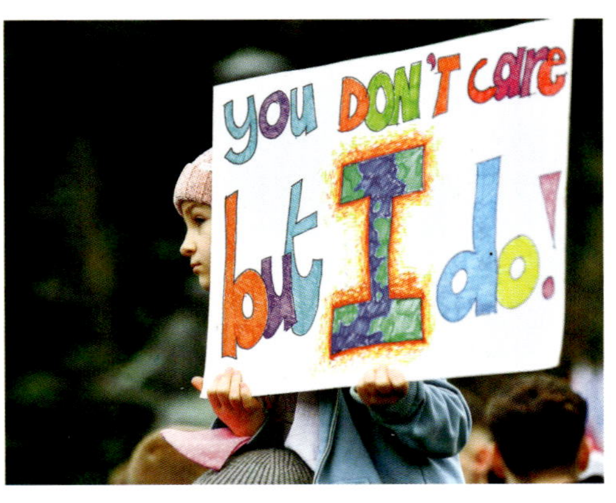

At the core of all their other virtues, handmade letters play a critical role in America's most important freedom. The First Amendment of the US Constitution declares the right of any citizen, alone or in a group, to write any opinion on a placard and hold it up anywhere. This protection continues to inspire ordinary people to turn their words into art.

Bold letters carry strong opinions.

For planning and keeping favorite letters from placards.

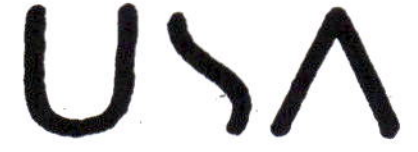
Minimalism

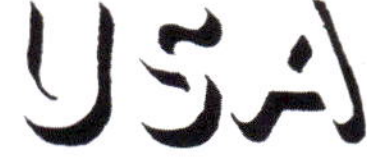
Optical illusion

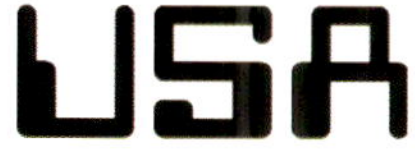
Machine readable

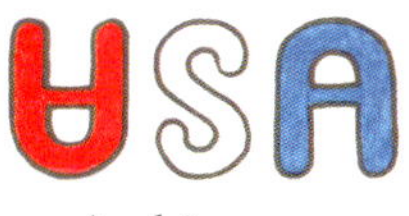
Ambigram

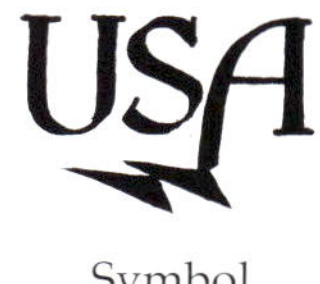
Symbol

TOMORROW

THE PATH TO TOMORROW'S ALPHABET is built on yesterday's letters. Even if most of them go out of style after a few years, a few have survived for decades, still new and eye-catching. A special quality, called *retro-futurism*, lets them show how tomorrow used to look.

- Minimalism inspires calligraphers to strip away everything possible, omitting serifs and leaving just enough strokes to keep the letters readable. Beginning with obvious capitals **A B D E P R**, it is easy to leave out strokes. And it works. The NASA logo, for instance, looks as modern today as it did when it was introduced in 1975.

- For centuries, optical illusions have fooled people into believing that a flat image has three dimensions. The human eye is so determined to look for edges that it "sees" them even where it knows they can not actually exist. A broad calligraphy pen stroke can create a convincing illusion of a solid letter.

- Although the magnetic ink character recognition font shown here (MICR) looks futuristic, its numerals have been in use since 1959 by banks to process checks. The lumps let machines read it, while the lines let humans read it. This style is easy to imitate with a blunt pen.

- Ambigrams suggest new ways to read. Polymath Scott Kim introduced the idea in 1981, expanding on the many letter pairs in the Roman alphabet that look like each other when they are rotated, like **u** and **n**, **p** and **d**, or mirrored, like **p** and **q**, **b** and **d**. More letters almost match. The author's last name, at left, transforms into her first name when the book is turned upside down.

- Alphabet styles have portrayed national progress throughout the twentieth century, when letter artists saw themselves as leading the world somewhere new. Starting with symbols of electricity itself, letters have suggested fast trains, skyscrapers, neon lights, atomic power, space travel, robots, pixelation, and computers. Some of these styles have stayed futuristic for decades.

Today's search for tomorrow's ABCs will always inspire letter artists. Despite knowing that they can't really be sure of what is coming next, American calligraphers and type designers will continue to dream of new alphabets for the future.

"Yesterday's weirdness is tomorrow's reason why."
~ *Hunter S. Thompson*

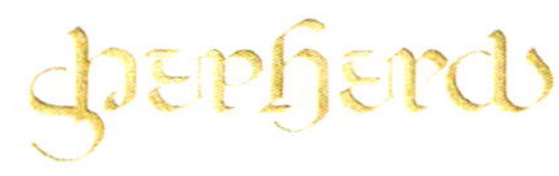

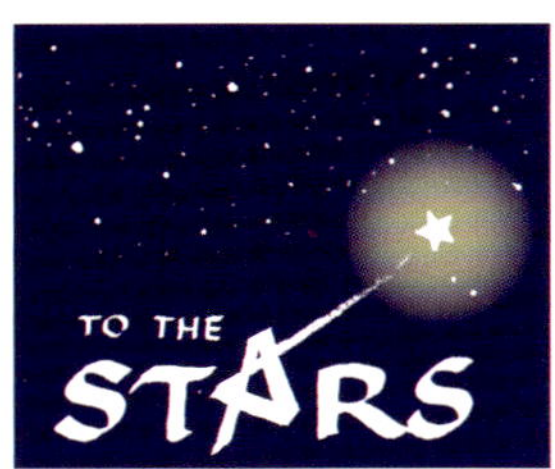

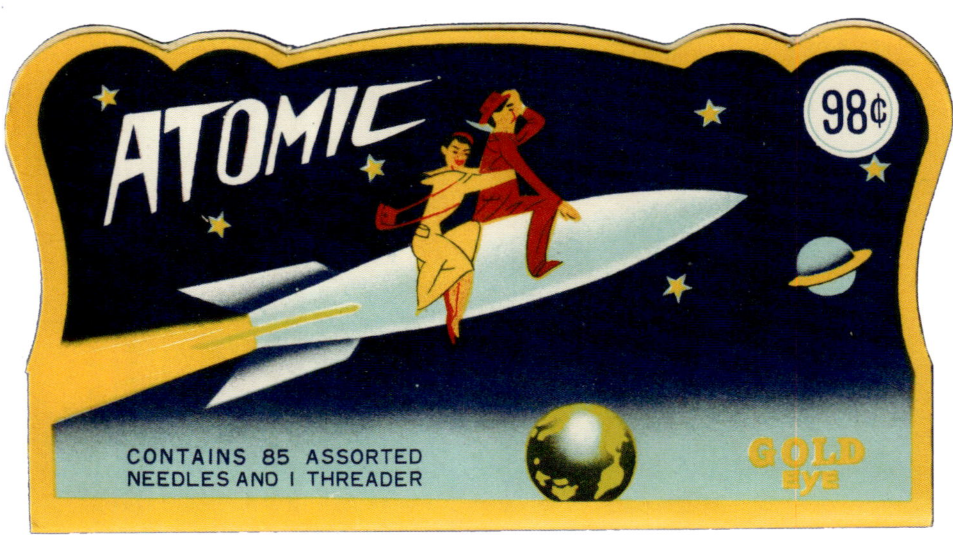

Made in Japan for the American market in the early 1950s, the futuristic letters in this design celebrate an era of faith in atomic power and space exploration.

IMAGE CREDITS

p vi: Jug, c 1797–1819, by Thomas W. Commeraw. Salt-glazed stoneware, cobalt oxide. 12" x 7 ¾". Purchased from Elie Nadelman. New-York Historical Society, 1937.820.

p vii: Keep on Truckin'. Used with permission from artist Robert Crumb.

FIRST AMERICANS

P1: Onondaga Nation. **P2:** Onondaga Nation, United States Mint. P3: Rick & Nora Bowers / Alamy Stock Photo. **P4:** National Museum of the American Indian, Smithsonian Institution (010617). Photo by NMAI Photo Services; Bureau of Land Management. **P5:** Haida raven art design by Lon French. Graphic based on Pacific NW art by Karin Clark. **P5 and P7:** Angel DeCora designs reproduced with kind permission of Letterform Archive. **P8:** (3) Digital Navajo. Thunderbird ©1999 by Cree artist Alvin Constant.

GOTHIC

P11: Istock. **P12:** Royal Danish Library, GKS 2232 kvart: Guamán Poma, Nueva corónica y buen gobierno (c 1615), page 828. **P14:** Courtesy of Princeton University. **P19:** Illustration from *Little Women*, Doubleday, 1947, artist Louis Jamber. **P20:** Photo ©Olivia Barrionuevo-Minkin. **P24:** Jennifer Parkhurst, on behalf of the Shire of Avonwood, c/o the Society for Creative Anachronism.

GRAFFITI

P29: Bob Wick, Bureau of Land Management. **P30:** Courtesy of therecordco.org. **P32:** www.vectorstock.com. **P34:** Evan Harrington / Alamy Stock Photo. **P35:** Z by Jasper Friend. **P36:** mural by Ian Staber.

HANDWRITING

PP41, 43: Alphabet and title by Chisato Uno. **P45:** Library of Congress. **P52:** Art by Zoë Friend. **P56:** Courtesy of Penn State Industries.

DOTS

P61: Mosaic, Courtesy of Texas State Library and Archives Commission, accession # 1992/180. Wampum belt Canadian Museum of History, LH2016.48.2, IMG2016-0267-250. **P62:** Sampler, The Speed Museum, Louisville, Kentucky, Gift of Mrs. Harry S. Frazier Jr. 2015.7.2. Sampler, *How Vain are All Things Here Below*, Rhode Island c 1835. Courtesy of the Rhode Island Historical Society, Providence, RI. RHi X17 1492. **P64:** Edwin E. Jack Fund. Adrienne Iselin Gilbert Memorial Fund and Susan Cornelia Warren Fund 2012.89, Museum of Fine Arts, Boston. **P65:** Courtesy Heritage House Museum, Hisham Ibrahimm / photo V / Alamy Stock Photo. **P66:** Photography by Alison Colby Campbell **P67:** Jannis Werner / Alamy Stock Photo. Joe Bird / Alamy Stock Photo. **P68:** The John Simmermaker Collection. M-Production / Alamy Stock Photo. From the collections at The National Museum of the American Coverlet. Gift of Jude Fera. The Kitty Bell and Ron Walter Collection **P69:** Ted Foxx / Alamy Stock Photo. **P70:**

Courtesy of Doug Greenway, The Corn Palace. Iowa State University Special Collections and University Archives.

ROMAN REVIVALS

P76: US Postal Service. **P78:** Tile courtesy of the Frank Lloyd Wright Foundation, Scottsdale, AZ All rights reserved. Frank Lloyd Wright, *The Architectural Forum*, Courtesy of the Frank Lloyd Wright Foundation, Scottsdale, AZ. All rights reserved. **P80:** Rea Irvin, The New Yorker, ©Conde Nast. **P82:** Library of Congress, Courtesy of the National Park Service. **P84:** Fox Searchlight Pictures / Photofest. **P86:** Artist Tina Shao.

FRAKTUR

P97: Courtesy of the Free Library of Philadelphia, Rare Book Department. **P99:** National Museum of American History, Smithsonian Institution. **P100:** Colonial Williamsburg Foundation. From the Collection of the Mercer Museum of the Bucks County Historical Society; Courtesy of the Free Library of Philadelphia, Rare Book Department. **P101:** Courtesy of Dennis Stephan. **P102:** Courtesy of Elizabeth Harris. Courtesy of Jake Rainis. **P105:** Border ©Dennis Stephan.

BLOCK

PP108–10: Photo, title, numerals, alphabet, and "NOW" variations by Kenji Nakayama. **P111:** Courtesy of Brigid Cowdrey Design. **P112:** Alaskan Photo by Sarah Friend. **P114:** Photo by Richard Herold. **PP116–117:** Courtesy of David Greer / https://woodtype.org/ **P117:** Ariel Molvig / The New Yorker Collection / The Cartoon Bank. Courtesy of Nick Sherman. **P120:** Missed Exit illustration ©SEPS licensed by Curtis Licensing Indianapolis, IN. All rights reserved. Marianne A. Campolongo / Alamy Stock Photo. Ken Koehler https://en.wikipedia.org/wiki/Burma-Shave. **P121:** Courtesy of Don Meeker. **P125:** ©Okefenokee Glee & Perloo, Inc. Used by permission. permissions@pogocomics.com. Calvin and Hobbes ©1992 Bill Watterson. Reprinted with permission of Andrews McMeel Syndication. All Rights Reserved. **P127:** BONE® by Jeff Smith ©2022.

AMATEUR

P131: The Art Institute of Chicago / Art Resource, NY / ©2022 Estate of Ben Shahn / Licensed by VAGA at Artists Rights Society (ARS) NY. **P138:** Associated Press; Streetsofsadness.com. **P140:** Corita Kent, *be, of love, (a little) more careful, than of everything*, series of four serigraphs, 1967. ©2022 Estate of Corita Kent / Immaculate Heart Community / Licensed by Artists Rights Society (ARS), New York. Kara Walker: *A Black Hole Is Everything a Star Longs to Be*, JRP | Editions & Kunstmuseum Basel, Geneva 2020. ISBN: 978-3-03764-557-4 Photo: JRP | Editions / Julien Gremaud. *Dr. No* poster, Saul Bass, with illustration and conception by Alain Bossuyt. **P141:** Art (2) by Zoë Friend. Xavier Bonghi / The Image Bank / Getty Images.

Images that have not been credited here are either in the public domain, or they were made by the author, or they come from her collection. Reasonable efforts have been made to find the original owner of each image's copyright and request permission to use it in this book.

BIBLIOGRAPHY

Alcott, Louisa May. *Little Women*. Illustrated by Louis Jamber. New York: Grosset & Dunlap, 1947.

Bird, Michael S. *Ontario Fraktur: A Pennsylvania-German Folk Tradition in Early Canada*. Toronto: M. F. Feheley, 1977.

Blachowicz, James. *From Slate to Marble: Gravestone Carving Traditions in Eastern Massachusetts 1770–1870*. Evanston, IL: Graver Press, 2006.

Bolton, Edith Stanwood, and Eva Johnston Coe. *American Samplers*. New York: Weathervane Books, 1973.

Chalfont, Henry, and James Prigoff. *Spraycan Art*. London and New York: Thames & Hudson, 1987.

Chastanet, François. *Cholo Writing: Latino Gang Graffiti in Los Angeles*. Stockholm: Dokument Press, 2015.

Cooper, Martha, and Henry Chalfont. *Subway Art*. New York: Thames & Hudson, 1982.

Cushman, Ellen. *The Cherokee Syllabary: Writing the People's Perseverance American Indian Literature and Critical Studies Series. Vol. 56*. Norman: University of Oklahoma Press, 2013.

Dawson, Barry. *Street Graphics* New York. London: Thames & Hudson, 2003.

Dubay, Inga, and Barbara Getty. *Write Now: The Complete Program for Better Handwriting*. Getty-Dubay Productions.

DuBosch, Carol. *Bone Script*. Greensboro, NC: John Neal Books, 2021.

Faust, Drew Gilpin. "Cursive Is History." *The Atlantic Monthly*. October 2022, 75–76.

Florey, Kitty Burns. *Script and Scribble*. Brooklyn and New York: Melville House, 2008.

Floyd, Pratt and Rounds. *Alphabets, Monograms, and Initials*. Potterton Books Sessay, UK. Facsimile reprint c 1900.

Fraser, Valerie. "The Artistry of Guamán Poma." *The Pre-Columbian, no. 29/30* (Spring–Autumn, 1996): 269–89.

Gaskell, George A. *Gaskell's Compendium of Forms*. Chicago: Fairbanks, Palmer & Co, 1880.

Gilbert, Jim, and Karin Clark. *Learning by Designing Pacific Northwest Coast Native Indian Art*. Vol. 1.; Raven, Union City, BC. 1999.

Gillon, Edmund Vincent Jr. *Early New England Gravestone Rubbings*. Mineola, NY: Dover, 1966.

Gray, Nicolete. *Lettering as Drawing: Contour and Silhouette*. Oxford and New York: Oxford University Press, 1970.

Gray, Nicolete. *Lettering as Drawing: The Moving Line*. Oxford and New York: Oxford University Press, 1970.

Guamán Poma de Ayala, Felipe. *The First New Chronicle and Good Government*. David L. Frye, translator and editor. Indianapolis and Cambridge: Hackett Classics, 2006.

Hartung, Ruthanne. *Fraktur: Tips, Tools, and Techniques for Learning the Craft. Heritage Crafts Today Series*. Mecanicsburg, PA: Stackpole Books, 2008.

Heller, Steven, and Louise Fili. *Slab Serif Type, A Century of Bold Letterforms*. London and New York: Thames & Hudson, 2016.

Henning, William. *An Elegant Hand: The Golden Age of American Penmanship and Calligraphy*. New Castle, DE: Oak Knoll Press, 2002.

Jabr, Ferris. "Why the Brain Prefers Paper." *Scientific American 309*, no. 5 (Nov. 2013): 48–53.

Jackson, Dick. *Copperplate Calligraphy*. Garden City, NY: Dover, 2015.

Jamra, Mark, "Learning to Design a Cherokee Syllabary with Mark Jamra." 2017. YouTube video.

Kelly, Rob Roy. *American Wood Type: 1828–1900: Notes on the Evolution of Decorated and Large Types*. Saratoga, CA: Liber Apertus Press. 2016; reissue of 1969 edition.

Lepore, Jill. *A is for American*. New York: Vintage, 2003.

Levine, Faythe, and Sam Macon. *Sign Painters*. Princeton, NJ: Princeton Architectural Press, 2013.

Minardi, Lisa. *Drawn with Spirit: Pennsylvania German Fraktur from the Joan and Victor Johnson Collection*. Ann Percy, contributor. New Haven, CT: Yale, 2015.

O'Donnell, Patrick. *The Knights Next Door: Everyday People Living Middle Ages Dreams*. New York; Lincoln, UK; and Shanghai: iUniverse, Inc, 2004.

Powers, Stephen. *The Art of Getting Over: Graffiti at the Millennium*. New York: St Martin's Press, 1999.

Renkl, Margaret. "The Nicest New Year's Resolution I Ever Made." *New York Times*. November 22, 2022.

Reynolds, Lloyd. *Calligraphy and Handwriting: Exercises and Text*. New York: Taplinger, 1969.

Ruben, Lee Rachel. *Well Met: Renaissance Fairies and the American Counterculture*. New York: NYU Press, 2012.

Russell, Laura. *Anything Helps*. Portland, OR: Simply Books Ltd., 2013.

Sassoon, Rosemary. *Handwriting of the Twentieth Century*. Abingdon on Thames, UK: Routledge, 1999.

Sealaska Heritage Institute. *Northwest Coast Formline Design, Artkit Textbook*. Edited by Kari Groven, Steve Brown, Annie Calkins, and Nancy Lehnhart. Juneau, AK: n.d.

Shahn, Ben. *Love and Joy About Letters*. New York: Grossman Publishers, 1963.

Shepherd, Margaret. *Calligraphy Alphabets*. New York: Perigree Books, 1986.

Shepherd, Margaret. *Learn Calligraphy*. New York: Random House, 2001.

Svaren, Jackie. *Written Letters: 33 Alphabets*. Rev. ed. New York: Taplinger Publishing Co., 1986.

INDEX